Human Enhancement Technologies and Healthcare Policy

Human enhancement (HE) is considered one of the most profoundly impactful effects of the Fourth Industrial Revolution. This book presents the definition, theory, scope, and main challenges of HE from a health policy and healthcare systems perspective. It offers a comprehensive view of the consequences of human enhancement disrupting the status quo in health service delivery and social coherence.

The book examines the latest achievements of HE, focusing on four forms of enhancement: cognitive, physical, mood, and moral. These forms are supported by the list of specific technologies and techniques used for HE. The book identifies the current trends in HE's development and analyses the challenges that HE poses to health policy and healthcare systems. It discusses the legal and financial aspects of HE, including regulation, and shows that the financing of HE goes far beyond the scope of universal health coverage, thus opening the door for private, voluntary insurance and/or out-of-pocket payments. This, in turn, leads towards growing inequalities, which may threaten social cohesion. Readers will receive a structured picture of the latest advances in HE and trends in the field, as well as a list of the challenges and problems that HE generates.

The book offers a concise picture of HE for students and researchers across the political sciences, public health, public sector management, and sociology. It will also find an audience among healthcare managers, policymakers, and those who are interested in social change.

Jacek Klich is an associate professor of economics in the Department for the Management of Public Organisations, Cracow University of Economics, Cracow, Poland.

Routledge International Studies in Health Economics
Edited by Charles Normand[1] and
Richard M. Scheffler[2]
[1]*Trinity College Dublin, Ireland*
[2]*School of Public Health, University of California, Berkeley, USA*

Public Policy and the Public Interest
Lok Sang Ho

Economics and HIV
The Sickness of Economics
Deborah Johnston

Medical Innovation
Science, Technology and Practice
Edited by Davide Consoli, Andrea Mina, Richard R. Nelson and Ronnie Ramlogan

Politics, Hierarchy, and Public Health
Voting Patterns in the 2016 US Presidential Election
Deborah Wallace and Rodrick Wallace

Equity and Healthcare Reform in Developing Economies
The Case of Turkey
Songül Çınaroğlu

The Digital Transformation of Healthcare
Health 4.0
Edited by Marek Ćwiklicki, Mariusz Duplaga and Jacek Klich

Social Finance and Health
Neil McHugh, Olga Biosca and Cam Donaldson

Artificial Intelligence and the Future of Healthcare
Jon-Arild Johannessen

Human Enhancement Technologies and Healthcare Policy
Jacek Klich

Human Enhancement Technologies and Healthcare Policy

Jacek Klich

Routledge
Taylor & Francis Group
LONDON AND NEW YORK

First published 2025
by Routledge
4 Park Square, Milton Park, Abingdon, Oxon OX14 4RN

and by Routledge
605 Third Avenue, New York, NY 10158

Routledge is an imprint of the Taylor & Francis Group, an informa business

British Library Cataloguing-in-Publication Data
A catalogue record for this book is available from the British Library

ISBN: 978-1-032-58316-7 (hbk)
ISBN: 978-1-032-58317-4 (pbk)
ISBN: 978-1-003-44958-4 (ebk)

DOI: 10.4324/9781003449584

Typeset in Sabon
by MPS Limited, Dehradun

Contents

List of abbreviations

ADHD	attention deficit hyperactivity disorder
AE	administrative efficiency
AI	artificial intelligence
AMGA	American Medical Group Association
AR	augmented reality
AWRU	Academic Ranking of World Universities
BCI	brain-computer interface
BD	big data
BNDF	brain-derived neurotrophic factor
BRICS	Brazil, Russia, India, China, and South Africa
CADD	computer-aided drug design
CAGR	compound annual growth rate
CAR-T	chimeric antigen receptor cell therapy
CBT	cognitive behavioural therapy
CDER	Center for Drug Evaluation and Research
CE	cognitive enhancement
CFTR	cystic fibrosis transmembrane conductance regulator
CDSS	clinical decision support system
CGMS	continuous glucose monitoring system
ChatGPT	Chat Generative Pre-Trained Transformer
CRISPR	clustered regularly-interspaced short palindromic repeats
CRT	cardiac resynchronisation therapy
CTR	clinical trials and research
CV	computer vision
DARPA	Defense Advanced Research Projects Agency
DBS	deep brain stimulation
DD	differential diagnosis
DDD	drug discovery and development
DDS	diagnosis and decision support
DL	deep learning
DT	digital twin

EE	emotive enhancement
EEG	electroencephalography
EF	epidemiological forecasting
EHCI	Euro Health Consumer Index
EMA	European Medicines Agency
sEMG	surface electromyography
FDM	fused deposition modelling
GE	genetic engineering
GMO	genetically modified object/crop
HE	human enhancement
HER	electronic health record
HET	human enhancement technology
HIE	human intracranial electrophysiology
HME	hot-melt extrusion
HNWI	high-net-worth individuals
HPE	human performance enhancement
IA	impact assessment
IA	Internet addictions
ICT	information and communication technologies
IoB	Internet of bodies
IoT	Internet of things
MBE	moral bioenhancement
MDD	major depressive disorder
MIA	medical imaging analysis
MlE	Moral enhancement
ML	machine learning
MODY	maturity-onset diabetes of the young
MRI	magnetic resonance imaging
MRT	mitochondrial replacement therapy
NDD	neurodevelopmental disorder
NFC	near-field communication
NLP	natural language processing
NSRD	National Security Research Division
NwHIN	nationwide health information network
OCD	obsessive-compulsive disorder
OLD	obesity and lifestyle diseases
PA	predictive analytics
PDSE	predicting drug side effects
PE	physical enhancement
PED	performance-enhancing drugs
PET	positron emission tomography
PHCPI	Primary Health Care Performance Initiative
PMM	patient monitoring and management
PPP	purchasing power parity
PT	personalised treatment

QUALY	quality-adjusted life years
R&D	research and development
RFID	radio-frequency identification
RM	remote monitoring
RTP	radiation therapy planning
SCID	severe combined immunodeficiency
SETI	Search for ExtraTerrestrial Intelligence
SMA	spinal muscular atrophy
SSWAD	smart somatosensory wearable assistive device
STO	Science and Technology Organization
TALEN	transcription activator-like effector nucleases
TDCS	transcranial direct current stimulation
TMS	transcranial magnetic stimulation
UHC	universal health coverage
UHNWI	ultra-high-net-worth individuals
VS	virtual screening
VSP	vital signs profile
WCD	wearable cardioverter defibrillator
WEF	World Economic Forum
WHO	World Health Organization
WONCA	World Organization of National Colleges, Academies and Academic Associations of General Practitioners/Family Physicians
4IR	Fourth Industrial Revolution

Introduction

The Fourth Industrial Revolution (4IR) is a multidimensional phenomenon which is emerging and developing before our eyes. It is resulting in unprecedented changes in terms of scale and depth in every dimension of human life including but not limited to economic, social, cultural, and environmental areas. This is one of the reasons why 4IR is the subject of intense interest of researchers representing various scientific disciplines. One of the areas of considerable and far-reaching impact of 4IR is the health sector considering from both societal (public health) and individual (health of individual people) perspectives. Here one can observe the emergence of a phenomenon which is directing *Homo sapiens* to a new and unknown area of human biology, changing the path of evolution aka human enhancement (augmentation). It is defined as an intervention (a human action of any kind) in the biology or psychology of a person that either increases species-typical normal functioning above the statistically typical levels or produces a new capacity that normal human beings do not possess. Keeping in mind that 4IR is considered a time of cyber-physical systems combined with a fusion of technologies that is blurring the lines between the physical, digital, and biological spheres (Schwab, 2016), one can maintain that HE is the essence of 4IR.

Human Enhancement Technologies and Health Care Policy aims to present the idea, scope, trends, and main challenges of HE in the contemporary world from the health policy and healthcare systems perspective, with an emphasis on economic (especially financial) and managerial determinants. Such an attempt contributes to the most recent of Coenen's finding that '… since the mid-2000s, human enhancement has been discussed widely in bioethics, neuroethics, and science and technology studies including technology assessment, and to some extent in research policy and sports policy' (Coenen, 2024, p. 27). The dominant role in researching HE played by Western bioethicists and philosophers is also acknowledged by others (Sachdev, 2022; López, 2023). This means that this book can be seen as a contribution to the current research on HE being done so far primarily by sociologists, anthropologists, political scientists, lawyers, and medical scientists.

The book consists of four chapters. The first chapter 'The Fourth Industrial Revolution and human enhancement'[1] shows how the Fourth

DOI: 10.4324/9781003449584-1

Industrial Revolution (4IR) is impacting healthcare systems through artificial intelligence (AI), information and communication technologies (ICT), new products, new services and innovative technologies, as well as big data (BD). Examples of new products include new medicines, medical devices, and implants, while new services are represented by telemedicine and eHealth. Examples of emerging technologies are genetic engineering, nanotechnologies, neurotechnologies, and nanorobotics. The chapter shows that all the above-mentioned 4IR outcomes with the exception being telemedicine and eHealth, directly impact human enhancement which is considered as the culmination of the 4IR, the best reflecting its *differentia specifica*.

The second chapter, Human enhancement: Scope, forms, and trends, presents HE as an emerging, heterogeneous, and difficult-to-monitor phenomenon. It introduces some limitations of HE measurement, monitoring, and assessment, followed by the identification of leading scientific journals' publications from 2020. The main body of the chapter is the presentation of four basic forms of HE: cognitive, physical, mood, and moral supported by the list of specific technologies and techniques used for HE. Trends and tendencies regarding HE concludes the chapter.

Chapter 3, Challenges of contemporary healthcare systems, aims to present the key challenges faced by national healthcare systems, especially their financing on global, supranational, and national levels. Two challenges are considered dominating: the growing demand for health services, and the rising costs. These are connected with the growing demand for high-quality health services (prices of which are leveraged by fast-growing markets of sophisticated medical devices and technologies), and the continuous pressure to increase efficiency and effectiveness.

Chapter 4, Human enhancement challenges, presents the most important challenges human enhancement is facing regarding legal, financial, social and societal, managerial, and technological spheres.

The book concludes that HE remains in the very first stage of development (*in statu nascendi*) and is intensively researched. Qualitative methods dominate. Economic analyses of HE are rare if existing. The phenomenon of HE is not unambiguously defined because its definitions vary, and despite its far-reaching consequences for individuals and societies, it is not regulated by current laws. HE has four main forms: *cognitive enhancement, physical enhancement, mood enhancement, and moral enhancement.* Cognitive enhancement: brain-computer interfaces (BCI), deep brain stimulations (DBS), optogenetics, transcranial direct current stimulations (TDCS), and transcranial magnetic stimulation (TMS) seems to possess a special meaning for individual people as well as societies, and countries. Rare HE procedures remain in an experimental phase and are financed either by governmental R&D programs or by individuals using private money since HE cannot be financed by standard health insurance schemes. The dominance of private financing of HE may lead to the deepening and further growth of social disparities and inequalities raising a serious challenge for health policy. HE procedures should be treated as inevitable since they are being pushed by technological development (that cannot be stopped) and are rooted in the competitive nature of humans (in its Darwinian sense which cannot be eliminated at the current stage of homo sapiens' evolution). Consequently, appropriate laws and/or regulations including adequate HE management must be elaborated and implemented without unnecessary delay. Research on HE should be intensified, with an emphasis on the use of quantitative methods. Noting the existence of an objective difficulty related to the legal regulation of a phenomenon that is not yet known and adequately described, it can be concluded that there is no other way.

The book is descriptive and is based on the recent publications stored in EBSCO, MEDLINE, ScienceDirect, and Web of Science. ChatGPT (OpenAI) was used in Chapter 1 and Chapter 2.

Note

1 This chapter is an extension and update of the article 'The Fourth Industrial Revolution and the healthcare system' (Klich, 2022).

References

Coenen, C. (2024). Spotlights on the history of human enhancement discourse. In Jotterand, F., Ienca, M. (Eds). *The Routledge Handbook of the Ethics of Human Enhancement*, Routledge, pp. 18–29.

Klich, J. (2022). The Fourth Industrial Revolution and the healthcare system. In Ćwiklicki, M., Duplaga, M., Klich, J. (Eds). *The Digital Transformation of Healthcare*, Routledge, pp. 1–16.

López, B.R. (2023). Experimental bioethics and the case for human enhancement. In Viciana, H., Gaitán, A., Aguiar, F. (Eds). *Experiments in Moral and Political Philosophy*, Routledge, pp. 270–289.

Sachdev, V. (2022). 'Beyond' human enhancement – taking the developing country's perspective seriously. *Asian Bioethics Review*, 14(2), 169–182, 10.1007/s41649-021-00193-z.

Schwab, K. (2016). The Fourth Industrial Revolution. What it means, how to respond, https://www.weforum.org/agenda/2016/01/the-fourth-industrial-revolution-what-it-means-and-how-to-respond, accessed 23.12.2023.

1 The Fourth Industrial Revolution and human enhancement

1.1 The meaning of the Fourth Industrial Revolution

The Fourth Industrial Revolution (4IR) is defined as an economic and social phenomenon driven, among others, by the development of artificial intelligence (AI) (Dahl, 2019; Chakraborty et al., 2022), robotics, the Internet of Things (IoT), autonomous vehicles, 3D printers, nanotechnology, additive manufacturing, neurotechnology, biotechnology, materials engineering, energy storage, quantum computers, etc. Although the 4IR is *in statu nascendi*, it is rapidly developing and is subject to intensive research. Research findings show that it is having an increasing impact on all dimensions and aspects of human life, including health. This process should be monitored and assessed especially concerning new and emerging technologies. Here various types of impact assessment (IA): social, environmental, human rights, ethical, health, technology, privacy, etc. should be used to analyse, evaluate, and manage the intended and unintended positive and negative consequences of planned interventions (Rodrigues, Diez Rituerto, 2022).

As Karl Schwab the founder of the World Economic Forum and the creator of the term the 'Fourth Industrial Revolution' puts it, we will have to 'understand and shape the new technology revolution, which entails nothing less than a transformation of humankind' (Schwab, 2016a, p. 7). The phrase 'transformation of humankind' is by no means an exaggeration in this context.

The 4IR entails far-reaching and system-wide changes due to its three essential characteristics: (1) fast pace, (2) breadth and depth of expansion, and (3) a sweeping impact on all spheres of human life. These changes result in, among other things, 'a fusion of technologies that is blurring the lines between the physical, digital, and biological spheres' (Schwab, 2016b).

The interpenetration of these three worlds with sophisticated technologies can be considered as the specific difference between the 4IR and the previous three industrial revolutions. In such a context, of key importance are the consequences of these processes, including in particular, the gradual disappearance of the boundary between man and machine. This is a two-way process, which involves, on the one hand, equipping machines with functions and characteristics inherent to humans (using AI) and, on the other

DOI: 10.4324/9781003449584-2

hand, equipping humans with a range of devices (including implants) and/or applications that expand their physical and cognitive capabilities to an unprecedented degree, known in the literature as human enhancement (HE).

1.2 4IR and healthcare systems

Health systems can be understood 'as comprising all the organizations, institutions and resources that are devoted to producing health actions' (WHO, 2000, p. xi). In an expanded definition, the World Health Organization (WHO) asserts that a health system 'consists of all organizations, people and actions whose primary intent is to promote, restore or maintain health' (WHO, 2007, p. 2) as well as compensating for permanent disabilities, regardless of whether health agents are public, governmental, nongovernmental, or private (Figueras, McKee, 2012).

Consequently, a health system is understood in this book as all the interrelated institutions, organisations, and resources whose primary purpose is to preserve and improve health by responding to the legitimate needs of patients and protecting them against the costs of ill-health (WHO, 2020).

This meaning of a healthcare system implies the responsive character of the system – since it protects, maintains, and/or restores health. In this view, good health is both the starting point and the goal of the system. The health system defined above covers the supply side of a healthcare system, i.e., healthcare providers and services they offer as well as all institutions involved in this process. The supply side of the system should be supplemented by the demand side of the system represented by the patients with their health needs. It is also worth emphasising how important stakeholders in the healthcare system are households. They can be placed on the demand side as well as on the supply side of the healthcare system. Households represent the primary demand for health services but very often they provide unpaid care to sick, disabled, or senior relatives and thus not only supplement the healthcare providers but simultaneously make an important contribution to the financing of the healthcare system by committing their resources. This important role of households in the healthcare system is also worth noting from the perspective of strengthening the position of the patient in the system, through a system of reciprocity in the process of diagnosis and treatment. The latter is fuelled by exponentially increasing access to information and decreasing information gaps between physicians and patients. Such a concept of the supply and demand side of the healthcare system in the context of 4IR influence is presented in Figure 1.1.

Staying with the responsive character of the healthcare system it is worth extending the analysis of a healthcare system. Here the point of departure may be the proposals of Figueras and McKee (2012) who develop a framework to understand the contribution of health systems to societal well-being. According to this framework, health systems would contribute to well-being in three ways: (1) producing health which in itself is a component

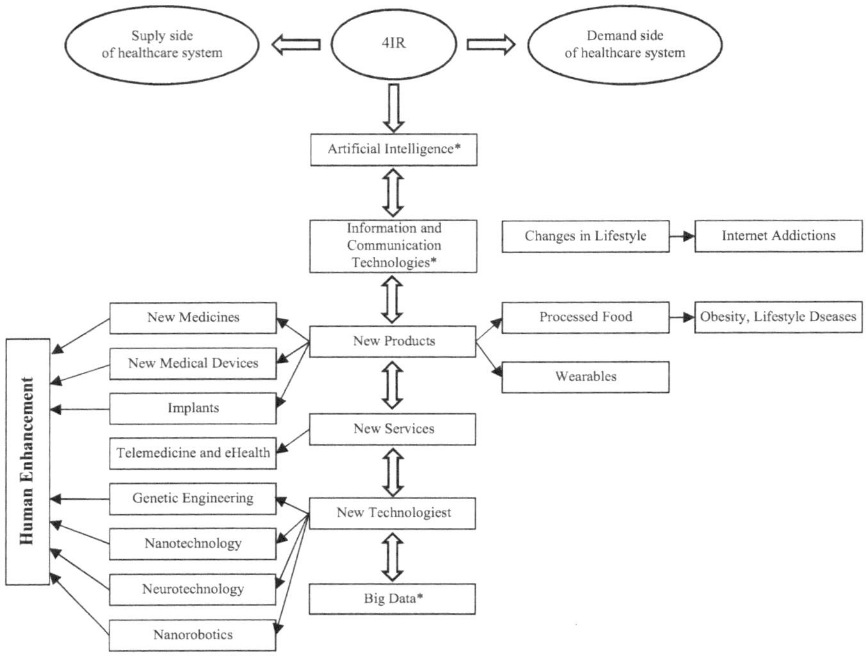

Figure 1.1 Directions of the impact of the Fourth Industrial Revolution on healthcare systems.

Source: Own elaboration based on Klich (2022), p. 3.

* Artificial intelligence, information and communication technologies and big data impact – on various degrees – nearly all the factors showed on the supply side of healthcare systems thus are not marked to make Figure 1.1. more transparent.

of well-being, (2) making health services a significant component of the economy and thus having health systems directly impact wealth, and (3) contributing directly to societal well-being '... because societies draw satisfaction from the existence of health services and the ability of people to access them, regardless of whether or not services are effective or indeed whether or not they are used' (Figueras, McKee, 2012, p. 8).

Naturally, societal well-being is also rooted in enhancing the health of individual people. Here we touch on an interesting question of whether or/and to what extent the healthcare system is responsible for improving the health of individual people. This in turn leads us to HE which can be interpreted as a tool for increasing individual well-being. For some of the researchers there is no structural conflict between individual and public context because HE '... should be a continuous project aiming to include everyone and maximize the public benefit' (Cabrera, 2017, p. 1). HE shows that a healthcare system does not just protect, maintain, and restore health but also enhances it. This can be seen as a new function of a healthcare system with a considerable impact on healthcare financing. HE and its financing will be elaborated on in the subsequent chapters.

The impact of 4IR on health is intensively researched. This is partly because of the progressive ethnicisation of medicine which is now a well-recognised phenomenon as the technical and technological advances themselves occur at an increasing pace, especially in surgery (Klipfel, 2017).

Among various publications on 4IR impact on health, one publication deserves special attention since the World Economic Forum (WEF) research on 4IR outperforms other institutions and research centres in this respect. The analysis of the developments between 2016 and 2018 allows the WEF to identify the following specific examples of breakthroughs:

- genetic engineering (especially genome editing) to cure genetic diseases, such as sickle cell disease and cystic fibrosis. Here germline editing has the potential to cure diseases with permanent intergenerational changes, while somatic genome editing can treat, control, and possibly cure acquired diseases,
- regenerative biology and medicine,
- tissue engineering,
- cancer genomics and immunotherapy,
- precision medicine,
- microbiome,
- optical imaging,
- optogenetics and brain-machine interface technology
- big data analytics,
- telehealth technologies (to send personal information to providers who can remotely diagnose health problems; IoT and other technologies will enable real-time monitoring; and technologies such as applications and wearables will help promote healthy behaviours and enable sustained behaviour modification),
- artificial intelligence (to transform all areas of health and medicine towards clinical decision-making) (Goy et al., 2019).

Khan et al. (2022) elaborate on the Digital Twin (DT) perspective of 4IR and the healthcare revolution. They present dozens of specific examples of the healthcare IoT, numerous applications of DT replicating the human body, which employs a large data set, and AI-powered models to replicate human physiology, machine learning (ML), deep learning (DL), and others.

As stated by researchers from the Global Future Council on the Future of Health and Healthcare, in the future humankind may expect two fundamental shifts that will reshape the healthcare industry.

> First, healthcare will be delivered as a seamless continuum of care, away from the clinic-centred point of care model and with a greater focus on

> prevention and early intervention. Second, health and healthcare delivery will focus on each person within their ecosystem, with a greater impact from people or patients themselves, often referred to as the consumerization of healthcare. (Goy et al., 2019, p. 5)

Although there are thousands of publications on 4IR the vast majority of them are focused on specific areas/fields of the healthcare system like home healthcare (Lee, Lim, 2017), occupational health (Min et al., 2019), clinical pharmaceutical services (Lobo Borba, Woranovicz Carvalho, 2023), clinical nutrition services (Kim, Seo, 2021), nursing as a profession (Aungsuroch, Gunawan, 2019), tumour images in diagnosing and treatment (Jayanthi et al., 2019), and healthcare management in the context of the growing amount of information (Jung, 2019). Comparatively scarce are publications aimed at the identification of the main direction and implications of such an impact (Melo e Castro, Araújo, 2020; Klich, 2021; Klich, 2022). This is partly because the 4IR is an emerging phenomenon and research on how it affects public health and the healthcare system is only gaining momentum. Melo e Castro and Araújo (2020) identify five key aspects of the 4IR on health:

- the impact on healthcare efficiency and effectiveness,
- the impact on government action,
- the impact on human resources,
- the impact on health system organisation,
- and the financial impact on the health sector.

One should notice, however, that the foundation behind this typology was interviews (consisting of four questions) with ten professionals (sic!) who had experience working in the health sector thus methodological soundness of their study remains problematic.

1.3 4IR impact on the healthcare sector

This book aims to contribute to the identification of the main ways 4IR affects healthcare systems. Based upon the characteristic traits of the 4IR and its impact documented in the literature it is possible to identify the main implications of the impact of the 4IR on the supply and demand side of healthcare systems (Figure 1.1).

It is assumed here that 4IR indirectly affects healthcare systems through the development of AI, information and communication technologies (ICTs), and big data (BD). The direct impact of 4IR is on the appearance of new products, services, and technologies. New products are represented by new medicines, new medical devices, and artificial implants. New services are telemedicine and eHealth and new technologies are represented by genetic engineering (GE), nanotechnology, neurotechnology, and nanorobotics. Needless to say, the factors listed above do not include the full list of directions of the impact of 4IR on health systems. As shown in Figure 1.1, all of these 4IR outcomes – except telemedicine and eHealth – affect HE which is, not without reason, the dominant element in Figure 1.1.

Figure 1.1 suggests that 4IR generally has a positive impact on a healthcare system because, on the demand side, we note obesity and lifestyle diseases (OLDs) (as a result of growing consumption of processed food), and internet addictions (IAs). There is electronic media, various gadgets, and stress and depression (broadly defined, including stress and depression resulting from job loss as a result of people being replaced by machines and/or computer applications in the workplace) standing behind these negative outcomes of 4IR on health. All these must be acknowledged, but will not be developed due to the profile of this book.

Now let us introduce factors placed on the supply side of a healthcare system. In Chapter 2 some of them will be developed further.

1.3.1 Artificial intelligence

Artificial intelligence (AI), not without reason, is considered as both one of the major outcomes of the 4IR and one of the most influential determinants (driving forces) of the 4IR. Setting aside the dilemma of whether AI might enable people to behave as if they have been cognitively enhanced or the opposite, AI technologies might make people less intelligent (Nyholm, 2023), let us focus on AI and healthcare (Chakraborty et al., 2022). Although issues related to the use of AI in medicine were discussed in the literature decades ago (Kaul et al., 2020), it is only in recent years that these discussions have accelerated significantly[1] and are researched in many centres, universities, and institutes.

Following John McCarthy's idea, the term 'artificial intelligence' is defined here as the art (not simply science) and engineering of making intelligent machines. There are the following subfields of AI identified in the literature:

- machine learning (ML),
- pattern identification and analysis,
- machines can improve with experience from provided data sets,
- deep learning (DL): composed of multi-layer neural networks that enable machines to learn and make decisions on their own,
- natural language processing (NLP): a process that enables computers to extract data from human language and make decisions based on that information, and
- computer vision (CV): a process by which a computer gains information and understanding from a series of images or videos (Kaul et al., 2020, p. 808).

AI can assist in data collection, processing, and use (Flores et al., 2023), including the identification of correlations which are notoriously difficult to capture using standard data and methods. This, in turn, can be of great importance, for example, in epidemiological research, and the personalisation of medicinal products and therapies. AI can be used also for patient involvement and commitment (Mukherjee et al., 2023).

Concerning the size of the market of AI in medicine, one may observe its impressive dynamic. In 2023, the anticipated market volume of AI in the health sector was $14.6 billion compared to estimated at $102.7 billion in 2028 (Statista, after Sen, 2024). In 2022, the medical and healthcare sectors attracted the most AI-related private investments ($6.05 billion) followed by data management, processing, and the cloud ($5.85 billion), and financial technology ($5.52 billion) (Sen, 2024).

Among the numerous ways of using AI in medicine, four leading sectors can be distinguished:

- medical imaging analysis (MIA),
- diagnosis and decision support (DDS),
- drug discovery and development (DDD),
- personalisation of treatment (PT).

MIA refers primarily to radiology and pathology. In radiology, AI algorithms can assist radiologists in detecting abnormalities in X-rays, magnetic resonance imagings (MRIs), and CT scans. They can help identify signs of diseases like cancer, fractures, and cardiovascular conditions. There are already several research studies suggesting that ML and DL models can perform as well as or better than humans at key healthcare tasks, such as diagnosing diseases and detecting malignant tumours from radiology images (Shandhi, Dunn, 2022, p. 2). In pathology, AI aids pathologists in analysing tissue samples and identifying patterns in slides for quicker and more accurate diagnoses. ML/DL models have been used to examine histopathology images which can contain billions of pixels and are difficult to process without computer-aided diagnosis (Shandhi, Dunn, 2022, p. 3).

DDS refers to clinical decision support systems (CDSS) and differential diagnosis (DD). In CDSS, AI can assist doctors in diagnosing diseases and suggesting treatment plans by analysing patient data, medical records, and the latest research (Thermolia et al., 2015; Braun et al., 2021; Herishanu, 2022). One should acknowledge, however, that there is still a lack of empirical evidence supporting the effectiveness of CDSS (Cresswell et al., 2023). In DD applications, AI systems help physicians consider a range of potential diagnoses based on symptoms and patient history (Skuban-Eiseler et al., 2023).

Within the framework of DDD, virtual screening (VS) and predicting drug side effects (PDSEs) play the leading role. In VS, computer-aided drug design (CADD), and other AI tools, synthesis has a positive impact on the discovery of natural moieties (*the part of a molecule or ion – excluding appended inactive portions that is responsible for the physiological or pharmacological action of a drug substance*) with therapeutic importance (Shreya et al., 2023). AI models predict the interaction between drug compounds and target proteins, helping identify potential drug candidates (Kang et al., 2022; Lin et al., 2018). AI is also used for drug database searches (Feng, Wei, 2023). In PDSE, AI is used to predict the potential adverse effects of drugs by analysing molecular structures and databases of known side effects (Khan et al., 2021).

PT can be further divided into personalised medicine (PM), drug dosage optimisation (DDO), and radiation therapy planning (RTP). Concerning PM, AI analyses genetic data to tailor treatment plans based on a patient's genetic makeup, enhancing precision and effectiveness (Shandhi, Dunn, 2022). For DDO, AI models calculate optimal drug dosages (Dasa et al., 2023) based on patient factors, such as age, weight, genetics, and other medical data. For RTP, AI helps oncologists plan radiation therapy by optimising treatment parameters and predicting potential side effects (Yang et al., 2022).

Apart from the four dominant sectors indicated above, there are a few other areas of AI applications that are used. Here epidemiological forecasting (EF) and clinical trials and research (CTR) deserve attention. EF AI models can predict disease outbreaks and trends by analysing large data sets, aiding public health authorities in planning interventions (Hutchinson et al., 2023; Onno et al., 2023). Since CTR involves large human and financial resources and requires complex legal solutions (apart from ethical dilemmas), the involvement of AI in optimising CTR is of great importance. AI optimises clinical trial designs, patient recruitment, and data analysis, accelerating the development of new treatments (Delso et al., 2021).

Among other applications of AI in medicine, one may mention patient monitoring and management (PMM), and NLP.

PMM can be divided into remote monitoring (RM) and predictive analytics (PA). RM has been already introduced in the form of medical devices. AI-powered wearables and sensors track patient vital signs, enabling remote monitoring and timely intervention for chronic conditions. While RM is reactive, PA is proactive. It translates streaming clinical data into a real-time visual estimation of patient risks and allows for evolving acuity assessments and detection of clinical deterioration while the patient is in a pre-symptomatic state (Keim-Malpass, Moorman, 2021). PA is used primarily in cardiology (Monfredi et al., 2023) and neurology (Pandit et al., 2022).

NLP is tightly connected to electronic health records (EHRs) and helps extract valuable insights from unstructured clinical notes (Liang et al., 2023), improving care coordination and research.

AI is also used for integrating uncertainty techniques in healthcare applications of ML and DL models. This can provide valuable insights and practical solutions to manage uncertainty in real-world medical data, ultimately improving the accuracy and reliability of medical diagnoses and treatment recommendations (Seoni et al., 2023).

Lastly, is the birth of the Chat Generative Pre-Trained Transformer (ChatGPT), generating great potential for healthcare applications. The current version of ChatGPT can provide accurate and practical information for doctors and patients, help healthcare professionals diagnose and treat, promote medical education, and improve the accuracy and efficiency of the healthcare system, etc. (Zhang et al., 2023).

1.3.2 Information and communication technologies

The role of information and communication technologies (ICTs) in health-care systems cannot be overestimated. ICTs play a crucial role in modern healthcare across various aspects, improving patient care, streamlining operations, and enhancing the overall healthcare system.

First, ICTs enable the creation of a system for obtaining, analysing and transferring basic information in the form of EHRs. An EHR provides healthcare professionals with easy access to patient histories, medications, and test results and enables the sharing of patient data among different healthcare providers and institutions. This serves to improve accuracy and reduce errors in patient care by ensuring that up-to-date information is available to all authorised personnel. EHRs can be supplemented by information such as heart rate, sleep patterns, and activity levels transferred from wearable health devices (WHD) like smartwatches and fitness trackers (WHDs will be discussed in more detail later in this chapter).

Second, ICTs contribute to health services provisions. Here one can distinguish between direct and indirect forms. In the first group, one can find medical imaging (ICT supports the storage and sharing of medical images such as X-rays, MRI, and computed tomography (CT) scans), and remote monitoring (ICT enables continuous monitoring of patients with chronic conditions). Healthcare providers receive real-time data, allowing for timely interventions and reduced hospital readmissions. The second group is represented by decision support systems (DSS). ICT tools offer clinical decision support through algorithms and data analysis. Healthcare professionals can access evidence-based guidelines and recommendations to assist in diagnosis and treatment decisions and adding to administrative efficiency. ICT streamlines administrative tasks, such as appointment scheduling, billing, and claims processing, reducing administrative costs and improving efficiency. Telemedicine connects doctors and patients (allowing for e-visits, e-prescriptions, and e-referrals but also for telesurgery), and doctors with each other (for image interpretation or consultations) and eHealth may be placed in between these two groups.

Third, ICT contributes to the dissemination of information. ICT supports health analytics and big data (BD), helping healthcare organisations analyse vast amounts of data to identify trends, predict disease outbreaks, and improve resource allocation, and research and education (ICT supports medical research by providing access to vast databases, promoting collaboration among researchers, and accelerating the development of treatments and therapies). ICT contributes to medical research by providing access to vast databases, promoting collaboration among researchers, and accelerating the development of treatments and therapies.

1.3.3 *New products*

The presentation of products originating from the 4IR and implemented in healthcare sectors will be limited to three broad categories: medicines, medical devices, and implants.

1.3.3.1 *New medicines*

The global pharmaceutical market is expected to grow in the upcoming years across the globe despite a recent slowdown in key markets. The reasons are simple: an ageing and growing population, rising income levels, emerging medical conditions, and the emergence of new diseases. The global pharmaceutical market has experienced significant growth in recent years. In 2022, the total global pharmaceutical market was estimated at $1.48 trillion (Mikulic, 2023a), and for 2023 it was estimated at $1.57 trillion. The pharmaceutical market plays a key role in how people get medications and what people pay for medication. However, some markets are better for pharmaceutical companies than others (ReportLinker, 2023).

Globally, the United States has emerged as the leading market for pharmaceuticals, followed by a group of emerging markets. Emerging markets can include middle and low-income countries such as Brazil, India, Russia, Colombia, and Egypt. Despite increasing revenues globally, the Latin American region accounts for the lowest share of the global pharmaceutical market's revenues.

The top pharmaceutical products sold globally include Humira, Eliquis, and Revlimid. Many of these pharmaceuticals are approved to treat multiple chronic conditions or cancers. Oncologics is the top therapeutic class for drug sales globally, followed by antidiabetics. However, the sales of drugs for autoimmune diseases and diabetes have experienced some of the largest growth in spending in recent years (Mikulic, 2023a). North America is expected to retain its leading position in the global pharmaceuticals market sales with a market share of 45.33% in 2023 improving on its market share compared to 2017. Europe on the contrary is expected to see a decline in its market share (sales) and be worth 20.24% of the global pharmamaceuticals industry in 2023. The Asia Pacific pharmaceuticals market is expected to retain its second position with a market share of 24.07% in sales in 2023. Latin America, the Middle East and Africa (MEA) regions are expected to retain 7.53% and 2.96% market share of the global pharmaceuticals sales market in 2023 (ReportLinker, 2023).

Oncology, pain therapy, and antidiabetics are among the drugs that bring in the most pharmaceutical revenue.

The largest global pharmaceutical markets are the United States and Europe. In the United States as of August 2023, according to the Center for Drug Evaluation and Research (CDER), there were 34 new drugs and therapeutic biological products approved[2] (as compared to 37 in 2022). It is worth remembering that in the United States, the number of newly registered drugs has shown an upward trend since 2008 (Mikulic, 2023b). The process of development of new drugs in the United States is intensive. As of December 2020, 560 new medicines were in development for pediatric conditions alone and hundreds of others for diabetes, neurological disorders, and mental health. The new drug development process is long and costly. In 1990, almost 15% of the revenue generated by the US pharmaceutical industry was spent on research and development for new medicines, and in 2021, the percentage stood at over 21% (Mikulic, 2023b). In 2021, research and development spending in the pharmaceutical industry[3] totalled some $238 billion globally compared to $137 billion in 2012 (Mikulic, 2023c). To cut the rising costs of new drug development, a growing number of drug manufacturers are outsourcing large parts of research and development (R&D), mostly to clinical research organisations. Another important development is the use of big data in clinical research. Thus, predictive modelling is possible which uses clinical and molecular data to develop safer and more efficient drugs. Particularly, real-time or real-world evidence is becoming a greater interest. This makes cooperation with technology companies necessary and includes data gathered from various sources, even social media (Mikulic, 2023c).

In Europe in 2022, the European Medicines Agency (EMA) recommended for authorisation 89 new medicines and 41 new active substances (European Medicines Agency, 2022). It should be noted that between 2020 and 2023 the number of marketing authorisation application evaluations decreased and in June 2023 there were 44 applications (out of which 35 were approved) (European Medicines Agency, 2023, p. 2). Taking into account the diminishing share of Europe in the global pharmaceutical market and the decreasing number of new drugs and substances approved by EMA, there is a ground to maintain that Europe is losing its position in the global pharmaceutical development market.

One should also acknowledge that the growing supply of new and innovative pharmaceuticals results in higher costs for healthcare systems and households.

Another distinct category worth mentioning when discussing the impact of the 4IR on the market for new pharmaceuticals and health technologies is drug personalisation and the individualisation of treatment (individual therapies). Thanks to advances in genomics personalised medicines are becoming more widely available. Personalised medicines or precision medicine refers to tailoring medical treatments, including drug therapies, to the individual characteristics of each patient. This approach takes into account factors such as a person's genetic makeup, molecular profile, medical history, and lifestyle to optimise the effectiveness and minimise the side effects of treatments. It would not be possible without the developments in immunotherapy. In recent years, immunotherapies have been developed that harness the body's immune system to fight diseases like cancer. Personalised medicine can help identify patients who are most likely to benefit from these treatments based on their immune profiles. Precision medicine can also help identify individuals at risk of adverse drug reactions or allergies based on their genetic predispositions. This knowledge allows healthcare providers to avoid prescribing medications that could cause harm. The goal is to provide the right treatment to the right patient at the right dose and time.

The size and scope of drug personalisation are continuously expanding as our understanding of genetics, molecular biology, and other relevant fields improves. Advances in technology, such as high-throughput sequencing and molecular profiling techniques, enable more comprehensive and precise personalisation.

As indicated earlier genetic information plays a significant role in drug personalisation. Genetic testing can identify variations in genes that impact how a person metabolises drugs, responds to treatments, and experiences side effects. An example is the use of pharmacogenomics to determine the optimal dosage of warfarin, a blood-thinning medication, based on a person's genetic profile.

Personalised medicines are used broadly but cardiology, oncology, neurology, and psychiatry are the leading disciplines focusing on personalised medicines. In cardiology, genetic factors can contribute to cardiovascular diseases. Personalised medicine can help identify individuals at higher risk and guide the selection of appropriate interventions. In oncology, tumour profiling helps identify specific genetic mutations or biomarkers that can guide the selection of targeted therapies, such as HER2-targeted treatments for breast cancer or BRAF inhibitors for melanoma. Genetic testing can assist in diagnosing and selecting treatments for neurological conditions like epilepsy, where the choice of antiepileptic drugs can be influenced by a person's genetic factors. Since genetic variations can affect susceptibility to infectious diseases and responses to treatments, personalised medicine approaches are being explored while fighting against infectious diseases in areas such as HIV and hepatitis C treatments.

However, it's important to note that while personalised medicine holds promise, challenges such as data privacy, ethical considerations, and the integration of complex genetic information into clinical decision-making still need to be addressed for its widespread adoption. This refers also to individual therapies.

Using sophisticated tools and techniques, targeted individual therapies are being identified for individual patients at the right time in a consistent and standards-based manner. As indicated above, personalised medicines enable personalised therapies.

Targeted therapies can be matched with developments in other technologies, which constitute 4IR starting from 3D printing and ending up with artificial intelligence. Successes in 3D printing technology may lead to intensive personalisation of treatment (Seoane-Viaño et al., 2021). 3D printing is constantly developed and as Khong Tan et al. (2018) showed hot-melt extrusion and fused deposition modelling can be combined into one integrated continuous processing platform for the use of advanced pharmaceutical applications.

One may allude to several examples of targeted individual therapies. As mentioned above, targeted cancer therapies focusing on specific molecular alterations in tumours are HER2 targeted therapy where HER2-positive breast cancers can be treated with drugs like trastuzumab (monoclonial antibody) that specifically target the HER2 protein overexpressed in these cancers and BRAF inhibitors. In another case, melanoma patients with BRAF mutations, drugs like vemurafenib target the mutated protein to inhibit cancer growth. One may also mention personalised cancer vaccines such as neoantigen-based cancer vaccines designed to target mutations unique to a patient's tumour.

Another kind of individual therapy could be pharmacogenomics-based dosage optimisation which determines the optimal drug dosage based on a patient's genetic makeup. An example could be warfarin dosage. Genetic testing can help determine the right dose of the blood thinner warfarin based on a patient's genetic variation in metabolising enzymes.

Immunotherapy, especially concerning cancer, is another example. Here one may find chimeric antigen receptor (CAR-T) cell therapy. It involves modifying a patient's immune cells to target cancer cells expressing specific antigens. It is the most advanced and personalised technology used in haemato-oncological treatment, which consists of producing medicine for each patient based on their lymphocytes (Stelmach, 2019).

Gene replacement therapies are another example. They treat genetic disorders by introducing functional copies of faulty genes. An example is spinal muscular atrophy (SMA). In this case, gene therapy like Zolgensma replaces the missing or mutated *SMN1* gene responsible for SMA.

One may point at some other individual therapies like tailoring diabetes treatment based on the patient's genetic and metabolic characteristics (like maturity-onset diabetes of the young – MODY), antiretroviral therapy in HIV-positive patients (individuals with a specific genetic mutation [CCR5 Delta32], cystic fibrosis therapies [cystic fibrosis transmembrane conductance regulator – CFTR] modulators where drugs like ivacaftor and tezacaftor/ivacaftor target specific CFTR gene mutations in individuals with cystic fibrosis), or Alzheimer's disease therapies aimed at ApoE4, a genetic risk factor for Alzheimer's disease that may guide personalised prevention strategies.

These examples illustrate personalised therapies across various medical fields and, of course, are not a representative sample.

1.3.3.2 New medical devices

New medical devices and appliances constitute a diverse and broad-ranging category thus in this book only selected issues are introduced.

The medical devices and equipment market is large and rapidly growing. In 2022, the global value of the medical devices and equipment market was $512.29 billion (Fortune Business Insights, 2023). The rising demand for medical devices is due to the rising prevalence of chronic diseases and the shift towards homecare settings (especially referring to portable devices). The global market is fragmented with players such as Medtronic, Johnson & Johnson Services, Inc., Abbott, and Skyter, accounting for a majority of the medical devices market share in 2022.

In this book, medical devices are divided into two groups based on the end user: medical devices *sensu stricto* (purchased mainly by hospitals and physicians) and wearable medical devices (purchased by patients and individuals). Such a dual division is arbitrary and simplified, because, for example, it does not cover the use of technologies known in other sectors and adopted/implemented in the healthcare sector. For example, virtual reality can be successfully used in the treatment of certain mental illnesses (Pons et al., 2022).

Coming back to our typology, the first group is composed of general surgical devices, in vitro diagnostics, cardiovascular devices, orthopaedic devices, diagnostic imaging, minimally invasive surgery, wound management, diabetes care, ophthalmic, dental, nephrology, and others. Some of them like wound management, diabetes care, and dental devices can be purchased also by individuals. This may also refer to robots which can be used for rehabilitation (Fareh et al., 2023).

Wearable medical devices constitute a large and heterogenous group. They have become increasingly popular as technology advances and people become more interested in tracking and improving their health. These devices come in various forms and serve different purposes. They can overlap in functionalities and features. Some of them are used for day-to-day treatment, and some of them are used for health improvement. An example of a wearable medical device used to treat people with visual impairments is the feelSpace belt. This belt can map information of the magnetic north to vibrotactile stimulation around the waist. This helps vision impaired and blind people with navigation and spacial orientation. The feelSpace users experienced substantial changes in their space perception. The belt's vibrating signal changed to a kind of spatial information over time while the belt's appeal and perceived usability increased. The belt also induced certain emotional states (Kaspar et al., 2014).

The choice of device depends on individual health goals and preferences. Additionally, advancements in technology continue to expand the capabilities of wearable health devices, blurring the lines between different types and offering more comprehensive health insights.

Based on their functionalities and purpose one may distinguish[4] between two broad categories: devices used directly in medical treatment and devices supporting health promotion.

The first group consists of medical monitoring devices. They play a crucial role in monitoring and managing various health conditions. Examples are blood pressure monitors, pulse oximeters, fetal monitors, continuous (i.e., throughout the day and night) glucose monitoring systems (CGMS), electrocardiogram (ECG/EKG) monitors, wearable cardioverter defibrillators (WCDs), respiratory monitors, home hemodialysis monitors, and home sleep study devices.

Blood pressure monitors help to monitor and manage hypertension. They provide readings of systolic and diastolic pressure, as well as pulse rate. Equally simple are pulse oximeters measuring oxygen saturation in the blood and pulse rate. They are commonly used to monitor respiratory conditions and overall oxygen levels. Fetal monitoring devices are used during pregnancy to monitor the heart rate and movement of the fetus. They help ensure the baby's well-being during pregnancy and labour. Slightly more complicated are CGMS. They use sensors inserted under the skin to transmit data to a device, reducing the need for frequent fingerstick tests. They can also be synchronised with insulin pumps. One of the latest inventions in this group of wearables is the wearable antenna built of textile material, it is highly comfortable to wear and has numerous benefits, such as lightweight, compact size, and low cost. The main purpose or application of this antenna is to observe three levels of glucose, i.e., hypoglycemia, hyperglycemia, and normal glucose (Ghodake, Hogade, 2023).

ECG monitors record the electrical activity of the heart over time. They can help detect irregular heart rhythms and other cardiac issues. WCDs are wearable devices that continuously monitor heart rhythms and deliver a shock if a life-threatening arrhythmia is detected. They provide a temporary solution while awaiting more permanent treatment. Respiratory monitors monitor lung function and help individuals with respiratory conditions such as asthma and chronic obstructive pulmonary disease (COPD) track their breathing patterns. Home hemodialysis monitors allow individuals with end-stage renal disease to perform hemodialysis at home while being monitored by medical professionals. From a technical perspective, medical professionals' monitoring can be included in virtually all wearable health devices depending on additional applications and health policies. However, one should mention remote patient monitoring systems. These comprehensive systems allow healthcare providers to remotely monitor patients' vital signs and health data. They can improve care for chronic conditions and postoperative care. Home sleep study devices monitor sleep patterns and breathing during sleep to diagnose sleep disorders like sleep apnea. They are often more convenient than in-lab sleep studies. Data obtained in this group of devices is often used by medical professionals.

The next group of wearable devices is composed of posture and activity correction devices and stress and relaxation devices. Both are used to improve health. The first category focuses on improving posture and overall body alignment. They often give feedback or reminders to help you maintain good posture and avoid prolonged inactivity. There are also wearables for rehabilitation like a smart somatosensory wearable assistive device (SSWAD) combined with wireless surface electromyography (sEMG) and exergame software and hardware technology (Chang et al., 2023). The second kind of wearables aims to manage stress through techniques like guided breathing, mindfulness, and relaxation exercises.

Since multifunctionality is nowadays an important driving force of innovation, it is logical that smart clothing and smartwatches appeared on the market. Smart clothing integrates technology directly into clothing and/or jewellery items. These garments can monitor various health metrics, including heart rate, breathing rate, body temperature, and posture. They offer a discreet way to track health without wearing a separate device. Smart clothing is on the rise, albeit still scarce (Ahsan et al., 2023). Smartwatches as versatile wearable devices offer health tracking along with other features like notifications, apps, and connectivity. They often include sensors for heart rate monitoring, GPS, and more. Data obtained in this group is used primarily by individuals themselves.

Activity trackers or fitness and sports-specific wearables constitute the last group. Activity trackers monitor your physical activity, including steps taken, distance travelled, and calories burned. They often include features like heart rate monitoring and sleep tracking. Fitness and sports-specific wearables are designed for specific sports or activities, such as running, cycling, swimming, and more. They often offer specialised features and metrics tailored to those activities. Data obtained is used for individual purposes, namely to measure (and compare) individual performance.

In the end, it is worth mentioning devices being prepared for production. For example, these are digestible microchips that signal whether the patient has taken the prescribed medication, and technologies capable of tracking a patient's gastric pH and transmitting relevant data (using Bluetooth technology) to his/her mobile phone and then to the monitoring centre, the attending physician or nurse. Another sophisticated measuring device is contact lenses for diabetics equipped with sensors that measure glucose levels in tears and relay this information to a smartphone and from there to a monitoring centre, etc.

All the above examples show that the impact of new technologies on medicine has been and will remain very strong. The progressive use of technology in medicine is now a well-recognised phenomenon as the technical and technological advances themselves occur at an increasing pace, especially in surgery (Klipfel, 2017).

1.3.4 Implants

Implants can refer to a wide range of medical devices or objects that are inserted into or attached to the human body for various purposes. Manufactured implants meet the criteria for medical devices and should therefore be subsumed under Section 1.3.3.2. The reason why they are discussed in a separate section reflects the growing importance of high-tech implants in blurring the boundary between man and machine. So it is not about simple dental implants – which continue to claim the largest share of the implant market – but extremely advanced ones, including those created using nanotechnology.

The global medical implants market size was valued at $90.24 billion in 2022 and is expected to reach $173.41 billion by 2032, poised to grow at a compound annual growth rate (CAGR) of 6.8% during the forecast period 2023 to 2032 (Precedence Research, 2023).

The global medical implants market is driven by the rising incidence of chronic diseases, improvements in surgical techniques and outcomes, patient acceptance of advanced medical implants, and an ageing population worldwide. Seniors are prone to various chronic diseases and consequently demand kidney implants, joints implants, eye implants, and heart implants (Precedence Research, 2023). The second factor in the growth of the global implant market is the desire to improve appearance (dental implants, breast implants, pectoral implants, deltoid implants, and cochlear implants) fuelled by growing disposable income (Precedence Research, 2023).

The largest implant market is the United States while Asia Pacific is the fastest-growing one. Leading companies on the global implant market are Medtronic Plc., Johnson & Johnson, Boston Scientific Corporation, Biotronik, LivaNova PLC, Globus Medical, Inc., NuVasive, Inc., Integra LifeSciences Holding Corporation, InstitutStraumann AG, and Conmed Corporation.

Based on product type the implant market can be divided into cardiovascular (pacemakers, defibrillators, implantable cardioverter-defibrillators, cardiac resynchronisation therapy [CRT] devices, stents, and artificial heart valves to treat heart-related conditions), orthopaedic (hip implants, knee implants, bionic hands, arms, legs, and feet), neurostimulators (deep brain stimulators, spinal cord stimulators, cochlear implants, and vagus nerve stimulators used to treat conditions like Parkinson's disease, chronic pain, and epilepsy), spinal (fusion implants, pedicle screw systems, artificial disc, interspinous process spacers, dynamic stabilisation implants, intradiscal, vertebroplasty and kyphoplasty, spinal cord stimulators), ophthalmic (intraocular lenses, retinal implants, bionic eyes), facial (for facial reconstruction, such as nose, ear, or eye implants for individuals who have lost facial features due to injury or illness or to enhance facial features, such as cheek, chin, or jaw implants), dental (surgically placing an artificial tooth root in the jawbone, microimplants), and breast (augmentation or reconstruction after mastectomy). If biomaterial is the criterium, one may distinguish between ceramic, metallic, polymers, and natural implants.

In the context of the 4IR, high-tech (bioelectronic or cybernetic) implants are particularly noteworthy. They refer to advanced medical devices or technologies that are surgically implanted into the human body to enhance or restore various functions. These implants can range from simple devices like pacemakers to complex systems that interface directly with the nervous system. They often incorporate electronics, sensors, and wireless communication to achieve their intended purposes. This group of medical devices includes technologically advanced cochlear implants aligned with speech recognition/processing software (Cosetti, Waltzman, 2011), the Gliadel Wafer intracranial implant (Ashby et al., 2016), which is a controlled-release formula for carmustine delivery directly into the space left after surgery to remove a portion of the brain. This new mode of delivery is expected to work better than other forms of carmustine and have fewer side effects.

From the human enhancement perspective, brain-computer interfaces (BCIs) and biohacking implants deserve special attention. BCIs are cutting-edge implants that establish a direct communication pathway between the brain and external devices. They have potential applications in assisting individuals with paralysis or neurological disorders. BCIs can enable users to control computers, and robotic limbs, or even communicate through thought alone like hands-free typing (Bosch, Mecacci, 2023). Research is ongoing to refine these technologies for various medical and non-medical purposes. Biohacking implants are examples of personal enhancement or experimentation. For example, radio-frequency identification (RFID) chips can be implanted for tasks like accessing secure areas, making contactless payments or storing medical data.

The application of 3D modelling in craniofacial surgery could be another example of the direct impact of 4IR on clinical practice. 3D modelling in craniofacial surgery changes the way surgeons are planning surgeries and graphic designers are designing custom implants.

> Advances in manufacturing processes and the ushering of additive manufacturing for the direct production of implants has eliminated the constraints of shape, size and internal structure and mechanical properties making it possible for the fabrication of implants that conform to the physical and mechanical requirements of the region of implantation. (Parthasarathy, 2014, p. 9)

A separate category of implants are such organs as hearts, livers, kidneys, and lungs obtained from genetically modified pigs for xenotransplantation (XT) in humans (Harisa et al., 2023).

The field of high-tech implants is rapidly evolving, driven by advancements in materials science, miniaturisation, wireless communication, and biotechnology. While these implants offer exciting possibilities for improving human health and capabilities, ethical and privacy considerations also come into play, particularly concerning data security, informed consent, and the potential long-term effects of implanting technology into the human body. Here an example could be a genetically engineered pig kidney attached in 2021 to a brain-dead patient who was sustained on life support. The kidney started working immediately for 54 hours (Fatima, Ebertz, 2021; Rabin, 2021). Another example of 2021 achievement could be an artificial heart with two ventricles (large chambers of the heart) and hydraulic pumps. The heart is made in parts of bovine heart tissue and is equipped with sensors and microprocessors. The sensors enable the heart to regulate blood flow according to the physical activities of the person, just as a normal heart would (Fatima, Ebertz, 2021).

1.3.5 *New services*

Among services which can be linked to the outcomes of 4IR, the most important are telemedicine and eHealth.

1.3.5.1 *Telemedicine and eHealth*

The 4IR contributes significantly to enhancing the service delivery process itself through eHealth and telemedicine. eHealth is an umbrella term defined broadly as the use of ICT for health (WHO, 2018). Telemedicine can be considered an important component of eHealth since it is defined as the performance of health services from a distance (WHO, 2022) by health professionals using ICT and the exchange of information to treat and educate patients to improve the quality of health. Consequently, various forms of telemedicine, each tailored to meet specific medical needs and situations can be divided into exchanging information and performing services from a distance. This distinction is not sharp because some activities can be placed in both of the above categories, but this does not disqualify the proposed division.

Exchanging information may have various forms:

1.3.5.1.1 STORE-AND-FORWARD (ASYNCHRONOUS TELEMEDICINE)

It involves the transmission of patient data, such as medical images, videos, lab results, or other diagnostic information, to a healthcare provider for later review and assessment (Das et al., 2022). This is particularly useful for specialists who need to analyse and provide recommendations without immediate patient interaction.

1.3.5.1.2 REMOTE PATIENT MONITORING

Remote patient monitoring (RPM) involves the use of devices to collect and transmit patient data to healthcare providers in real time (Kruklitis et al., 2022). This data can include vital signs, blood glucose levels, heart rate, blood pressure, and more. RPM is especially beneficial for managing chronic conditions like diabetes (De Luca et al., 2023; Jendly et al., 2023) and postoperative care.

1.3.5.1.3 MOBILE HEALTH (MHEALTH) APPLICATIONS

Mobile applications allow patients to communicate with healthcare providers, schedule appointments, access medical records, receive medication reminders, and even engage in video consultations through their smartphones or tablets. Although these applications are important for all, they are especially important for seniors (Lee et al., 2023).

1.3.5.1.4 REMOTE SURGICAL ASSISTANCE

Surgeons can use telemedicine to provide guidance and advice during surgical procedures conducted by other healthcare professionals in distant locations. This requires – among other things – adequate surgeons' education and preparation (Stone et al., 2022).

1.3.5.1.5 ONLINE HEALTH PORTALS ALLOW PATIENTS TO ACCESS ONLINE PLATFORMS TO REVIEW MEDICAL RECORDS, LAB RESULTS, AND OTHER HEALTH-RELATED INFORMATION

This empowers patients to take a more active role in managing their healthcare.

If the main goal of a patient is to receive treatment, to be diagnosed or to get a prescription, the following forms of performing services from a distance (synchronous telemedicine) can be used.

1.3.5.1.6 TELESURGERY – REMOTE SURGICAL SERVICE

It is an emerging surgical tool that utilises both robotic technology (example being DaVinci Surgical System) and wireless networking to connect patients and surgeons who are geographically distant. The future of surgery is transforming with the integration of such components of 4IR as the fifth-generation (5G) internet, AI, haptic feedback technology, 3-dimensional (3D) printing, nanotechnology, and high-definition (3D) cameras. 3D cameras allow a surgeon to see close-up views of the surgery site, not easily accessible. Robotic arms make it possible to access the areas in the body that are very hard to access. Accelerometer technology is useful to cancel out a surgeon's physiological tremor and help the surgeons' anxiety, resulting in improved surgical accuracy and overcoming the limitations associated with surgeons' dexterity. Improved surgical accuracy reduces the chances of damaging surrounding structures, and remarkably lessens the risks of blood loss, transfusions, and less risk of infection (Mohan et al., 2021). The main utility of telesurgery is its ability to overcome the limitations of conventional surgery, namely the geographical inaccessibility of rapid and high-quality surgical care, a surgeon shortage/logistical limitations of surgeon schedules, financial costs, and long-distance travel.

1.3.5.1.7 E-CONSULTATIONS AND TELEPHONIC CONSULTATIONS

Here we have real-time video consultations (live, interactive video communication between a patient and a healthcare provider, for example in cardiology (Khanji et al., 2023) or dermatology (Linkous et al., 2023) conducted remotely through a smartphone, a computer, or tablet. There are also traditional telephone calls between patients and healthcare providers that match this category (Perham, Keskar, 2023; Samia et al., 2023). While not as visually interactive as video consultations, telephonic consultations are a simple and effective way to provide medical advice and guidance which occurred to be intensively used during the COVID-19 pandemic (Carrera-Muñoz et al., 2023). Pharmacists can provide medication counselling, prescription reviews, and medication management services over the phone or through video calls (Ahmed et al., 2023; Lobo Borba, Woranovicz Carvalho, 2023).

Telemedicine and eHealth offer numerous benefits, such as increased accessibility to healthcare services, reduced travel and wait times, and improved convenience for patients. It should be acknowledged, that telemedicine played a fundamental role during the COVID-19 pandemic. The pandemic leveraged the usage of telemedicine to an unprecedented level. It is also worth mentioning that ICT, interactive chatbots, WhatsApp, and Facebook were used from the very beginning by WHO to communicate about various aspects of the COVID-19 pandemic.

1.3.6 New technologies

The list of new technologies originating from 4IR is extensive thus here it will be limited to genetic engineering, nanotechnology, neurotechnology, and nanorobotics.

1.3.6.1 Genetic engineering

Genetic engineering (GE) is a leading technology. It is a process that uses laboratory-based technologies to alter the DNA makeup of an organism. This may involve changing a single base pair (A-T or C-G), deleting a region of DNA or adding a new segment of DNA (NHGRI, 2023). Genetic engineering aims to modify the genes to enhance the capabilities of the organism beyond what is normal (which leads us to human enhancement discussed later). GE has been the leader in a wide range of achievements with significant impacts across various fields (Rehana, 2020) such as medical applications (e.g., mass-produced insulin, human growth hormones, follistim [for treating infertility], human albumin, monoclonal antibodies, antihaemophilic factors, vaccines, and many other drugs), gene therapy in cystic fibrosis, haemophilia, and certain types of blindness, and cancer treatments –

for example, Chimeric Antigen Receptor cell Therapy (CAR-T cell therapy), agricultural advancements (genetically modified crops, GMOs or *Golden Rice* – engineered rice able to produce beta-carotene), industrial and environmental applications (bioremediation, biofuel production), synthetic biology (creating novel organisms) or biological computers. GE helps to understand genetic contributions to diseases. It plays a role in uncovering the genetic components of various diseases, leading to a deeper understanding of their underlying mechanisms and potential avenues for treatment.

Among examples of GE applications in medicine one may find the following.

1.3.6.1.1 GENE THERAPY FOR GENETIC DISORDERS

Gene therapy involves introducing functional genes into cells to replace or correct defective ones (Li et al., 2023a; Zhang, Wu, 2023; Kumar et al., 2024). For instance, treatments have been developed for certain inherited diseases like severe combined immunodeficiency (SCID), and some types of inherited blindness. The spectacular Lulu and Nana case (see further) fits into this category. Gene therapy is considered an opportunity in many medical disciplines (Li et al., 2023a).

1.3.6.1.2 CLUSTERED REGULARLY-INTERSPACED SHORT PALINDROMIC REPEATS (CRISPR)-CAS9 GENE-EDITING TOOL

It was ranked second in the Global Top Ten Engineering Achievements in 2021 (Cui, 2021). Working like genetic scissors, this technology allows extremely precise and efficient genome editing. The CRISPR/Cas9 gene editing technology[5] has revolutionised molecular biology and holds profound potential for gene and tumour therapy, gene screening and detection, and the breeding and genetic modification of animals and plants. Researchers have used it to edit genes in human embryos to study various genetic conditions. However, this also raised ethical concerns about altering the germline (inheritable) DNA.

1.3.6.1.3 MITOCHONDRIAL REPLACEMENT THERAPY

Mitochondrial replacement therapy (MRT) aims to prevent the transmission of mitochondrial diseases from mother to child by replacing defective mitochondria with healthy ones from a donor egg (Sharma et al., 2020). This technique has been used in a limited number of cases but is considered as possessing considerable potential (Liu et al., 2023).

1.3.6.1.4 IMPROVED GENETIC DIAGNOSTICS

Advances in genetic engineering have led to more accurate and accessible genetic diagnostics, aiding in the identification of various diseases (Elander et al., 2022) and conditions, and enabling personalised treatment plans (Mota et al., 2017).

GE continues to play an important role in the personalisation of therapy and human enhancement. In China, in 2018, scientist He Jiankui claimed to have created the first genetically edited babies. It was revealed to the media that two girls nicknamed Lulu and Nana whose genomes had been edited were born. He Jiankui used CRISPR-Cas9 to edit embryos, disabling a gene that allows HIV to enter cells. The idea was to try to make the children resistant to AIDS (the girls' father was HIV positive). From the very beginning, this case was widely debated (Termanini, 2023) and restricted access to information about this procedure fuelled it even further. Some critics maintained that He Jiankui had no expertise in gene editing. He was sentenced to three years in a Chinese prison for practising medicine without a license. In 2023, after serving the sentence, he faced obstacles and critics as he tried to re-enter science. He Jiankui reported about his plans to develop affordable gene therapies for rare diseases, starting with the muscle-wasting condition Duchenne muscular dystrophy. In August 2023, it was unclear how the three children (it was a third child known as Amy) who grew from the embryos were doing (Ungar, 2023).

Apart from Lulu, Nana, and Amy's case, several successful landmark interventions have also been reported in recent years, including the correction of a defective gene in a patient with Hunter syndrome (mucopolysaccharidosis type II – a genetic disorder caused by a deficiency of the enzyme I2S), the genetic alteration of T-lymphocytes in cancer patients to prime them to attack and kill cancer cells. For the first time, a genetically modified bacteriophage was used to treat a bacterial infection in an antibiotic-resistant individual. A completely new form of DNA was also obtained, called Hachimoji DNA, which consists of four natural and four synthetic nucleobases. Animal research has also entered a new phase, as pig-monkey chimaeras (pigs with a proportion of monkey cells) were created in 2019. Interestingly enough while the latter raises a lot of ethical concerns, novel immunogenic chimaera protein (Saleki et al., 2022) or similar substances do not catch special attention.

GE raises ethical concerns, especially for chimaeras. The scientific community were working on developing guidelines and ethical frameworks for responsible genetic engineering (Sankar, Cho, 2015; Sandel, 2017). International summits and discussions took place to establish common standards.

1.3.6.2 Nanotechnology

Nanotechnology underpins what constitutes the *differentia specifica* of the 4IR, namely the blurring of the boundaries between man and machine. Nanotechnology can be perceived as an integration of multiple disciplines of science to develop advanced products in such sectors as manufacturing, agriculture, energy, textiles, or the environment. Concerning medicine, nanotechnology is utilised mainly for novel diagnostic modalities, novel therapeutics, and different nanotechnologies for improved theranostics (i.e., therapy and diagnostics). Nanotechnology refers to all the structures that are roughly in the range of 1–100 nm in size in at least one dimension. Even with this size limit, nanotechnology is generally designated to structures that are up to some hundred nanometres in size which are fabricated by bottom-up or top-down methods (Khurana et al., 2023, p. 1). Nanotechnology is based on nanomaterials which are engineered materials with nanoscale structures that exhibit unique properties compared to their bulk counterparts. They are used in various industries, including electronics, coatings, and medicine. Raffa et al. (2010) classified nanomaterials and found 11 current medical uses of nanotechnology (Raffa et al., 2010, p. 134). There are three main forms of nanomaterials broadly used: nanoparticles, nanotubes, and nanowires. Nanoparticles are tiny particles with dimensions on the nanoscale, used for drug delivery, imaging, and catalysis. Nanotubes are cylindrical carbon or other materials with remarkable electrical, mechanical, and thermal properties. Nanowires are ultra-thin wires with nanoscale diameters, used in electronics and sensors. Haleem et al. (2023, p. 72) present a more elaborate classification consisting of ten classes of nanotechnology-based materials, including, among others, dendrimers, liposomes, metal nanoparticles, polymer nanocomposites, and biodegradable polymers. It appears that the greatest opportunities for nanotechnology to cross the boundary between man and machine may come from nanosystems and molecular nanosystems, nano-bio-generators and nano-scaffoldings. Although the applications of nanotechnology may be diverse, it is not without reason that some see human health and the health sector as nanotechnology's most important domains (Jha et al., 2014).

Nanotechnology has the potential to revolutionise medicine by enabling precise diagnostics (Li et al., 2023b), targeted drug delivery (Mitra et al., 2017), and enhanced imaging techniques. Haleem et al. (2023) indicated wound treatment, antibacterial treatments, minimising damage to healthy cells, and nanomedicine diagnostic techniques as classical associated features and characteristics of nanotechnology for the medical domain (Haleem et al., 2023, p. 73).

There are several applications of nanotechnology in medical practice. They can be illustrated by the following examples.

1.3.6.2.1 NANOPARTICLE DRUG DELIVERY

Nanoparticles have a significant surface-area-to-volume ratio due to their nanoscale size, which allows them to absorb vast amounts of medications and move quickly throughout the bloodstream. Their increased surface area gives them distinct capabilities, as it increases their mechanical, magnetic, optical, and catalytic qualities, allowing them to be used in more pharmaceutical applications. Nanoparticles are classified into three areas based on their chemical composition: organic, inorganic, and carbon-based (Haleem et al., 2023, pp. 71–72). They may transport medicines to the exact place required, substantially improving their efficacy and restricting toxicity to other tissues in the body. Liposomes, polymer-based nanoparticles, and lipid nanoparticles are some examples. These nanoparticles can release drugs gradually, enhancing their therapeutic effect (Hsu et al., 2023).

1.3.6.2.2 TARGETED DRUG DELIVERY

It can be treated as a part of nanoparticle drug delivery. Nanoparticles can be functionalised with molecules that specifically bind to receptors on certain cells, allowing for targeted drug delivery (Ellipilli et al., 2023). This approach increases drug accumulation at the intended site and reduces off-target effects (Sharma et al., 2022).

1.3.6.2.3 CANCER TREATMENT

Nanoparticles can operate as molecular imaging agents within those devices and input cancer-related genetic alterations and tumour cell functional features. Gold nanoparticles, for instance, can be used to enhance the effects of radiation therapy (Ayyanaar, Kesavan, 2023). They can accumulate in cancer cells and enhance radiation damage while sparing healthy tissues. Additionally, targeted nanoparticles can deliver chemotherapeutic agents directly to tumour cells (Zhang et al., 2022; Bhardwaj, Rasool, 2023; Chandra et al., 2023; Gulia et al., 2023).

1.3.6.2.4 DIAGNOSTIC NANOPARTICLES

Quantum dots, inorganic type of nanoparticles, which are tiny semi-conductor particles, can be engineered to emit specific wavelengths of light. They can be used in imaging to detect and track cellular processes, tumours, and other disease-related changes more precisely than traditional imaging methods (Hejazi et al., 2023).

1.3.6.2.5 MOLECULAR IMAGING

Nanoparticles can be designed to carry contrast agents (Cai et al., 2023) for imaging techniques like MRI and CT scans. These agents enhance the visibility of specific tissues or cellular structures, aiding in disease diagnosis. This is critical in the case of imaging of the brain (McAteer, Choudhury, 2009; Sala et al., 2023). The advantage of molecular imaging over conventional imaging (concerning prostate cancer) is well documented (Sutera et al., 2023).

1.3.6.2.6 THERANOSTICS

Theranostic nanoparticles can be used to both deliver treatment and monitor its effectiveness in real time. This approach allows doctors to adjust treatments as needed for optimal results (Sharma et al., 2023). There are positive examples of the integration of pharmacogenomics and theranostics with nanotechnology which leads to novel dosage forms for effective drug therapy (Jhawat et al., 2020).

1.3.6.2.7 REGENERATIVE MEDICINE

Nanomaterials can be used to create scaffolds for tissue engineering, providing a supportive structure for cells to grow and regenerate damaged tissues (Li et al., 2022). Nanoparticles can also be used to deliver growth factors and bioactive molecules to enhance tissue regeneration (Lowe et al., 2019). In the next few decades, revolutionary approaches in regenerative medicine will be applied based on artificial intelligence and wireless data exchange, soft intelligence biomaterials, nanorobotics, and even living robotics capable of self-repair (Lowe et al., 2019).

1.3.6.2.8 ANTIBACTERIAL NANOPARTICLES

Nanoparticles with antimicrobial properties can be used to combat bacterial infections (Shanmugan et al., 2022; Dousari et al., 2023). Silver nanoparticles, for example, have been explored for their ability to inhibit bacterial growth and biofilm. Silver nanoparticles green-synthesised can also be used for breast cancer treatment (Xu et al., 2023).

1.3.6.2.9 NEUROLOGICAL APPLICATIONS

Nanotechnology can aid in the delivery of drugs across the blood-brain barrier, a challenge in treating neurological disorders. Nanoparticles can also be used for neural stimulation and monitoring in conditions like Parkinson's disease (Tryphena et al. 2023).

1.3.6.2.10 DIAGNOSTICS AND MONITORING

Nanoscale biosensors can detect minute concentrations of disease markers, such as proteins or nucleic acids. This could lead to early detection and monitoring of diseases like diabetes, rheumatoid arthritis (Zhao et al., 2021), cardiovascular disorders (Li et al., 2023b), and infectious diseases.

1.3.6.2.11 NANOBIOSENSORS

These nanoscale devices can detect specific biomarkers or molecules associated with diseases, offering rapid and sensitive diagnostic capabilities. They can be used for early disease detection (Shandilya et al., 2019; Razlansari et al., 2022) and monitoring (Kurlinkus et al., 2020).

All the above demonstrate the diverse applications of nanotechnology in medicine, showing its potential to revolutionise diagnostics, treatment, and monitoring of various diseases. One may share the opinion that nanotechnology will have a crucial role to play in personalised medicine and that nanomedicine is the most promising use of nanorobotics (Haleem et al., 2023, p. 76).

Significant upcoming areas for nanotechnology applications in the medical field cover: diagnostics, tissue engineering and cell treatment, therapy development, drug delivery, disease detection, detection of body oxygen, economical healthcare, improvement of the efficiency of medicine, management of illness, fight against cancer, helpful for cardiovascular disease, nanobots,[6] better preventive procedure, and radiation therapy (Haleem et al., 2023, pp. 73–75).

1.3.6.3 Neurotechnology

Neurotechnology is a multidisciplinary field that combines neuroscience, engineering, and computer science to develop technologies that interact with the nervous system. It consists of a set of diagnostic (e.g., MRI, functional MRI – fMRI, positron emission tomography – PET, and electroencephalography – EEG), and therapeutic (e.g., neuroprosthetics devices, artificial limbs, sensory organs, neural implants that can replace or enhance lost or impaired sensory or motor functions) tools designed to record and stimulate electrical activity in the nervous system (Cometa et al., 2022). Neurotechnology has significantly expanded its range of applications thanks to the development of flexible, stretchable, and injectable electronics (Fanelli, Ghezzi, 2021), novel materials, molecules (Cai et al., 2023), and techniques (Vitale et al., 2022). Speaking about recent developments in neurotechnology, one may mention transient electronics, i.e., devices disappearing in the environment after a programmed time and leaving minimal and harmless traces after their disposal. They can be fabricated from natural food and foodstuffs, among other materials, introducing the concept of edible electronics, which exploit disposable and harmless materials, easy and safe to ingest. Transient neurotechnology reduces the side effects of chronic implants and transforms inert devices into bio-active and bio-responsive structures. There is a solid ground to perceive transient neurotechnology as a new and safer tool for advanced diagnostics and therapy (Fanelli, Ghezzi, 2021).

As indicated above, neurotechnology encompasses a wide range of techniques and devices aimed at diagnosing, treating, or enhancing the functioning of the nervous system, including the brain and peripheral nervous system. Neurotechnology is used to treat neurodevelopmental disorders (NDDs) (Jung et al., 2023) and can be used for forensic psychiatric and psychological assessment in criminal justice (Kempes, 2023).

Neurotechnology represents huge potential concerning human enhancement. Here *brain-computer interfaces* – BCIs (devices that establish a direct communication pathway between the brain and external devices, such as computers or prosthetic limbs), *cognitive enhancement* (improving memory, attention, or learning abilities), and *neuromodulation* (techniques involving the use of electrical or chemical stimulation to modify the activity of neural circuits like deep brain stimulation, transcranial magnetic stimulation, and optogenetics could be mentioned as leading tools and methods. In addition, these approaches are used in treating conditions like Parkinson's disease, depression, and epilepsy (OpenAI, 2023). Some of these issues will be further elaborated in Chapter 2.

1.3.6.4 Nanorobotics

Nanorobotics is an emerging field of nanotechnology at the intersection of nanotechnology and robotics which deals with the design and construction of devices at an atomic, molecules, or cellular level (Tripathi, Kumar, 2018), typically, nanometres to micrometres in size. Nanorobots are often designed to interact with and manipulate individual molecules or cells (Nistor, Rusu, 2019). Nanorobots hold great promise for several applications, including diagnostics to detect specific biomarkers or abnormalities in the body, enabling early diagnosis of diseases such as cancer or infections by travelling through the bloodstream and transmitting real-time data to external devices for analysis. Drug delivery nanorobots deliver drugs or therapeutic agents directly to targeted cells or tissues within the body reducing side effects and increasing the efficiency of treatment. Surgery nanorobots can be used for precise procedures, such as clearing blocked arteries or removing tumours, with minimal damage to surrounding tissues. Nanorobots can be used for monitoring the body's internal environment and transmitting data to healthcare providers, and for treatment of various diseases (nanorobots can work in conjunction with nanoparticles for various therapeutic purposes, such as hyperthermia heating targeted tissues for cancer treatment. Nanorobots can be used as carriers for gene therapies. They could be also used to repair damaged cells or tissues by delivering nanoparticles or biological materials to facilitate regeneration, for example, concerning spinal cord injuries or neurodegenerative diseases, wound healing, etc. (Manickam et al., 2023). From a human enhancement perspective, special attention should be given to BCIs, where nanorobots could interface with the brain to treat neurological disorders, enhance cognitive function, or enable direct communication between the brain and external devices. The potential of nanorobots notwithstanding, one may acknowledge that they are still largely in the experimental and theoretical stages. Researchers envision applications such as dentistry (Verma, Chauhan, 2014), cancer treatment (Tripathi, Kumar, 2018; Pedrero et al., 2022), diabetes (Cavalcanti et al., 2008), or regenerative medicine (Altyar et al., 2023).

Many technical challenges remain, including ensuring the safety of these nanorobots, their biocompatibility, and reliable control mechanisms.

1.4 Big data

Big data (BD) is a term that describes large, hard-to-manage volumes of data both structured and unstructured, multiplied continuously by 4IR achievements.

BD in health care describes massive volumes of information created by the adoption of digital technologies that collect patients' records and help in managing hospital performance; otherwise too large and complex for traditional technologies (Calzon, 2023). Although not directly named and not separately analysed, BD is present in the background of most of the outcomes of 4IR presented above. It should be noted here that in even positive results of BD in various applications notwithstanding, BD remains a challenge (Lin et al., 2018) not only from a technical/engineering perspective but also because of data privacy and regulatory compliance.

1.5 Technical progress and innovations in medicine and healthcare systems

4IR is carried out at high speed, which means a growing number of inventions and innovations applicable to health. Consequently, it is hard to identify the most current breakthrough innovations in medicine. Looking back, one may point out that some technologies are changing the way medicine will be practised in the future. Bajwa (2014) points out a few significant: smartphones, tablet PCs, touch screens, digital ink, voice recognition, electronic health records (EHRs), personal health records (PHRs), health information exchange, nationwide health information network (NwHIN), patient portals, nanomedicine, genome-based personalised medicine, GPS, RFID, telemedicine, CDSS, mobile home healthcare, cloud computing, and social media.

Searching for an updated list of modern medical technologies one may look at what engineers and technicians consider the most important. Tech Business News (2022) has created a list of the ten most important modern medical technologies and innovations in 2022, which included:

- wearable health monitoring devices,
- DNA sequencing and genomics research,[7]
- robotics in medicine,
- electronic health and medical records,
- telemedicine and remote patient care,
- mRNA technology,[8]
- technology in mental health,[9]
- precision medicine,
- neurotechnology,
- virtual reality,[10]
- artificial intelligence.

For 2023, a similar list was prepared by Pacific Asia Consulting Expertise. It consisted of eight of the same elements as listed above and introduced two new[11] ones: 3D printing, and CRISPR (Pacific Asia Consulting Expertise, 2023).

Tulp (2022) adds to the above artificial organs, robotic prosthetic limbs, applications of biophotonics on patients affected by previously incurable infections and disorders such as hepatitis, HIV, and other maladies, less invasive treatments of cancer (clarifying the difficulties in getting chemotherapeutic agents into the tumour, and getting cancer out by utilising basic biochemical mechanisms and the biochemical alterations of the tumour cell), brain-to-tech interface (which uses EEG to decode and transform brain signals into an electrical pattern through a high-tech computer algorithm to convey brain signals to wires attached to the legs, essentially replacing some of the jobs of the spinal cord), and high-resolution 3D images of flexible DNA structures to appear as a nanoscale 'jump ropes'.

Even a cursory analysis and assessment of the scope and pace of changes in technologies that have (and may have) applications in the healthcare sector can be said, without hesitation, that this progress is significant and the related changes in the security sector are increasing.

The chapter shows how broad and intense the impact of the outcomes of the 4IR: AI, ICT, new products (drugs, medical devices, implants), new services (telemedicine and eHealth), new technologies (genetic engineering, nanotechnology, neurotechnology, robotics), and BD on the healthcare system is. As shown in Figure 1.1, all of the above-mentioned outcomes, but telemedicine and eHealth, directly impact human enhancement. This phenomenon fits perfectly with a *differentia specifica* of the 4IR which is crossing the lines between the physical, digital, and biological spheres. In other words, HE can be seen as a perfect example of a fundamental, far-reaching outcome of 4IR. Human enhancement as a multidimensional phenomenon will be presented in the following chapter.

Notes

1 In ScienceDirect alone on August 31, 2023, when *AI in medicine* phrase was used for searching, there were 182,350 results out of which in 2021 and 2023 there were, respectively, 7,971 and 8,597 results.
2 As of August 17, 2023, https://www.fda.gov/drugs/new-drugs-fda-cders-new-molecular-entities-and-new-therapeutic-biological-products/novel-drug-approvals-2023, accessed 19.08.2023.
3 Pharmaceutical R&D includes all steps from the initial research of disease processes, compound testing over pre-clinical, and all clinical trial stages. At a certain point in the process – mostly during the pre-clinical phase – a governmental authority is involved to overview, regulate, and ultimately approve the drug. In the United States, the Food and Drug Administration is the principal agency associated with processes.
4 Based on OpenAI typology as of August 17, 2023.
5 Emmanuelle Charpentier and Jennifer A. Doudna who discovered it were awarded the Nobel Prize in chemistry in 2020.
6 The authors use such a term but their goals and functions presented (pp. 74–75) allow for considering them as nanorobots.
7 The Nobel Prize winner in physiology or medicine was in 2022 Svante Pääbo, awarded for his 'research in the field of genomes of extinct hominins and human

evolution'. It is also worth mentioning some developments in gene therapy. Between 2019 and 2021 the US Food and Drug Administration approved several gene therapies for rare genetic diseases, for example, Zolgensma for spinal muscular atrophy and Luxturna for a rare form of inherited blindness.

8 The successful use of mRNA technology in COVID-19 vaccines paved the way for potential applications in other vaccines and therapies, including those for cancer and other infectious diseases.

9 AI allows patients to complete their intakes and receive a preliminary diagnosis through mental health applications that utilise AI. Chatbots can assist patients in practising their cognitive behavioural therapy (CBT) strategies by using smartphone applications to detect emotional distress based on a patient's voice and speech patterns. Digital symptom tracking is crucial for future mental health care to optimise efficiency. Patients are prompted to share data online, and providers are alerted in real-time if there are any warning signs based on an AI algorithm's analysis of the data. Also, video games like EndeavorRx, the first and only FDA-cleared video game treatment approved in 2020, or Minecraft can help. The game is used to improve the attention span of children 8–12 years old with ADHD and requires a prescription (Kulman, 2021).

10 VR is also used in psychiatry (Pons et al., 2022).

11 Not entirely new since both were introduced earlier and CRISPR can be treated as a part of 'DNA sequencing and genomics research'.

References

Ahmed, N.J., Almalki, Z.S., Alsawadi, A.H., Alturki, A.A., Bakarman, A.H., Almuaddi, A.M., Alshahrani, S.M., Alanazi, M.B., Alshehri, A.M., Albassam, A.A., Fatani, S., Alahmari, A.K., Aldosari, S.A., Alamer, A.A. (2023). Knowledge, perceptions, and readiness of telepharmacy among community pharmacists. *Saudi Pharmaceutical Journal*, 31(9), 101713, 10.1016/j.jsps.2023.101713.

Ahsan, M., Haider, J., Hashmi, S. (2023). Current advancements and future perspectives in electronic materials for developing smart clothing. *Encyclopedia of Materials: Electronics*, 3, 507–516, 10.1016/B978-0-12-819728-8.00094-2.

Altyar, A.E., El-Sayed, A., Abdeen, A., Piscopo, M., Mousa, S.A., Najda, A., Abdel-Daim, M.M. (2023). Future regenerative medicine developments and their therapeutic applications. *Biomedicine & Pharmacotherapy*, 158, 114131, 10. 1016/j.biopha.2022.114131.

Ashby, L.S., Smith, K.A., Stea, B. (2016). Gliadel wafer implantation combined with standard radiotherapy and concurrent followed by adjuvant temozolomide for treatment of newly diagnozed gigh-grade glioma: A systematic literature review. World Journal of Surgical Oncology, 14, 225, https://doi.org/10.1186/s12957-016-0975-5.

Aungsuroch, Y., Gunawan, J. (2019). Viewpoint: Nurses preparation in the era of the Fourth Industrial Revolution. *Belitung Nursing Journal*, 5(1), 1–2, 10.33546/bnj.744.

Ayyanaar, S., Kesavan, M.P. (2023). One-pot biogenic synthesis of gold nanoparticles@ saponins niosomes: Sustainable nanomedicine for antibacterial, anti-inflammatory and anticancer therapeutics. *Colloids and Surfaces A: Physicochemical and Engineering Aspects*, 676(Part A), 132229, 10.1016/j.colsurfa.2023.132229.

Bajwa, M.I. (2014). Emerging 21st century medical technologies. *Pakistan Journal of Medical Sciences*, 30(3), 649–655, 10.12669/pjms.303.5211.

Bhardwaj, M., Rasool, S. (2023). Nanotechnology for the treatment of cancer: Progress and challenges. In Yadav, M.K., Babu, P.J.S., Song, J.J., Kharat, A.S. (Eds).

Nanotechnology and Human Health: Current Research and Future Trends, Elsevier, pp. 285–307, 10.1016/b978-0-323-90750-7.00010-7.

Bosch, V., Mecacci, G. (2023). Eyes on the road: Brain computer interfaces and cognitive distraction in traffic. *Frontiers Neuroergonomics*, 4, 10.3389/fnrgo.2023.1171910, accessed 30.08.2023.

Braun, M., Hummel, P., Beck, S., Dabrock, P. (2021). Primer on an ethics of AI-based decision support systems in the clinic. *Journal of Medical Ethics*, 47(12), e3, 10.1136/medethics-2019-105860.

Cabrera, L.Y. (2017). Reframing human enhancement: A population health perspective. *Frontiers in Sociology*, 2(4), 10.3389/fsoc.2017.00004.

Cai, Y., Ren, J., Jin, J., Shao, H., Wang, P., Cheng, K., Jiang, P., Jiang, P., Zhu, S., Zhu, G., Zhang, L. (2023). Novel affibody molecules as potential agents in molecular imaging for MAGE-A3-positive tumor diagnosis. *Environmental Research*, 237(Part 1), 116895, 10.1016/j.envres.2023.116895.

Calzon, B. *24 Examples of Big Data Analytics in Healthcare That Can Save People*, https://www.datapine.com/blog/big-data-examples-in-healthcare, accessed 3.09.2023.

Carrera-Muñoz, I., Romero-Fábrega, J.C., Vilchez-Carrillo, R.M., Madrid-Navarro, C.J., Ruiz-Giménez, J., Escamilla-Sevilla, F., Mínguez-Castellanos, A. (2023). Electronic consultation (e-consultation) between primary care and the neurology department: One-year experience in a healthcare area in Andalusia, Spain. *Neurology Perspectives*, 3(1), 10010, 10.1016/j.neurop.2023.100109.

Cavalcanti, A., Shirinzadeh, B., Kretly, L.C. (2008). Medical nanorobotics for diabetes control. *Nanomedicine: Nanotechnology, Biology and Medicine*, 4(2), 127–138, 10.1016/j.nano.2008.03.001.

Chakraborty, U., Banerjee, A., Saha, J.K., Sarkar, N., Chakraborty, C. (2022). *Artificial Intelligence and the Fourth Industrial Revolution.* Jenny Stanford Publishing Pte. Ltd.

Chandra, J., Hasan, N., Nasir, N., Wahab, S., Thanikachalam, P.V., Sahebkar, A., Ahmad, F.J., Kesharwani, P. (2023). Nanotechnology-empowered strategies in treatment of skin cancer. *Environmental Research*, 235, 116649, 10.1016/j.envres.2023.116649.

Chang, C.-H., Lien, W.-C., Chiu, T.-P., Yang, T.-H., Wei, C.-C., Kuo, Y.-L., Yeh, C.-H., Liu, B., Chen, P.-J., Lin, Y.-C. (2023). A novel smart somatosensory wearable assistive device for older adults' home rehabilitation during the COVID-19 pandemic. *Frontiers in Public Health*, 11, 10.3389/fpubh.2023.1026662.

Cometa, A., Falasconi, A., Biasizzo, M., Carpaneto, J., Horn, A., Mazzoni, A., Micera, S. (2022). Clinical neuroscience and neurotechnology: An amazing symbiosis. *iScience*, 25(10), 105124, 10.1016/j.isci.2022.105124, accessed 8.09.2023.

Cosetti, M.K., Waltzman, S.B. (2011). Cochlear implants: Current status and future potential. *Expert Review of Medical Devices*, 8(3), 389–401.

Cresswell, K., Rigby, M., Magrabi, F., Scott, P., Brender, J., Craven, C.K., Wong, Z.S.-Y., Kukhareva, P., Ammenwerth, E., Georgiou, A., Medlockk, S., De Keizerk, N.F., Nykänen, P., Prgome, M., Williams, R. (2023). The need to strengthen the evaluation of the impact of artificial intelligence-based decision support systems on healthcare provision. *Health Policy*, 136, 104889, 10.1016/j.healthpol.2023.104889.

Cui, J. (2021). Global top ten engineering achievements 2021. *Engineering*, 7(12), 1651–1652, 10.1016/j.eng.2021.11.00.

Dahl, M. (2019). Niemcy jako europejski i światowy ośrodek badań nad rozwojem sztucznej inteligencji. Studia Europejskie - Studies in European Affairs, 2, 153–162.

Das, S., Su, M.Y., Kvedar, J.C., Smith, G.P. (2022). Asynchronous telemedicine for isotretinoin management: A direct care pilot. *Journal of the American Academy of Dermatology*, 86(1), 184–186, 10.1016/j.jaad.2021.01.039.

Dasa, S.K., Maheshwari, R.A., Chakraborty, J., Roya, S.D., Shil, D. (2023). Enhancing drug related problem (DRP) management in Indian healthcare through AI integration: An insight view. *Intelligent Pharmacy*, 1(4), 175–178, 10.1016/j.ipha.2023.08.006.

Delso, G., Cirillo, D., Kaggie, J.D., Valencia, A., Metser, U., Veit-Haibach, P. (2021). How to design AI-driven clinical trials in nuclear medicine. *Seminars in Nuclear Medicine*, 51(2), 112–119, 10.1053/j.semnuclmed.2020.09.003.

De Luca, V., Bozzetto, L., Giglio, C., Tramontano, G., De Simone, G., Luciano, A., Lucibelli, L., Maffettone, A., Riccio, M., Romano, G., Rossi, E., Chiatti, C., Berler, A., Berler, A., Iaccarino, G., Illario, M., Annuzzi, G. (2023). Clinical outcomes of a digitally supported approach for self-management of type 2 diabetes mellitus. *Frontiers in Public Health*, 11, 10.3389/fpubh.2023.1219661.

Dousari, A.S., Hosseininasab, S.S., Akbarizadeh, M.R., Naderifar, M., Satarzadeh, N. (2023). *Mentha pulegium* as a source of green synthesis of nanoparticles with antibacterial, antifungal, anticancer, and antioxidant applications. *Scientia Horticulturae*, 320, 112215, 10.1016/j.scienta.2023.112215.

Elander, J., Ullmark, T., Ehrencrona, H., Jonson, T., Piccinelli, P., Samuelsson, S., Löwgren, K., Falkenius-Schmidt, K., Ehinger, J., Stenfeldt, K., Värendh, K. (2022). Extended genetic diagnostics for children with profound sensorineural hearing loss by implementing massive parallel sequencing. Diagnostic outcome, family experience and clinical implementation. *International Journal of Pediatric Otorhinolaryngology*, 159, 111218, 10.1016/j.ijporl.2022.111218.

Ellipilli, S., Wang,H., Binzel, D.W., Shu, D., Guo, P. (2023). Ligand-displaying-exosomes using RNA nanotechnology for targeted delivery of multi-specific drugs for liver cancer regression. *Nanomedicine: Nanotechnology, Biology and Medicine*, 50, 102667, 10.1016/j.nano.2023.102667.

European Medicines Agency (2022). *Human medicines highlights 2022*. https://www.ema.europa.eu/en/about-us/what-we-do/authorisation-medicines/medicine-evaluation-figures, accessed 28.08.2023.

European Medicines Agency (2023). *Monthly statistics report: June 2023*. https://www.ema.europa.eu/en/about-us/what-we-do/authorisation-medicines/medicine-evaluation-figures#ema-inpage-item-8614, accessed 29.08.2023.

Fareh, R., Elsabe, A., Baziyad, M., Kawser, T., Brahmi, B., Rahman, M.H. (2023). Will your next therapist be a robot? – A review of the advancements in robotic upper extremity rehabilitation. *Sensors*, 23, 5054. 10.3390/s23115054.

Fanelli, A., Ghezzi, D. (2021). Transient electronics: New opportunities for implantable neurotechnology. *Current Opinion in Biotechnology*, 72, 22–28, 10.1016/j.copbio.2021.08.011.

Fatima, T., Ebertz, A. (2021). *Rewind 2021 – The biotech advancements at the beginning of a new decade*, https://the-dna-universe.com/2021/12/23/rewind-2021/, accessed 26.08.2023.

Feng, H., Wei, G.-W. (2023). Virtual screening of DrugBank database for hERG blockers using topological Laplacian-assisted AI models. *Computers in Biology and Medicine*, 153, 106491, 10.1016/j.compbiomed.2022.106491.

Figueras, J., McKee, M. (2012). *Health systems, health, wealth and societal well-being: Assessing the case for investing in health systems*. Open University. European Observatory on Health Systems and Policies.

Flores, L., Kim, S., Young, S.D. (2023). Addressing bias in artificial intelligence for public health surveillance. *Journal of Medical Ethics*, May 2023, 2022–108875, 10.1136/jme-2022-108875.

Fortune Business Insights (2023). *Medical devices market size, share & COVID-19 impact analysis*, https://www.fortunebusinessinsights.com/industry-reports/medical-devices-market-100085, accessed 2.01.2024.

Ghodake, A., Hogade, B. (2023). Wearable textile antenna for glucose level monitoring. *International Journal of Electronics and Telecommunications*, 69(2), 219–224, https://journals.pan.pl/dlibra/publication/144353/edition/127349/content.

Goy, A., Nishtar, S., Dzau, V., Balatbat, C., Diabo, R. (2019). *Health and Healthcare in the Fourth Industrial Revolution: Global Future Council on the Future of Health and Healthcare 2016–2018. Insight Report*. World Economic Forum, April 2019, https://apo.org.au/node/235506, accessed 17.08.2023.

Gulia, M., Nishal, S., Maddiboyina, B., Dutt, R., Desu, P.K., Wadhwa, R., Jhawat, V. (2023). Physiological pathway, diagnosis and nanotechnology based treatment strategies for ovarian cancer: A review. *Medicine in Omics*, 8, 100020, 10.1016/j.meomic.2023.100020.

Haleem, A., Javaida, M., Singh, R.P., Rab, S., Suman, R. (2023). Applications of nanotechnology in medical field: A brief review. *Global Health Journal*, 7(2), 70–77, 10.1016/j.glohj.2023.02.008.

Harisa, G.I., Faris, T.M., Sherif, A.Y., Alzhrani, R.F., Alanazi, S.A., Kohaf, N.A., Alanazi, F.K. (2023). Gene-editing technology, from macromolecule therapeutics to organ transplantation: Applications, limitations, and prospective uses. *International Journal of Biological Macromolecules*, 127055, 10.1016/j.ijbiomac.2023.127055.

Hejazi, M., Arshadi, S., Amini, M., Baradaran, R., Shahbazi-Derakhshi, P., Sameti, P., Soleymani, J., Mokhtarzadeh, A., Tavangar, S.M. (2023). Hyaluronic acid-functionalized gold nanoparticles as a cancer diagnostic probe for targeted bioimaging applications. *Microchemical Journal*, 193, 108953, 10.1016/j.microc.2023.108953.

Herishanu, S.A. (2022). AI-based clinical decision support system for treatment of chronic lymphocytic leukemia/small lymphocytic lymphoma (CLL/SLL) and prediction of treatment efficiency. *Blood*, 140(1), 12393–12394, 10.1182/blood-2022-159349.

Hsu, C.-Y., Rheima, A.M., Kadhim, M.M., Ahmed, N.N., Mohammed, S.H., Abbas, F.H., Abed, Z.T., Mahdi, Z.M., Abbas, Z.S., Hachim, S.K., Ali, F.K., Mahmoud, Z.H., Kianfar, E. (2023). An overview of nanoparticles in drug delivery: Properties and applications. *South African Journal of Chemical Engineering*, 46, 233–270, 10.1016/j.sajce.2023.08.009.

Hutchinson, D., Kunasekaran, M., Quigley, A., Moa, A., MacIntyre, C.R. (2023). Could it be monkeypox? Use of an AI-based epidemic early warning system to monitor rash and fever illness. *Public Health*, 220, 142–147, 10.1016/j.puhe.2023.05.010.

Jayanthi, P., Iyyanki, M., Mothkuri, A., Vadakattu, P. (2019). Fourth Industrial Revolution: An impact on health care industry. In Ahram, T. (Ed.). *Advances in Artificial Intelligence, Software and Systems Engineering*. AHFE 2019. Advances in Intelligent Systems and Computing, Springer, Vol. 965, pp. 58–69, 10.1007/978-3-030-20454-9_6.

Jendly, M., Santschi, V., Tancredi, S., Konzelmann, I., Raboud, L., Chiolero, A. (2023). eHealth profile of patients with diabetes. *Frontiers in Public Health*, 11, 10.3389/fpubh.2023.1240879, accessed 27.08.2023.

Jha, R.K., Jha, P.K., Chaudhury, K., Rana, S.V.S., Guha, S.K. (2014). An emerging interface between life science and nanotechnology: present status and prospects of reproductive healthcare aided by nano-technology. *Nano Reviews*, 5(1), 22762.

Jhawat, V., Gulia, M., Gupta, S., Maddiboyina, B., Dutt, R. (2020). Integration of pharmacogenomics and theranostics with nanotechnology as quality by design (QbD) approach for formulation development of novel dosage forms for effective drug therapy. *Journal of Controlled Release*, 327, 500–511, 10.1016/j.jconrel.2020.08.039.

Jung, M. (2019). Digital health care and the Fourth Industrial Revolution. *The Health Care Manager*, 38(3), 253–257, 10.1097/HCM.0000000000000273.

Jung, Y., Ibrahim, G.M., McDonald, P.J. (2023). Invasive neurotechnology for neurodevelopmental disorders. In Gibbard, W.B. (Ed.). *Developments in Neuroethics and Bioethics*, Academic Press, Elsevier, Vol. 6, pp. 147–164, 10.1016/bs.dnb.2023.06.002.

Kang, K.M., Lee, I., Nam, H., Kim, Y.-C. (2022). AI-based prediction of new binding site and virtual screening for the discovery of novel P2X3 receptor antagonists. *European Journal of Medicinal Chemistry*, 240, 114556, 10.1016/j.ejmech.2022.114556.

Kaspar, K., König, S., Schwandt, J., König, P. (2014). The experience of new sensorimotor contingencies by sensory augmentation. *Consciousness and Cognition*, 28, 47–63, 10.1016/j.concog.2014.06.006.

Kaul, V., Enslin, S., Gross, S.A. (2020). History of artificial intelligence in medicine. *Gastrointestinal Endoscopy*, 92(4), 807–812, 10.1016/j.gie.2020.06.040.

Keim-Malpass, J., Moorman, L.P. (2021). Nursing and precision predictive analytics monitoring in the acute and intensive care setting: An emerging role for responding to COVID-19 and beyond. *International Journal of Nursing Studies Advances*, 3, 100019, 10.1016/j.ijnsa.2021.100019.

Kempes, M. (2023). Added value of neurotechnology for forensic psychiatric and psychological assessment. In Swaab, H., Meynen, G. (Eds). *Handbook of Clinical Neurology*, 197, 217–232, 10.1016/B978-0-12-821375-9.00015-3.

Khan, S., Arslan, T., Ratnarajah, T. (2022). Digital twin perspective of Fourth Industrial and Healthcare Revolution. *IEEE Access*, 10, 25732–25754, 10.1109/ACCESS.2022.3156062.

Khan, S.R., Rijjal, D.A., Piro, A., Wheeler, M.B. (2021). Integration of AI and traditional medicine in drug discovery. *Drug Discovery Today*, 26(4), 982–992, 10.1016/j.drudis.2021.01.008.

Khanji, M.Y., Gallagher, A.M., Rehill, N., Archbold, A. (2023). Remote consultations: Review of guiding themes for equitable and effective delivery. *Current Problems in Cardiology*, 48(8), 101736, 10.1016/j.cpcardiol.2023.101736.

Khong Tan, D., Maniruzzaman, M., Nokhodchi, A. (2018). Advanced pharmaceutical applications of hot-melt extrusion coupled with fused deposition modelling (FDM) 3D printing for personalised drug delivery. *Pharmaceutics*, 10(4), 203, 10.3390/pharmaceutics10040203.

Khurana, I., Allawadhi, P., Neeradi, D., Banothu, A.K., Thalugula, S., Naik, R.R., Packirisamy, G., Bharani, K.K., Khurana, A. (2023). Introduction to nanoengineering and nanotechnology for biomedical applications. In Ahmad, N., Packirisamy, G. (Eds). *Emerging Nanotechnologies for Medical Applications: Micro and Nano Technologies*. Elsevier, pp. 1–34, 10.1016/B978-0-323-91182-5.00002-4.

Kim, G.Y., Seo, J.-S. (2021). A new paradigm for clinical nutrition services in the era of the Fourth Industrial Revolution. *Clinical Nutrition Research*, 10(2), 95–106, 10.7762/cnr.2021.10.2.95.

Klich, J. (2021). Kierowana i rzeczywista odpowiedzialność państwa. Studium sektora ochrony zdrowia państw postsocjalistycznych. Wydawnictwo Naukowe SCHOLAR, 2021.

Klich, J. (2022). The Fourth Industrial Revolution and the healthcare system. In Ćwiklicki, M., Duplaga, M., Klich, J. (Eds). *The Digital Transformation of Healthcare: Health 4.0*. Routledge, pp. 1–16.

Klipfel, A. (2017). La technicisation de la chirurgie représente-t-elle un danger? Entre regret et perspectives d'avenir. *Journal international de bioéthique et d'éthique des sciences*, 2(28), 131–143, https://www.cairn.info/revue-journal-international-de-bioethique-et-d-ethique-des-sciences-2017-2-page-131.htm.

Kruklitis, R., Miller, M., Valeriano, L., Shine, S., Opstbaum, N., Chestnut, V. (2022). Applications of remote patient monitoring. *Primary Care: Clinics in Office Practice*, 49(4), 543–555, 10.1016/j.pop.2022.05.005.

Kulman, R. (2021). Video games can help kids with ADHD – if you choose wisely, *ADDitude*, Updated on May 20, 2021, https://www.additudemag.com/video-games-help-adhd/?src=embed_ss, accessed 3.09.2023.

Kumar, S., Schroeder, J.A., Shi, Q. (2024). Platelet-targeted gene therapy induces immune tolerance in hemophilia and beyond. *Journal of Thrombosis and Haemostasis*, 22(1), 23–34, 10.1016/j.jtha.2023.07.025.

Kurlinkus, B., Ger, M., Valius, M., Petrulionis, M., Strupas, K., Šileikis, A. (2020). Novel nanobiosensor for pancreatic cancer protein biomarkers concentration and visualization. *Pancreatology*, 20(1), S129, 10.1016/j.pan.2020.07.237.

Lee, J.Y., Lim, J.Y. (2017). The prospect of the Fourth Industrial Revolution and home healthcare in super-aged society. *Annals of Geriatric Medicine and Research*, 21(3), 95–100, 10.4235/agmr.2017.21.3.95.

Lee, T., Seohyun, K., Park, S. (2023), Mobile health applications for communication between caregivers of community-dwelling older adults: A scoping review. *Geriatric Nursing*, 52, 172–180, 10.1016/j.gerinurse.2023.06.011.

Li, D., Liu, Y., Wu, N. (2022). Application progress of nanotechnology in regenerative medicine of diabetes mellitus. *Diabetes Research and Clinical Practice*, 190, 109966, 10.1016/j.diabres.2022.109966.

Li, B., Tan, W., Wang, Z., Zhou, H., Zou, J., Li, Y., Yoshida, S., Zhou, Y. (2023a). Progress and prospects of gene therapy in ophthalmology from 2000 to 2022: A bibliometric analysis. *Heliyon*, 9(7), e18228, 10.1016/j.heliyon.2023.e18228.

Li, F., Shao, H., Zhou, G., Wang, B., Xu, Y., Liang, W., Chen, L. (2023b). The recent applications of nanotechnology in the diagnosis and treatment of common cardiovascular diseases. *Vascular Pharmacology*, 152, 107200, 10.1016/j.vph.2023.107200.

Liang, J., Xie, J., He, Y., Fan, X., Liu, Y., Wen, Q., Shen, D., Xu, J., Gu, S., Lei, J. (2023). Mining electronic health records using artificial intelligence: Bibliometric and content analyses for current research status and product conversion. *Journal of Biomedical Informatics*, 146, 104480, 10.1016/j.jbi.2023.104480.

Lin, M.-C., Pharm, U.I., Li, Y.-C. (2018). AI in medicine: Big data remains a challenge. *Computer Methods and Programs in Biomedicine*, 164, A1, 10.1016/j.cmpb.2018.08.015.

Linkous, C., Pagan, A.D., Shope, C., Andrews, L., Snyder, A., Ye, T., Valdebran, M. (2023). Applications of laser speckle contrast imaging technology in dermatology. *JID Innovations*, 3(5), 100187, 10.1016/j.xjidi.2023.100187.

Liu, M., Ji, W., Zhao, X., Liu, X., Hu, J.-F., Cui, J. (2023). Therapeutic potential of engineering the mitochondrial genome. *Biochimica et Biophysica Acta (BBA) – Molecular Basis of Disease*, 1869(7), 166804, 10.1016/j.bbadis.2023.166804.

Lobo Borba, H., Woranovicz Carvalho, D.M. (2023). Impact of the Fourth Industrial Revolution on clinical pharmaceutical services: A scoping review. *Research in Social and Administrative Pharmacy*, 19(2), 235–242, 10.1016/j.sapharm.2022.09.008.

Lowe, T.L., Agrahari, V., Kannan, R.M., Kannan, S. (2019). Nanotechnology enabled regenerative medicine for neurological disorders. *Advanced Drug Delivery Reviews*, 148, 1–2, 10.1016/j.addr.2019.11.006.

Manickam, P., Vashist, A., Sadasivam, M., Shinde, R., Kanagavel, V. (2023). Mobile nanorobotics for biomedical applications. In Kaushik, A.K., Kumar, S., Chaudhary, G.R. (Eds). *Engineered Nanostructures for Therapeutics and Biomedical Applications*. Woodhead Publishing Series in Biomaterials, pp. 297–311, 10.1016/B978-0-12-82124 0-0.00003-2, accessed 8.09.2023.

McAteer, M.A., Choudhury, R.P. (2009). Applications of nanotechnology in molecular imaging of the brain. *Progress in Brain Research*, 180, 72–96, 10.1016/S0079-6123(08)80004-0.

Melo e Castro, J.A.G., Araújo, N.M.F. (2020). Impact of the Fourth Industrial Revolution on the health sector: A qualitative study. *Health Informatics Research*, 26(4), 328–334, 10.4258/hir.2020.26.4.328.

Mikulic, M. (2023a). *Pharmaceutical market: worldwide revenue 2001–2022*, https://www.statista.com/statistics/263102/pharmaceutical-market-worldwide-revenue-since-2001, accessed 13.12.2023.

Mikulic, M. (2023b). *Number of novel drugs approved annually by CDER 2008–2022*. Statista, January 25, 2023, https://www.statista.com/statistics/817534/annual-novel-drug-approvals-by-cder, accessed 4.09.2023.

Mikulic, M. (2023c). *Total global pharmaceutical R&D spending 2014–2028*. Statista, August 29, 2023, https://www.statista.com/statistics/309466/global-r-and-d-expenditure-for-pharmaceuticals, accessed 4.09.2023.

Min, J., Kim, Y., Lee, S., Jang, T.-W., Kim, I., Song, J. (2019). The Fourth Industrial Revolution and its impact on occupational health and safety, worker's compensation and labor conditions. *Safety and Health at Work*, 10(4), 400–408, 10.1016/j.shaw.2019.09.005.

Mitra, A.K., Cholkar, K., Mandal, A. (Eds). (2017). *Emerging Nanotechnologies for Diagnostics, Drug Delivery, and Medical Devices*. Micro & Nano Technology Series, Elsevier.

Mohan, A., Wara, U.U., Shaikh, M.T.A., Rahman, R.M., Zaidi, Z.A. (2021). Telesurgery and robotics: An improved and efficient era. *Cureus*, 13(3), e14124. 10.7759/cureus.14124.

Monfredi, O.J., Moore, C.O., Sullivan, B.A., Keim-Malpass, J., Fairchild, K.D., Loftus, T.J., Bihorac, A., Krahn, K.N., Dubrawski, A., Lake, D.E., Moorman, J.R., Clermont, G. (2023). Continuous ECG monitoring should be the heart of bedside AI-based predictive analytics monitoring for early detection of clinical deterioration. *Journal of Electrocardiology*, 76, 35–38, 10.1016/j.jelectrocard.2022.10.011.

Mota, A., Colás, E., García-Sanz, P., Campoy, I., Rojo-Sebastián, A., Gatius, S., García, A., Chiva, L., Alonso, S., Gil-Moreno, A., González-Tallada, X., Díaz-Feijoo, B., Vidal, A., Ziober-Malinowska, P., Bobiński, M., López-López, R., Abal, M., Reventós, J., Matias-Guiu, X., Moreno-Bueno, G. (2017). Genetic analysis of uterine aspirates improves the diagnostic value and captures the intra-tumor heterogeneity of endometrial cancers. *Modern Pathology*, 30(1), 134–145, https://pubmed.ncbi.nlm.nih.gov/27586201.

Mukherjee, J., Sharma, R., Dutta, P., Bhunia, B. (2023). Artificial intelligence in healthcare: A mastery. *Biotechnology and Genetic Engineering Reviews*, 10.1080/02648725.2023.2196476.

NHGRI (2023). National Human Genome Research Institute, https://www.genome.gov/genetics-glossary/Genetic-Engineering, accessed 24.08.2023.

Nistor, M.T., Rusu, A.G. (2019). Nanorobots with applications in medicine. In Vasile, C. (Ed.). *Polymeric Nanomaterials in Nanotherapeutics. Micro and Nano Technologies*. Elsevier, pp. 123–149.

Nyholm, S. (2023). Artificial intelligence and human enhancement: Can AI technologies make us more (artificially) intelligent? *Cambridge Quarterly of Healthcare Ethics*, 1–13, 10.1017/S0963180123000464.

Onno, J., Khan, F.A., Daftary, A., David, P.-M. (2023). Artificial intelligence-based computer aided detection (AI-CAD) in the fight against tuberculosis: Effects of moving health technologies in global health. *Social Science & Medicine*, 327, 115949, 10.1016/j.socscimed.2023.115949.

OpenAI (2023). ChatGPT (August 3 Version) [Large language model]. https://chat.openai.com, accessed 28.08-30.10.2023.

Pacific Asia Consulting Expertise (2023). *Top 10 new medical breakthroughs of 2023*, https://pacificasiaconsultingexpertise.com/top-10-new-medical-breakthroughs-of-2023, accessed 4.09.2023.

Pandit, A.S., Toma, A.K., Jalal, A.H., Nachev, P. (2022). An AI-enabled predictive analytics dashboard for acute neurosurgical referrals. *Brain and Spine*, 2(2), 101373, 10.1016/j.bas.2022.101373.

Parthasarathy, J. (2014). 3D modeling, custom implants and its future perspectives in craniofacial surgery. *Annals of Maxillofacial Surgery*, 4(1), 9–18, 10.4103/2231-0746.133065.

Pedrero, M., Gamella, M., Serafín, V. (2022). Nanomachines and nanorobotics: Improving cancer diagnosis and therapy. In Ozkan, S.A., Bakirhan, N.K., Mollarasouli, F. (Eds). *The Detection of Biomarkers. Past, Present and the Future Prospects*. Academic Press, Elsevier, pp. 503–543, 10.1016/B978-0-12-822859-3.00015-8.

Perham, A., Keskar, M. (2023). Patient experience and satisfaction with telephone consultations in maternity POAC – a service evaluation at Musgrove Park Hospital Taunton. *BJA Open*, 6, 100192, 10.1016/j.bjao.2023.100192.

Pons, P., Navas-Medrano, S., Soler-Dominguez, J.L. (2022). Extended reality for mental health: Current trends and future challenges. *Frontiers in Computer Science*, 4, 10.3389/fcomp.2022.1034307, accessed 30.08.2023.

Precedence Research (2023). *Medical implants market*, https://www.precedenceresearch.com/medical-implants-market, accessed 5.09.2023.

Rabin, R.C. (2021). In a first, surgeons attached a pig kidney to a human, and it worked. *The New York Times*, https://www.nytimes.com/2021/10/19/health/kidney-transplant-pig-human.html, accessed 2.09.2023.

Raffa, V., Vittorio, O., Riggio, C., Cuschieri, A. (2010). Progress in nanotechnology for healthcare. *Minimally Invasive Therapy & Allied Technologies*, 19(3), 127–135.

Razlansari, M., Ulucan-Karnak, F., Kahrizi, M., Mirinejad, S., Sargazi, S., Mishra, S., Rahdar, A., Díez-Pascual, A.M. (2022). Nanobiosensors for detection of opioids: A review of latest advancements. *European Journal of Pharmaceutics and Biopharmaceutics*, 179, 79–94, 10.1016/j.ejpb.2022.08.017.

Rehana, K.K. (2020). A research on genetic engineering in different fields. *Middle East Journal of Applied Science & Technology*, 3(2), 49–64, https://ssrn.com/abstract=3714738.

ReportLinker (2023). *Global pharmaceuticals industry analysis and trends 2023*, https://www.reportlinker.com/p05750669/Global-Pharmaceuticals-Industry-Analysis-and-Trends.html, accessed 28.11.2023.

Rodrigues, R., Diez Rituerto, M. (2022). Socio-economic impact assessments for new and emerging technologies. *Journal of Responsible Technology*, 9, 100019, 10.1016/j.jrt.2021.100019.

Sala, A., Lizarraga, A., Caminiti, S.P., Calhoun, V.D., Eickhoff, S.B., Habeck, C., Jamadar, S.D., Perani, D., Pereira, J.B., Veronese, M., Yakushev, I. (2023). Brain connectomics: Time for a molecular imaging perspective? *Trends in Cognitive Sciences*, 27(4), 353–366, 10.1016/j.tics.2022.11.015.

Saleki, K., Alijanizade, P., Moradi, S., Rahmani, A., Banazadeh, M., Mohamadi, M.H., Shahabi, F., Nouri, H.R. (2022). Engineering a novel immunogenic chimera protein utilizing bacterial infections associated with atherosclerosis to induce a deviation in adaptive immune responses via Immunoinformatics approaches. *Infection, Genetics and Evolution*, 102, 105290, 10.1016/j.meegid.2022.105290.

Samia, P., Sahu, J.K., Ali, A., Caraballo, R.H., Chan, J., Coan, A.C., Fortini, P.S., Gwer, S., Jocic-Jakub, B., Kissani, N., Rivera, Y., Sarfo, F.S., Singh, M.B., Trinka, E.,

Yoo, J.Y., Hsiang-Yu Yu, H.-Y., Zelano, J., Cross, J.H. (2023). Telemedicine for individuals with epilepsy: Recommendations from the International League Against Epilepsy Telemedicine Task Force. *Seizure*, 106, 85–91, 10.1016/j.seizure.2023.02.005.

Sandel, M.J. (2017). The case against perfection. What's wrong with designer children, bionic athletes, and genetic engineering? In Murray, T.H., Chuan, V.T. (Eds). *The Ethics of Sports Technologies and Human Enhancement*. Routledge, pp. 329–338.

Sankar, P.L., Cho, M.K. (2015) Engineering values into genetic engineering: A proposed analytic framework for scientific social responsibility. *The American Journal of Bioethics*, 15(12), 18–24, 10.1080/15265161.2015.1104169.

Schwab, K. (2016a). *The Fourth Industrial Revolution*. World Economic Forum.

Schwab, K. (2016b). *The Fourth Industrial Revolution: What it means, how to respond*, https://www.weforum.org/agenda/2016/01/the-fourth-industrial-revolution-what-it-means-and-how-to-respond, accessed 9.04.2021.

Sen, M. (2024). *5 steps to put healthcare on the AI fast-track*, https://www.weforum.org/agenda/2024/01/healthcare-ai/?utm_source=sfmc&utm_medium=email&utm_campaign=2819770_WeeklyAgenda5January2024&utm_term=&emailType=Agenda%20Weekly, accessed 5.01.2024.

Seoane-Viaño, I., Januskaite, P., Alvarez-Lorenzo, C., Basit, A.W., Goyanes, A. (2021). Semi-solid extrusion 3D printing in drug delivery and biomedicine: Personalised solutions for healthcare challenges. *Journal of Controlled Release*, 332, 367–389, 10.1016/j.jconrel.2021.02.027.

Seoni, S., Jahmunah, V., Salvi, M., Barua, P.D., Molinari, F., Acharya, U.R. (2023). Application of uncertainty quantification to artificial intelligence in healthcare: A review of last decade (2013–2023). *Computers in Biology and Medicine*, 165, 107441, 10.1016/j.compbiomed.2023.107441.

Shandhi, M.H., Dunn, J.P. (2022). AI in medicine: Where are we now and where are we going? *Cell Reports Medicine*, 3, 1–5, 10.1016/j.xcrm.2022.100861.

Shandilya, R., Bhargava, A., Bunkar, N., Tiwari, R., Goryacheva, I.Y., Mishra, P.K. (2019). Nanobiosensors: Point-of-care approaches for cancer diagnostics. *Biosensors and Bioelectronics*, 130, 147–165.

Shanmugan, S., Selvaraju, P., Nagaraj, J., Sivakumar, S., Ravichandran, S. (2022). Biogenic silver nanoparticles of antibacterial activities for poly-herbal extracts in novel medicine. *Materials Today: Proceedings*, 51(1), 1107–1114, 10.1016/j.matpr.2021.07.107.

Sharma, A., Sharma, N., Singh, S., Dua, K. (2023). Review on theranostic and neuroprotective applications of nanotechnology in multiple sclerosis. *Journal of Drug Delivery Science and Technology*, 81, 104220, 10.1016/j.jddst.2023.104220.

Sharma, H., Singh, D., Mahant, A., Sohal, S.K., Kesavan, A.K., Samiksha, (2020). Development of mitochondrial replacement therapy: A review. *Heliyon*, 6(9), e04643, 10.1016/j.heliyon.2020.e04643.

Sharma, P., Dhanjal, D.S., Chopra, C., Tambuwala, M.M., Sohal, S.S.S., van der Spek, P.J., Sharma, H.S., Satija, S. (2022). Targeting eosinophils in chronic respiratory diseases using nanotechnology-based drug delivery. *Chemico-Biological Interactions*, 365, 110050, 10.1016/j.cbi.2022.110050.

Shreya, S., Dagur, P., Rakshit, G., Ghosh, M. (2023). Virtual screening of phytochemicals for drug discovery. In Egbuna, C., Rudrapal, M., Tijjani, H. (Eds). *Phytochemistry, Computational Tools and Databases in Drug Discovery. Drug Discovery Update*. Elsevier, pp. 149–179, 10.1016/B978-0-323-90593-0.00006-X.

Skuban-Eiseler, T., Orzechowski, M., Denkinger, M., Kocar, T.D., Leinert, C., Steger, F. (2023). Artificial intelligence – based clinical decision support systems in

geriatrics: An ethical analysis. *Journal of the American Medical Directors Association*, 24(9), 1271–1276.e4, 10.1016/j.jamda.2023.06.008.
Stelmach, M. (2019). Po raz pierwszy w Polsce zastosowano innowacyjną terapię CAR-T. *Termedia*, http://www.termedia.pl/mz/Po-raz-pierwszy-w-Polsce-zastosowano-innowacyjna-terapie-CAR-T,36223.html, accessed 2.01.2024.
Stone, N.N., Wilson, M.P., Griffith, S.H., Immerzeel, J., Debruyne, F., Gorin, M.A., Brisbane, W., Orio, P.F., Kim, L.S., Stone, J.J. (2022). Remote surgical education using synthetic models combined with an augmented reality headset. *Surgery Open Science*, 10, 27–33. https://doi/10.1016/j.sopen.2022.06.004.
Sutera, P., Song, Y., Van der Eecken, K., Shetty, A.C., English, K., Hodges, T., Chang, J., Fonteyne, V., Rana, Z., Ren, L., Mendes, A.A., Lumen, N., Delrue, L., Verbeke, S., De Man, K., Song, D.Y., Pienta, K., Feng, F.Y., Joniau, S., Lotan, T., … Tran, P.T. (2023). Clinical and genomic differences between advanced molecular imaging-detected and conventional imaging-detected metachronous oligometastatic castration-sensitive prostate cancer. *European Urology*, 84(6), 531–535, 10.1016/j.eururo.2023.04.025.
Tech Business News (2022). *Top 10 medical technologies 2022: Innovations in the medical field*, https://www.techbusinessnews.com.au/top-10-medical-technologies-2022-innovations-in-the-medical-field/#extended-summary, accessed 3.09.2023.
Termanini, R. (2023). *Biomedical Defense Principles to Counter DNA Deep Hacking*. Academic Press.
Thermolia, C., Bei, E., Petrakis, E. (2015). AI-care: A clinical decision support system with application in bipolar disorder. *European Psychiatry*, 30(1), 1905, 10.1016/S0924-9338(15)31457-7.
Tripathi, R., Kumar, A. (2018). Application of nanorobotics for cancer treatment. *Materials Today: Proceedings*, 5(3), Part 1, 9114–9117, 10.1016/j.matpr.2017.10.029.
Tryphena, K.P., Singh, G., Jain, N., Famta, P., Srivastava, S., Singh, S.B., Khatri, D.K. (2023). Integration of miRNA's theranostic potential with nanotechnology: Promises and challenges for Parkinson's disease therapeutics. *Mechanisms of Ageing and Development*, 211, 111800, 10.1016/j.mad.2023.111800.
Tulp, O.L. (2022). Innovations in science and medical technology in the 21st century: Excerpts from a recent commencement address. *MedCrave Online Public Health*, 1(1), 54–56, 10.15406/mojph.2022.11.00375.
Ungar, L. (2023). The man who claimed he genetically engineered babies just got out of a Chinese prison for practicing without a license and he's eyeing a comeback. *FortuneWell*, February 28, 2023, https://fortune.com/well/2023/02/28/gene-edited-babies-scientist-comeback, accessed 28.08.2023.
Verma, S.K., Chauhan, R. (2014). Nanorobotics in dentistry: A review. *Indian Journal of Dentistry*, 5(Supplement), 62–70, 10.1016/j.ijd.2012.12.010.
Vitale, F., Gelinas, J.N., Cabrera, L.Y. (2022). Neurotechnology: Bridging the dialogue between engineers, material scientists, clinicians, and ethicists. *iScience*, 25(11), 105432, 10.1016/j.isci.2022.105432.
WHO (2000). *The world health report 2000. Health systems: Improving performance*. WHO.
WHO (2007). *Everybody's business: Strengthening health systems to improve health outcomes. WHO's framework for action*. WHO.
WHO (2018). *Digital health: Digital health in the Western Pacific*, August 15, 2018, https://www.who.int/westernpacific/health-topics/e-health, accessed 31.08.2023.
WHO (2020). *Health system. Health systems strengthening glossary*. World Health Organization, https://www.who.int.healthsystems/hss_glossary/en/index5.html, accessed 2.03.2020.
WHO (2022). *Consolidated telemedicine implementation guide*. World Health Organization.

Xu, X., Amraii, S.A., Toushmalani, R., Almasi, M. (2023). Formulation of a modern anti-human breast cancer drug from silver nanoparticles green-synthesized using *Allium saralicum*. *Journal of Engineering Research*. Available online June 27, 2023. In Press, Corrected Proof, 10.1016/j.jer.2023.100136.

Yang, D., Murr, C., Yoo, S., O'Neill, L., Catalano, S., Blitzblau, R.C., McDuff, S., Yin, F.F., Wu, Q.J.J., Sheng, Y. (2022). Prospective clinical integration of AI based treatment planning tool for whole breast radiation therapy (WBRT): A single institution's three-year experience. *International Journal of Radiation Oncology, Biology, Physics*, 114(3), S33, 10.1016/j.ijrobp.2022.07.389.

Zhang, J., Jiang, S., Li, S., Jiang, J., Mei, J., Chen, Y., Ma, Y., Liu, Y., Liu, Y. (2022). Nanotechnology: A new strategy for lung cancer treatment targeting pro-tumor neutrophils. *Engineering*, Available online December 19, 2022. In Press, Corrected Proof, 10.1016/j.eng.2022.11.006.

Zhang, Y., Pei, H., Zhen, S., Li, Q., Liang, F. (2023). Chat generative pre-trained transformer (ChatGPT) usage in healthcare. *Gastroenterology & Endoscopy*, 1(3), 139–143, 10.1016/j.gande.2023.07.002.

Zhang, Y., Wu, Z.-Y. (2023). Gene therapy for monogenic disorders: Challenges, strategies, and perspectives. *Journal of Genetics and Genomics*, 10.1016/j.jgg.2023.08.00.

Zhao, J., Chen, X., Ho, K.-H., Cai, C., Li, C.-W., Yang, M., Yi, C. (2021). Nanotechnology for diagnosis and therapy of rheumatoid arthritis: Evolution towards theranostic approaches. *Chinese Chemical Letters*, 32(1), 66–86, 10.1016/j.cclet.2020.11.048.

2 Human enhancement

Scope, forms, and trends

2.1 The concept of human enhancement as an outcome of the Fourth Industrial Revolution

The phenomenon of human enhancement (HE) has been studied for decades. Over the years, reflections on HE have become more mainstream and have been discussed from a variety of scientific perspectives (Koops et al., 2013; Bateman et al., 2015), including bioethics. The fact is there are ethics and philosophy which lead the research on HE (Clarke et al., 2016; Forsberg et al., 2017; Juengst, Moseley, 2019; Fisher, 2021). Within philosophy, several specialities and fields of study can be distinguished such as philosophical anthropology, philosophy of technology, and philosophy of risk (Coeckelbergh, 2013). One cannot ignore religion either (Mercer, Trothen, 2015; Trothen, Mercer, 2017). Over time, the number of studies has been growing (Buchanan, 2011) so today the publications available are aimed at a wider audience than just academic circles. One may maintain that HE is an intensively explored area gaining increasing attention from academia and society at large.

Due to the multidimensionality of HE, there is no single, universally accepted definition of this phenomenon (Moore, 2008; Chadwick, 2024). This is partly because it covers a wide spectrum of phenomena and objects. This refers to a wide range of devices and systems starting from smart pills, plastic surgery, through genetic selection, computer brains, and ending up with clones and chimeras (Koops, 2013, p. 184).

In the ethics and philosophical literature, HE is usually defined as interventions leading to biological changes in human bodies and brains, using pharmaceutical, surgical, or genetic techniques. Juengst and Moseley (2019) distinguish between four fields HE could be implemented:

- cosmetic surgery and the use of biosynthetic growth hormone to increase stature,
- 'blood doping' and steroid use to improve athletic endurance and strength,
- psychopharmaceutical approaches increasing memory, elevating mood, and improving cognitive capacities,

DOI: 10.4324/9781003449584-3

- potential genetic and neurological manipulations to increase the human life span, acquire new sensory-motor abilities, and, through 'moral enhancement', live together in more peaceable, generous, and just ways (Juengst, Moseley, 2019, p. 2).

For this book, we have adopted a definition of HE using the elements of Sandberg's proposal as cited by Moore (Moore, 2008, p. xi) and Buchanan's proposition (Buchanan, 2011, p. 5).

Thus, human enhancement is defined as an intervention/modification – a human action of any kind – in the biology or psychology of a person that either increases species-typical normal functioning above the statistically typical levels, or produces a new capacity that normal human beings do not possess. This definition matches one of the most current concepts of HE perceiving it as '... means raising physical, cognitive or emotional human capacities or the performance of these capacities above levels of normality by technology or supported by technology' (Kamenjasevic, 2022, p. 10). It should be added that some authors use *human enhancement* and *human augmentation* interchangeably (Raisamo et al., 2019; Daniel, 2020) so it is also in this book.

HE can be seen as synonymous with biomedical enhancement and may affect the body or the mind (Canellopoulou-Bottis, 2018, p. 1). Human enhancement should not be associated with therapy (i.e., actions aimed at curing a disease or protecting against one) (Canellopoulou-Bottis, 2018) although the line between these two terms is blurring (Evans et al., 2021; Martín et al., 2023; Garasic, Lavazza, 2024) and needs clarification in the future regulations (Almeida, Diogo, 2019). Consequently, hearing aids, vision restoration technologies, or artificial organs (assuming that their functionality does not surpass natural biological organs) are not considered human enhancements. They serve to restore the features/functions lost due to illness/accident, rather than augment them. Leaving aside the details and issues related to the impossibility of unambiguously assigning a particular HE treatment to one of these two categories, in this book, HE is not considered as a therapy or/and curing activity. Consequently, HE does not belong to a list of treatments covered by a typical healthcare insurance coverage thus it is not financed from health insurance plans (this issue will be developed in Chapter 4).

All the above show that HE is an emerging heterogeneous phenomenon that eludes an unambiguous and clear, precise definition thus making it difficult to research. There is no single doubt that HE deserves close attention from scientists, researchers, and society at large. HE's humanistic values, complexity and heterogeneous character and all its profound impact on humans are powerful incentives to explore HE. One may acknowledge a growing interest in research on transhumanism's ideals of achieving super-intelligence, super longevity, and super well-being through human enhancement technologies (HETs) and their relations with other aspects of human existence, for example, services marketing principles (Lima, Belk, 2022). It is also worth acknowledging that debates on HE, although mostly focused on its benefits, do not ignore the attendant threats, which include the widening gap between the rich and the poor, and corruption (Buchanan, 2011). This issue will be developed in Chapter 4.

Consequently, it is worth starting by presenting some institutional research on HE in an organised and continuous manner, giving certain guarantees of methodological correctness and soundness as well as the appropriate quality of the outcomes of the research.

2.2 Institutional dimension of research on HE

There are many institutions of various statuses, ranks, goals, and profiles that research HE. They can be classified according to various criteria, but for this book, a dual division into non-military and military institutions will be adopted, which seems to be the right solution given the genesis of HE research.

2.2.1 Non-military institutions/organisations

Many prestigious universities and institutions research HE. It is no coincidence that all three of the highest-ranking universities in the Shanghai Academic Ranking of World Universities (ARWU) in 2022 were Harvard University, Stanford University, and Massachusetts Institute of Technology research HE. Additional research is carried out in specialised institutes and university organisational units which include but are not limited to:

- *Wyss Institute for Biologically Inspired Engineering.* The institute conducts interdisciplinary research at the intersection of engineering, biology, and medicine. Researchers work on projects related to regenerative medicine, synthetic biology, and wearable devices that enhance human capabilities.
- *Human enhancement ethics and policy project.* Stanford University has a project dedicated to the ethical factors editing, cognitive enhancement, and the social and ethical ramifications of these technologies.
- *MIT Media Lab – Biomechatronics Group.* The Group at MIT focuses on developing advanced prosthetic limbs and wearable technologies to enhance human physical abilities. They work on projects that push the boundaries of human-machine integration.

HE is researched also at the University of Oxford (ranked 7th in 2022) in the Future of Humanity Institute. This institute explores various aspects of human enhancement, including the ethical and societal implications of emerging technologies like artificial intelligence and genetic engineering. Consequently, HE is researched in specialised organisational settings in four out of ten best world universities (as of 2022).

Top universities are not the only places of scientific inquiry on HE. The list can be extended to some prestigious research centres such as the Max Planck

Institute for Human Cognitive and Brain Sciences which conducts studies on cognitive enhancement, neuroscience, and human brain function where topics related to brain-computer interfaces (BCIs) and neurofeedback are studied. The Center for Bioethics at the University of Pennsylvania is another example. Here researchers focus on ethical issues in biomedicine and technology and the legal, and social implications of various HETs.

Apart from classic academic institutions, there are also independent research centres such as the Hastings Center (examining ethical issues related to human enhancement, including genetic editing, cognitive enhancement, and human enhancement in sports), Future of Life Institute (focusing on ensuring that emerging technologies, including those related to human enhancement, are developed and used in ways that benefit humanity), or the Transhumanist Movement (a global community of individuals and organisations interested in the enhancement of human capabilities through technology and science engaging in discussions and debates about the future of human enhancement) (OpenAI, 2023).

One cannot ignore the RAND Corporation (and its National Security Research Division), a powerful and influential non-profit corporation. It can be treated separately not only because of its origin[1] but also because of its wide and heterogeneous scope of activities undertaken globally.

So there are universities, independent research centres, various organisations, communities, and the society at large, interested and/or involved in the process of studying HE. Although all these organisations possess the status of civilian entities, they may be involved through outsourcing in various military projects conducted by resourceful and powerful military institutions.

2.2.2 *Military institutions and organisations*

The idea of HE has a nearly 40-year institutional history and apparent military origin, as it was the US Army Research Institute that originally requested the National Research Council of the National Academy of Sciences to establish an institute to study human enhancement (Druckman, Bjork, 1994, p. vii).

The military institutions and organisations fully desire to be treated separately not just because they were founding fathers of human enhancement, but due to their outstanding financial and organisational capacity.

As mentioned earlier, human enhancement has a profound military dimension (Taraska, 2017). This can be seen in the 2021 report for the US Department of Defense and Intelligence Community officials on enhancing human performance prepared by the RAND National Security Research Division (NSRD). The report places HPE among such strategic and far-reaching topics like quantum technology, semiconductor technology, the intersection of artificial intelligence and cybersecurity, deepfake generation and detection, and the use of patent data to assist in understanding global trends in emerging technologies (Blumenthal et al., 2021, p. iii).

As indicated in the previous chapter, it was the US Army Research Institute which initiated research on human enhancement and paved the way for intensive exploration of HE. There is sufficient ground to maintain that the United States is at the top among countries with the greatest achievements regarding HE. Nowadays, a division of the US Department of Defense, the Defense Advanced Research Projects Agency (DARPA) and its Defense Science Office and Biological Technologies Office oversee much of the research on HE. It should be noted, however, that there is limited open-sourced information on DARPA and its activities (Taraska, 2017, p. 180).

There is no sufficient information about the achievements and projects in other countries. Judging by appearances, Russia, China, the United Kingdom, and Israel can be seen as important players in the global market of HE. The Russian military has experimented with exoskeletons and advanced prosthetics. The Chinese People's Liberation Army has been researching genetic engineering techniques. Exoskeletons have also been explored by the UK Ministry of Defence and Israel Defense Forces. The UK Ministry of Defence also invests in wearable technologies. Various other countries have shown interest in HE technologies, although specific details might not be publicly available. These countries include France, Germany, and South Korea, among others (OpenAI, 2023).

Also, NATO through its Science and Technology Organization (STO), a subsidiary body, and the Collaborative Programme of Work (CPoW), is involved in human enhancement. Here exoskeletons and BCIs take the lead (NATO, 2023).

Needless to say, the specificity of the functioning and objectives of military research institutes means that both the projects they carry out and the results are secret or top secret, which results in, among other things, difficulties or an inability to familiarise the public with these issues.

Staying with the institutional arrangement, one phenomenon attracts attention. For decades, research on HE and emerging technological applications/interventions was performed in conventional settings, for example, research institutes (Coenen, 2024) and through conventional regulated and controlled procedures (e.g., clinical trials). However, the last decade has witnessed an emergence of scientific activities being performed in unconventional settings (e.g., households, community labs), often through unconventional unregulated and uncontrolled procedures (e.g., self-administration of substances; Gaspar et al., 2019). One may interpret this as an outcome of the democratisation of knowledge leveraged by growing access to information. This issue will be further developed in Chapter 4.

2.3 Measuring human enhancement: key determinants

Estimation of the scope of HE (see Section 2.4) must be preceded by methods and specific measures of its measurement. In the case of HE, which is a multidimensional phenomenon, such a procedure is difficult and complicated. Researching HE raises important questions regarding its measuring, monitoring, and assessment, especially in the context of the emerging character of this phenomenon. Some key points are raised below.

2.3.1 Measuring

The point of departure of HE measuring lies on an individual level, that is, relates to various aspects of an individual's cognitive, physical, or emotional abilities (Kitporntheranunt, Kitporntheranunt, 2022) before and after a specific intervention or enhancement technique. HE is a social phenomenon and has also a wider societal dimension. In this context, all individual abilities should be collected, aggregated, and analysed when one draws the picture of HE.

The measurement of HE should be preceded by a short methodological introduction. Here one may distinguish five steps/elements.

First, a fundamental question of what is *the purpose of HE* should be asked. What are the specific goals and objectives of the human enhancement intervention? What do we want to improve or enhance, and why?

Second, we should establish *a baseline measurement* of the individual's abilities or attributes before the enhancement intervention. Depending on what we want to improve, a baseline measurement may concern three fields indicated above: cognitive enhancement (CE), physical enhancement (PE), and emotive enhancements (EE) (Taraska, 2017).

Third, one must decide on *the appropriate metrics*. This could involve quantitative measures (e.g., reaction time, memory tests, physical strength) or qualitative assessments (e.g., self-reported well-being, subjective experiences). Due to the very nature of HE, it is inevitable to include subjective assessments (surveys, interviews, self-report questionnaires) from individuals undergoing enhancement to gauge their perception of improvement and overall well-being.

Fourth, if it is possible, *a control group* or individuals who do not undergo HE intervention should be established and monitored. This will allow us to assess the true impact of the enhancement.

Fifth, after the enhancement intervention, it is necessary to conduct (under similar conditions to minimise confounding variables) *a follow-up assessment* using the same metrics and methods as the baseline assessment.

It is also worth noting that due to the very nature of human enhancement and its ongoing and evolving process, it is necessary to pay special attention to two things: one is long-term effects (*Do the enhancements persist over time? Are there side effects?*) and the second is iteration and improvement (*measurement methods and techniques should be continuously refined based on feedback and new knowledge*) (OpenAI, 2023).

Looking at the above-mentioned points, one may perceive them as demanding. Some may express reasonable doubts about whether they fully apply to the day-to-day operation of HE. Indeed, measuring HE shows weaknesses in each of the five steps/stages highlighted above.

Problems start from the very beginning, from *the purpose of HE.* Simplifying and generalising, one may say that HE procedures are used by individuals to gain an advantage over other people simply because competition is embedded in humans. This can be also justified by strong HE military roots since better physical and cognitive abilities, communication and coordination, and predictive analytics and planning (Pawar et al., 2023) determine victory on the battlefield. HE procedures aimed at these traits are perceived as a proper goal to achieve competitive advantage on the battlefield.

Since striving to compete and wanting to stand out from others is very human, baseline measurement and the appropriate metrics are individual and subjective and thus difficult to measure. Partly due to this subjectivity, it is questionable whether the establishment of a control group could improve HE measuring.

Of special importance is *a follow-up assessment* of HE or rather a lack of it. From the point of view of human evolution as a species, the lack of such systematic assessment carried out over a long period can be treated as a potential threat to homo sapiens.

It can therefore be concluded that the measurement of HE is in the initial phase. A supporting argument could be the fact that at the time of this publication, there were no scientific publications specifically on HE measurement. It seems that the most challenging issue at this stage is the objectification of measurement procedures, tools, and methods partly because HE has its immanent, strong subjective character.

2.3.2 Monitoring

Bearing in mind the difficulties of measuring HE, one can move on to the issue of monitoring it. Monitoring a phenomenon difficult to measure is by definition, very complicated. Following the distinction between non-military and military institutions researching HE, one may make a distinction between HE of primarily military and civil (with individual choices) character. Monitoring this first category of HE is hardly possible due to the lack of open-access to appropriate information. Concerning the second category, valuable sources of information are publications in scientific journals and what is published by think tanks and other independent centres and available on the internet. Due to the scarce literature, gathering information about HE is a challenge and this is acknowledged in the literature (Gaspar et al., 2019).

Monitoring HE can be done through the review and analysis of scientific publications, proceedings from international conferences, tailored scientific programmes, and special reports. Supplementary to these could be sources available on the internet (when treated with due caution).

At the time of this publication, there was a limited number of scientific journals devoted to HE or specialising in HE. Table 2.1 shows a subjective and non-representative list of journals[2] publishing papers on HE between 2020

Table 2.1 Selected scientific journals covering research and experiments related to HE

Title (year of the first issue publication)	*Profile/topics*	*The most recent* volume is numbered as*	*No. of articles** from 2020*
Brain-Computer Interfaces (2014)	Theoretical and practical advances in brain-computer interface (BCI) technology, biomedical engineering, computer science and engineering, electrical engineering, human factors, industrial and systems engineering, machine learning, mechanical engineering, neuroscience, neurosurgery, psychology, rehabilitation engineering	10	32
Journal of Genetic Engineering and Biotechnology (2003)	Microbial biotechnology, industrial biotechnology, medical biotechnology, genomics, proteomics, and bioinformatics	21	0
The American Journal of Human Genetics (1949)	Human genetics and biological processing	110	0
American Journal of Medical Genetics Part A (1977)	Biological and medical aspects of genetic disorders and birth defects, in-depth documentation of phenotype analysis within the current context of genotype/phenotype correlations, experimental and molecular approaches to cancer genetics and cytogenetics, clinical molecular genetics (linkage, mapping, and gene sequencing), neuropsychiatric genetics	191	0
Human Molecular Genetics (1992)	All topics related to human molecular genetics, two 'special review' issues are published each year	32	0
Molecular Genetics and Genomics (1908)	All areas of genetics and genomics, any approach to the study of genes and genomes (experimental, theoretical or synthetic), research on all organisms that is of broad interest to those working in the fields of genetics, genomics, biology, medicine, and biotechnology	298	0
Biotechnology and Genetic Engineering Reviews (1984)	Major reviews covering the important state-of-the-art developments in industrial, agricultural, and medical applications of biotechnology and therapeutics	39	8
Journal of Posthuman Studies: Philosophy, Technology, Media (2017)	Consequences of enhancement, especially bio enhancement, transhumanist, and posthumanist accounts of 'the human'	6 (December 2022)	3
Journal of NeuroEngineering and Rehabilitation (from 2004)	Neuroscience and biomedical engineering, rehabilitation and human movement augmentation	20	3

Journal of Medical Ethics (1975)	Ethical aspects of health care	49	9
Neuroethics (2008)	Ethical issues posed by new technologies, psycho-pharmaceuticals, practice of neuroscience, regulation of neuroscientific technologies	16	13
Frontiers in Human Neuroscience (2007)	A wide range of specialities and disciplines in the field of neuroscience	8,710 articles since beginning	1
New Genetics and Society: Critical Studies of Contemporary Biosciences (1982)	Sociological perspectives on contemporary genetics and related biological sciences	42	7
Ethics and Information Technology (1999)	Technology assessment, cultural studies, public policy analysis and public administration, cognitive science, social and anthropological studies in technology, mass communication, and legal studies	25	5
Augmented Human Research (2016)	Augmented musculoskeletal system and rehabilitation; exoskeletons and human technologies; BCIs, muscle interfaces and implanted interfaces; wearable computing and ubiquitous computing; smart objects and smart textiles augmenting humans; interfaces, services, and applications for human enhancement; cognitive augmentation of the human intellect; augmented health care, quality of life and well-being; hardware, material, substances and sensors for human augmentation; safety, trust, privacy, and security of augmented human technologies; applications of artificial intelligence and virtual reality in health care and sports***	7 (December 2022)	8
Journal of Genetic Engineering and Biotechnology Research (2019)	Synthetic genomes and genomics; human genetic enhancement; genomic data mining; mapping of genomes	5	1

Source: Author's own elaboration

* In the vast majority of cases as of September 2023.

** Web pages of all journals included in Table 2.1 were searched. The key term for searching was 'human enhancement'. In addition, papers dealing with factors also indirectly connected with human enhancement as indicated in Figure 1.1 were also counted.

*** https://www.springer.com/journal/41133/aims-and-scope

and mid-2023. Out of these 15 journals only two titles: *Brain-Computer Interfaces* (published in 2014) and *Augmented Human Research* (launched in 2016) seem to be focused on HE.

Notes

Table 2.1 shows that HE is present in the most recent publications mainly in journals from social (sociology) and humanistic (philosophy and ethics) disciplines. Although before 2020 all of the listed in Table 2.1 journals published papers on HE, those specialising in genetics did not report new papers directly related to HE. This in turn confirms the opinion presented earlier that HE issues are addressed mainly in the social sciences and humanities, and to a lesser extent in medical or engineering sciences. This in turn allows us to maintain that HE is being researched based mainly on qualitative methods, the quantitative ones remaining rare.

One should add that some journals included HE as their research topics, an example is *ELSI*[3] *in Human Enhancement: What Distinguishes It from Therapy* (Greenbaum, Cabrera, 2020).

In addition to scientific journals, there are also books on HE published by recognised academic and scientific publishing houses where Routledge, Elsevier, and Springer take the lead.

Apart from publications, there are other academic initiatives and actions regarding HE such as research projects,[4] workshops,[5] and seminars.[6]

An important component of academic activities is scientific meetings and conferences focused on HE. Peter Joosten on his web page dedicated HE among information a list of nine international meetings aimed at human enhancement (https://www.peterjoosten.org/human-enhancement-research), including the Augmented Humans (AHs) International Conference.[7]

One may conclude that there are several international scientific journals which publish articles on human enhancement. Various aspects of HE are the subjects of international conferences, workshops, and seminars as well as scientific projects, including international ones. As of the time of writing, there is no scientific journal specialising in HE and publishing empirical studies on quantitative aspects of HE.

2.3.3 Assessment

Given the objective and subjective limitations and shortcomings of the methodology for measuring HE, it is obvious that this makes it difficult and complicated to assess HE (Chadwick, 2024). But the latter refers mainly to practical aspects and empirical research and study, since on the level of scientific reflection and in normative terms, HE is the subject of in-depth studies and assessment mainly from the perspective of the humanities and social sciences: philosophy (primarily ethics), psychology, and sociology. One may conclude that, as indicated above, at the current stage of the study on HE, its assessment is almost exclusively qualitative. The quantitative dimension of HE research remains a challenge.

2.4 Scope of HE

The paucity of quantitative analyses of HE significantly limits and makes it difficult to determine the scope of this phenomenon. Here we are doomed to disordered and fragmentary data on HE. In the absence of reliable and complete information on the use of HE in clinical practice,[8] we are forced to provide only random data related to the examples of various forms of HE which will be presented below.

2.5 Forms of HE

As shown in Figure 1.1, the Fourth Industrial Revolution (4IR) can affect human enhancement through multiple channels and devices. As a result, HE can be achieved in various ways (Bostrom, Sandberg, 2009).

One should also notice that different HE forms may not be mutually exclusive, and some may necessitate other configurations. This refers to nearly all of the forms presented below.

There are different kinds of HE. It can be classified and structured according to the type of *ability/feature* they are intended to improve or *the intervention* and *technology used* to that end. Biomedical enhancements can improve motor traits, such as physical strength, speed, and endurance as well as cognitive ones, cognitive ability, mood, temperament, emotional capacity, or longevity (Buchanan, 2011, p. 5). These traits can be enhanced through *the ingestion of chemicals*, *exposure to a special device*, or *surgical intervention.*

Daniel (2020) distinguishes between three types of human enhancement:

- *replicating* (these are HEs that restore or replicate typical human abilities like prosthetic limbs for the disabled, hearing aids for the deaf, and voice synthesisers for the mute),
- *supplementing* (HEs that improve our ability to do something like devices that artificially increase our strength, enhance our sight beyond normal limits, or increase our intelligence), and
- *exceeding* (HEs that allow us to do things that we cannot do on our own like the ability to fly, breath underwater, see ultraviolet or infrared light, and smell chemicals not currently detectable by the human olfactory sense) (Daniel, 2020, p. 5).

One should acknowledge, however, that Daniel's typology does not fit with our definition of HE since only *supplementing* (but only partially) and *exceeding* apply to it.

HE forms can be classified and distinguished according to various criteria. Such criteria can be a human body (as a place of intervention), or environment and hardware/software.[9] Using the first criterion one may distinguish between internal interventions like gene therapy, nano-implants (Gaspar et al., 2019), nano-robots, etc., and external ones like various devices/materials/substances, for example, external exosenses (Gauttier, 2019).

Human enhancement can also be achieved through a smart environment, for example, digital or virtual environments (Coeckelbergh, 2011, 2013) or through hardware/software, for example, brain-machine interface (BMI) (Jebari, 2013).

For decades, this type of research and emerging technological applications/interventions were performed in conventional settings (e.g., research institutes) and through conventional regulated and controlled procedures (e.g., clinical trials) (Coenen, 2024). However, the last decade has witnessed an emergence of scientific activities being performed in unconventional settings (e.g., households, community labs), often through unconventional unregulated and uncontrolled procedures (e.g., self-administration of substances (Gaspar et al., 2019).

The typology of HE forms differs, but it is possible to identify common elements. Based on what already exists in the literature, Taraska proposes a tripartite division of HE forms into *cognitive enhancement, physical enhancement*, and *emotive enhancement* (Taraska, 2017).

Anomaly (2020) proposes a slightly different typology of HE but the first four categories – *cognitive enhancement, moral enhancement, aesthetic enhancement*, and *immuno-enhancement* – correspond to Taraska's division since *aesthetic enhancement*, and *immuno-enhancement* can be classified as a kind of *physical enhancement*. The most striking is Anomaly's fifth category labelled *creating life from scratch*, which means (in common language) a laboratory creation of various forms of living creatures.

Erden and Brey (2022) propose the following types of HE (they may not be mutually exclusive, and some may necessitate others): physical enhancements (improving physical abilities or introducing new ones, including for performance or endurance), cognitive enhancements (enhancing cognitive function, such as intelligence or memory), moral enhancements (modulating or fostering attitudes and behaviours that are considered morally or socially acceptable), cosmetic enhancements (improving the appearance or traits of a human being), and longevity enhancements (improving durability and that extending life span) (Erden, Brey, 2022, p. 836).

In this book, four forms of HE: *cognitive enhancement, physical enhancement*, mood *enhancement*, and *moral enhancement* are presented following the typology by Jotterand and Ienca (2023). Such a fourfold division is adopted here, not only because this publication was one of the most recent at the time of publication, but also because it distinguishes moral enhancement, which has a considerable research record partly due to the contribution of philosophers and social scientists.

2.5.1 Cognitive enhancement

Cognitive enhancement (CE) has a long tradition since the idea of augmenting the human intellect is over 60 years old. The term was coined by Engelbart in 1962 (Engelbart, 1962). CE can be defined as any augmentation of core information processing systems in the brain, including the mechanisms underlying perception, attention, conceptualisation, memory, reasoning, and motor performance (Luber, Lisanby, 2014).

To have a broader picture of CE let us refresh our understanding regarding brain functioning. The brain receives information from five senses: sight, smell, sound, touch, and taste. It also receives inputs including vibration, pain, and temperature from the rest of the human body as well as autonomic (involuntary) inputs from human organs. It interprets this information so a person can understand and associate meaning with what goes on around him/her. Consequently, the brain enables the following functions: thoughts and decisions, memories and emotions, movements (motor function), balance and coordination, perception of various sensations including pain, automatic behaviour such as breathing, heart rate, sleep and temperature control, regulation of organ function, speech and language functions, and fight or flight response (stress response).

Cognitive enhancement can be achieved through technologies that aim to improve human empirical abilities such as thinking, quick and effective decision-making, memory, attention, focus, understanding, learning, pain management, and enhancing sensory abilities, such as vision, hearing, or smell, using artificial sensors or implants.

Several methods are leading to cognitive enhancement. These methods can be achieved either through medical or non-medical methods.

2.5.1.1 Medical methods

Medical methods can be divided into invasive groups such as BCIs, deep brain stimulation (DBS) and optogenetics or non-invasive ones like transcranial direct current stimulation (TDCS) and transcranial magnetic stimulation (TMS).

Invasive methods require a part of the skull be exposed to remove appropriate pieces of physical objects. These interventions are often difficult, messy, expensive, and usually leave the patient with severe trauma. DBS involves electrodes that are permanently placed in certain brain regions. The electrodes are connected to a small device, which sends low electrical currents to the electrodes in a programmed rhythm. DBS is successfully used in patients with Parkinson's disease as well as other conditions, including severe chronic depression, Tourette syndrome and severe obsessive-compulsive disorders. As the names suggest, TDCS works using electrical stimulation, TMS by magnetic stimulation and optogenetics by light stimulation. In TDCS, electrodes are placed on the outside of the skull and a weak electrical current is emitted. Initially, this technology was developed to improve cognitive function (Joosten, 2023).

Applying the criterion of an entity undertaking an action, HE methods can be divided into those utilised by medical staff (medical interventions) and those undertaken by the patients themselves (autonomous) by using nootropics (*a diverse group of medicinal substances whose action improves human thinking, learning, and memory*) and pharmaceuticals.

2.5.1.1.1 INVASIVE METHODS: MEDICAL INTERVENTIONS

In this category, one may find BCIs, DBS, and optogenetics. BCIs are advanced technologies that enable direct communication between the brain and external devices or computer systems.

Brain-computer interfaces Among examples of BCIs, one may find *neurorehabilitation*, *neurofeedback*, and *mind-controlled devices*.

In *neurorehabilitation*, BCIs are used to help patients recover from conditions such as stroke or spinal cord injuries. They can assist in regaining motor functions by enabling users to control robotic exoskeletons or prosthetic limbs through their thoughts. In the context of controlling robotic exoskeletons, one may speculate that the next step of the development of neurorehabilitation may lead beyond treatment, to human enhancement. Such a scenario may also apply to neurofeedback.

Nowadays BCIs can be used for *neurofeedback* training to help individuals manage stress, anxiety, and other mental health conditions (Cai Chen et al., 2023). Users can learn to control their brain activity patterns and improve their mental well-being. Further developments in this field may result in curbing stress to an unprecedented scale.

Mind-controlled devices are now limited to a variety of assistive devices, such as wheelchairs, home automation systems, and communication devices. Users can navigate their environment and control appliances with their thoughts. The list of devices controlled by the mind can be extended thus BCIs can assist in human enhancement.

Deep brain stimulation Deep brain stimulation (DBS) is a medical procedure that involves the implantation of electrodes into specific regions of the brain to deliver electrical impulses. DBS involves time-specific electrical stimulation of the brain via implanted electrodes but electrical currents spread non-selectively, such that fibres in the vicinity of electrodes are activated along with the targeted cells, making it difficult to estimate the actual volume of stimulated tissue (Adamczyk, Zawadzki, 2020). DBS has been used to treat a variety of neurological and psychiatric conditions such as essential tremor, dystonia, obsessive-compulsive disorder (OCD), epilepsy, major depressive disorder (MDD), Tourette syndrome, pain management, Huntington's disease (experimental stage), and severe tinnitus. It should be noted that DBS can also lead to unpredictable changes in the experience of self and personal identity (Gallagher, 2021). The above list suggests that DBS is used nearly exclusively for treatment, not for enhancement. However, depression and pain management possess a certain potential for human enhancement development.

It is important to notice that the efficacy of DBS against mental illness has not been confirmed due to the absence of publications on randomised, controlled trials (RCTs) (Schläpfer et al., 2021).

Optogenetics Optogenetics can be defined as an invasive neuromodulation technology involving the use of light to control the activity of individual neurons (Adamczyk, Zawadzki, 2020). It can be also treated as a technological platform consisting of development and a combined implementation of optical and genetic methods for studying neural contributions to behaviour (Michaelides, Bonci, 2022). Optogenetics enables the user not only to record but also to manipulate the activity of individual neurons in living tissue with the use of light and to observe the effects of such manipulation in real time (Adamczyk, Zawadzki, 2020). Optogenetics enables far more precise and selective neural control than any other existing neuromodulation technique.

Artificial intelligence (AI) is treated as a potential form of cognitive enhancement (Nyholm, 2023) and can be called intellectual augmentation (Erler, Müller, 2021). There is no consensus in the literature regarding AI assignment to the group of invasive methods. This is legitimate, however, if for its operation AI uses various nanotechnology products/outcomes implanted in the human body.

One may conclude that specific mechanisms underlying brain stimulation remain unclear, despite the demonstrated efficacy in several nervous system diseases (Hoang et al., 2017). Also, the effectiveness of adaptive brain implants can vary widely depending on the individual, the specific application, the technology used, and the level of support and rehabilitation provided. While brain implants have shown promise in restoring lost functions and improving the quality of life for individuals with certain medical conditions, it is still an evolving field, and ongoing research is essential to further enhance their effectiveness and safety (OpenAI, 2023).

Invasive HE methods should be approached with caution, and the decision to undergo such procedures should involve careful consideration of the risks, benefits, and ethical implications. Additionally, the effectiveness of these methods can evolve as medical technology advances and research continues to refine these interventions (OpenAI, 2023). At this point, we revisit the issue of the lack of legal regulations on HE.

2.5.1.1.2 NON-INVASIVE METHODS

Two leading non-invasive methods of HE are TDCSs and TMSs.

Transcranial direct current stimulation Transcranial direct current stimulation (TDCS) is a non-invasive brain stimulation technique that uses weak electric currents (usually between 1 mA and 2 mA) to modulate brain activity by affecting neuronal membrane excitability. It has several advantages over other brain stimulation techniques. It is safe, it is characterised by the highest tolerability among brain stimulation techniques as it causes minimal discomfort to participants, is cost-effective (the price of TDCS devices and applications are 10 to 100 times lower than other treatment options), and is easy to use, and therefore has a high potential to be applied even in home-based settings (Bjekić et al., 2021). However, the effectiveness of the enhancement due to TDCS is still controversial (Lavazza, 2019) but it seems to have a large potential for improvement. TDCS can reduce fear (Vicario et al., 2020) and lead to associative and working memory improvement (Bjekić et al., 2021).

Transcranial magnetic stimulation Transcranial magnetic stimulation (TMS) uses very brief high-intensity magnetic fields to induce currents and thus depolarise neurons in small regions of the cortex. It modulates cortical networks in ways that might produce performance enhancements in healthy individuals by accelerating skill acquisition (Luber, Lisanby, 2014) and thus can be seen as a classical tool for human enhancement. A few dozen reports of TMS performance enhancement show that TMS '… increases our understanding of enhancement mechanisms such as addition-by-subtraction, potentiating oscillatory behaviour, and promotion of Hebbian-type learning …' (Luber, Lisanby, 2014, p. 964).

2.5.1.2 Non-medical methods

Since both invasive and non-invasive methods indicated above can be classified as medical interventions, non-medical methods will be limited to nootropics and pharmaceuticals.[10]

Human enhancement drugs, also known as cognitive enhancers or nootropics, are substances that people use to improve various aspects of their mental and physical performance. These drugs or supplements are not used to treat medical conditions but are instead taken to enhance cognitive function, alertness, memory, focus, or physical capabilities. It should be noted here that pharmacological cognitive enhancement may lead to a dilemma for users (Gordon, Dunn, 2021).

2.5.1.2.1 NOOTROPICS

They are substances that are claimed to enhance cognitive function, memory, creativity, or motivation. Some popular nootropics include racetams, choline supplements, and herbal extracts like *ginkgo biloba* and *bacopa monnieri*. Studies show that nicotine can have nootropic effects, such as improved alertness and attention, especially in people with naturally poor attention spans (Poltavski, Petros, 2006, after Julson, 2023).

2.5.1.2.2 STIMULANTS

Like *caffeine* (the most widely consumed psychoactive substance in the world), amphetamines, and modafinil are often used to increase alertness and concentration. They can help users stay awake and focused for extended periods. Caffeine works by blocking adenosine receptors in your brain, making you feel less tired. *Amphetamines* (such as Adderall) is a prescription medication that contains highly stimulating properties that speed up messages travelling between the brain and body. It's most commonly prescribed to treat attention deficit hyperactivity disorder (ADHD) and narcolepsy, but it's increasingly taken by healthy adults to improve attention and focus. *Bacopa monnieri* is an ancient herb used in Ayurvedic medicine to enhance brain function. Several studies have found that *Bacopa monnieri* supplements can speed up information processing in your brain, reduce reaction times and improve memory (Pase et al., 2012; Kongkeaw et al., 2014, both after Julson, 2023) *L-theanine* is a naturally occurring amino acid found in tea, but it can also be taken as a supplement. Taking even just 50 mg – the amount found in roughly two cups of brewed tea – has been found to increase alpha waves in the brain, which are linked to creativity. *Modafinil* commonly sold under the brand name Provigil, modafinil is a prescription drug that is often used to treat narcolepsy, a condition that causes uncontrollable drowsiness. Its stimulating effects are similar to those of amphetamines or cocaine. Yet, animal studies suggest it has a lower risk of dependence. Several studies have shown that modafinil significantly reduces feelings of fatigue and improves memory in sleep-deprived adults. It also enhances executive functioning, or the ability to properly manage your time and resources to accomplish your goals.

2.5.1.2.3 SMART DRUGS

They are pharmaceutical drugs improving cognitive function. *Modafinil* and *Adderall* are examples, although they are typically prescribed for medical conditions like narcolepsy and ADHD. *Methylphenidate* (Ritalin) is another prescription drug used to manage symptoms of ADHD and narcolepsy. Like *Adderall*, it's a stimulant (Tomasi et al., 2011) and increases dopamine and noradrenaline concentrations in the brain. However, it does not contain *amphetamines*. In healthy adults, *Ritalin* improves short-term memory, information-processing speed and attention (Linssen et al., 2014, after Julson, 2023). Like *Adderall*, *Ritalin* is widely abused, especially by people aged 18–25. The most common side effects of *Ritalin* include insomnia, stomach ache, headache, and loss of appetite. It can also cause hallucinations, psychosis, seizures, heart arrhythmias and high blood pressure, particularly when taken in high doses. *Ritalin* is a smart drug that enhances information processing, memory, and attention. It's only available with a prescription. *Noopept* is a synthetic smart drug that can be purchased as a supplement. Unlike some of the natural nootropics, the effects of Noopept can be felt within minutes, rather than hours, days, or weeks, and typically last for several hours (Vorobyov et al., 2011, after Julson, 2023). Animal studies have shown that Noopept speeds up how quickly the brain forms and retrieves memories by boosting levels of brain-derived neurotrophic factor (BDNF), a compound that promotes the growth of brain cells (Ostrovskaya et al., 2007; Ostrovskaya et al., 2008, both after Julson, 2023). Human research has found that this smart drug helps people recover more quickly from brain injuries, but more studies are needed to understand how it might be used as a nootropic in healthy adults (Neznamov, Teleshova, 2009). *Piracetam* is another synthetic nootropic molecule that's very similar to Noopept in structure and function. It has been shown to improve memory in people with age-related mental decline but does not seem to have much benefit in healthy adults (Leuner et al., 2010, after Julson, 2023). During the 1970s, a few small, poorly designed studies suggested that piracetam may improve memory in healthy adults (Mindus et al., 1976; Wilsher et al., 1979, both after Julson, 2023), but these findings have not been replicated. *Piracetam* is marketed as a nootropic supplement, but research supporting its effectiveness is lacking. *Phenotropil*, also known as *phenylpiracetam*, is a synthetic smart drug that is widely available as an over-the-counter supplement. It's similar in structure to piracetam and Noopept and helps the brain recover from various injuries like stroke, epilepsy, and trauma. One study in rats found that phenotropil slightly enhanced memory, but research to support its use as a smart drug in healthy adults is unavailable (Zvejniece et al., 2011, after Julson, 2023).

2.5.1.2.4 MEMORY ENHANCERS

The presentation of several examples of memory enhancers must be preceded by an important note namely that there are conceptual and neurobiological differences between memory systems so talking about 'memory' in general is too imprecise to be helpful (Fox et al., 2016, p. 376). Memory enhancers, such as *donepezil* and *memantine*, are prescribed to treat Alzheimer's disease but may be misused to enhance memory and cognitive function in healthy individuals. *Creatine* is an amino acid, which your body uses to make protein. It's a popular bodybuilding supplement that promotes muscle growth but is also beneficial for your brain. After it's consumed, creatine enters your brain where it binds with phosphate, creating a molecule that your brain uses to quickly fuel its cells. This increased availability of energy for your brain cells is linked to improved short-term memory and reasoning skills, especially in vegetarians and highly stressed people.

2.5.1.2.5 NUTRITIONAL SUPPLEMENTS

They are vitamins, minerals, and herbal supplements marketed as cognitive enhancers. Examples include *omega-3 fatty acids*, *vitamin B complex*, and various *adaptogenic herbs*. One may also place *Panax ginseng root* and extracts from the leaves of the *Ginkgo biloba* here. *Panax ginseng root* is an ancient medicinal plant used to boost brain function. Taking a single dose of 200–400 mg of *Panax ginseng* has been shown to reduce brain fatigue and significantly improve performance on difficult tasks like mental math problems; however, it's unclear how *Panax ginseng* boosts brain function. It may be due to its strong anti-inflammatory effects, which help protect your brain from oxidative stress and enhance its function (Reay et al., 2006, after Julson, 2023). Extracts from the leaves of the *Ginkgo biloba* tree may also have positive effects on your brain. *Ginkgo biloba* supplements have been shown to improve memory and mental processing in healthy older adults when taken daily for six weeks (Kaschel, 2011, after Julson, 2023). Taking *Ginkgo biloba* before a highly stressful task also reduces stress-related high blood pressure and decreases levels of cortisol, a type of stress hormone.

2.5.1.2.6 PERFORMANCE-ENHANCING DRUGS

They are substances commonly associated with athletes and bodybuilders to enhance physical performance. Examples include anabolic *steroids*, *Human Growth Hormone* (HGH), and *Erythropoietin* (EPO). There is a considerable number of other substances for enhanced physical performance, some of them of natural origin in the stage of clinical trials like Astaxanthin (Hecht et al., 2021).

2.5.1.2.7 MOOD STIMULANTS

Rhodiola rosea is an adaptogenic herb that helps your body handle stress more effectively. Several studies have found that *Rhodiola rosea* supplements can improve mood and decrease feelings of burnout in both anxious and highly stressed individuals (Olsson et al., 2009, after Julson, 2023). Taking small daily doses of *Rhodiola rosea* has been shown to reduce mental fatigue and increase feelings of well-being in college students during stressful exam periods (Spasov et al., 2000, after Julson, 2023).

Even with the increasing medical studies, the use of human-enhancement drugs remains a complex and controversial topic in society.

The forms of HE presented above and classified as invasive and non-invasive, and medical and non-medical do not exhaust the topic. One may add to the items above other forms of non-invasive products and activities which indirectly impact human enhancement through learning and education (here one may mention online learning platforms: technological platforms offer personalised and interactive learning experiences, enhancing educational outcomes and augmented reality (AR) and virtual reality (VR). These technologies can create immersive educational environments, improving engagement and understanding, social and communication (examples being social media and networking platforms). These platforms allow for enhanced communication and connection with others on a global scale and language translation technologies (here example is of real-time translation tools that can bridge language barriers and enhance cross-cultural communication).

Talking about additional non-invasive methods of influencing mood one must mention military and psychological resilience training, which seeks to assess and instil resilience in soldiers and their families through techniques developed in the discipline of positive psychology (Howell, 2015).

It is also worth acknowledging that cognitive enhancement turns out to be a multifaceted concept and that cognitive enhancers differ in their mode of action, the cognitive domain they target, the time scale they work on, their availability, their side effects, and how they differentially affect different groups of subjects (Dresler et al., 2019).

Research into cognitive enhancement is highly controversial, and arguments for and against it have failed to identify the logical fallacy underlying this debate: the fallacy of composition. The fallacy of composition is a lesser-known fallacy of ambiguity, but it has been explored and applied extensively to other fields, including economics. The fallacy of composition, which occurs when the characteristics of the parts of the whole are incorrectly extended to apply to the whole itself, and the conclusion is false, should be addressed in the debate on cognitive enhancement and within education. Within cognitive enhancement, the premise that individual distinct cognitive processes can be enhanced by cognitive enhancers leads to the conclusion that they must enhance overall cognition, and this idea is pervasive in the literature. If the goal of cognitive enhancement is to enhance cognition or learning, and not merely individual cognitive processes, then this is a clear example of the fallacy of composition. The ambiguity of 'cognitive', 'cognition', and 'enhancement' only perpetuates this fallacy and creates more confusion surrounding the purposes and goals of enhancement. Identifying this fallacy does not threaten the existing body of research. However, it provides a novel framework to explore new avenues for research, education, and enhancement, particularly through education reform initiatives. Education enhances and facilitates learning, and improvements to education could be considered cognitive enhancements. Furthermore, the same fallacy is ubiquitous in education; educators commit it by 'teaching to the test' and prioritising memorisation over generalisable skills such as critical thinking and problem-solving. We will explore these new avenues for research and highlight principles of learning success from other disciplines to create a clearer understanding of the means and ends of cognitive enhancement. Recognising the pervasiveness of composition fallacy in cognitive enhancement and education will lead to greater clarity of normative positions and insights into student learning that steer away from fallacious reasoning (Edgren, Dubljević, 2023).

2.5.2 *Physical enhancement*

The interest in physical enhancement (PE) from society at large one may point to two social groups especially motivated to proceed with physical enhancement. They are uniformed service personnel (army, police, firefighters, etc.) and sportsmen (Ryan et al., 2023).

One may distinguish between the following forms of PE.

2.5.2.1 *Gene editing technologies (GETs) and gene therapy*

While still largely experimental, gene editing technologies have the potential to treat genetic disorders and enhance certain physical traits. Among gene editing technologies one may distinguish RNAi (RNA interference which is the silencing of gene expression by the administration of double-stranded RNA – dsRNA), ZNFs (Zinc-finger proteins), TALEN (transcription activator-like effector nucleases; restriction enzymes that can be engineered to cut specific sequences of DNA), and CRISPR, including CRISPR/Cas9 (clustered regularly interspaced short palindromic repeats). Out of these four, CRISPR/Cas9 has higher editing efficiency and targeting specificity compared to other GETs to insert, delete, modify, or replace the gene at a specific location in the host genome (Harisa et al., 2023). Some authors maintain that safe and effective gene editing remains well beyond technological capabilities (Sparrow, 2019). GETs are promising for the production of molecular, cellular, and organ therapies. As noticed in Chapter 1, genetically modified pigs are used in clinical trials as a source of heart, liver, kidneys, and lungs for xenotransplantation (XT) in humans. One should note, however, that the use of GETs as XT is still in the early stage as well and it has ethical and biosafety issues (Harisa et al., 2023). Ethical concerns and biosafety issues apply entirely also to CRISPR (Kubikova et al., 2023).

2.5.2.2 *Biomechanical enhancements (BE)*

This involves the integration of mechanical or electronic components (or both) with the human body to enhance physical abilities. Examples include prosthetic limbs, exoskeletons, and wearable devices that augment strength and mobility.

Biomechanical enhancement is widely used in therapy like fracture healing (Claes, 2022) or reconstruction of extensor mechanism (EM) following total knee arthroplasty with a synthetic mesh (Naveen et al., 2020). Along with orthopedics and in cardiology, BE is used in treatment. Here one may mention devices enhancing the biomechanics of a failing heart such as atrial shunts, ventricle expanders, stimulation therapy, and mechanical circulatory support, or like in the case of atrioventricular (AV) valve disease, corresponding devices that alter the geometry, mechanics or hemodynamics of annuli, chords, leaflets and papillary muscles (Rosalia et al., 2022).

Research shows that electric fields induced by piezoelectric biological materials in humans direct tissue development, repair, and regeneration. Biodegradable piezoelectric polymers for skin, skeletal, and nerve tissue engineering occurred to lead to enhanced bone formation in bone repair via activation of signalling cascades responsible for matrix production, cell growth and tissue repair, neurite directional outgrowth filling in gaps in nerve tissue repair and accelerated wound closure and reduced scarring in skin tissue engineering (Goonoo, Bhaw-Luximon, 2022).

Transient electronics (Cheng, Vepachedu, 2016; Shim et al., 2021) can contribute significantly to BE. Transient electronics are an emerging class of electronics with the unique characteristic of completely dissolving within a programmed period. It can be seen as a crucial asset for next generation neurotechnology. It eliminates surgery for device removal and reduces infection potential. Bioresorbable neural interfaces have been developed for neural recording, neural stimulation and monitoring of biological parameters, and biodegradable neural implants could cover both short- and long-term applications by adjusting their degradation rate (Fanelli, Ghezzi, 2021).

BE is used in elite athletic training (Glazier, 2021) and the development of innovative materials in sports equipment and design (Shan, 2023) which can be treated also as forms of HE. As indicated in the literature, there is room for artificial intelligence to enhance biomechanical modelling (David et al., 2022).

2.5.2.3 *Performance enhancements*

Human performance enhancement (HPE) can be interpreted as 'any implantable, ingestable, wearable invasive or non-invasive technology that can temporarily or permanently change or promote human function' (Shao, Wu, Zhou, 2021, p. 1). Within HPE, three fields can be distinguished: perceptive enhancement, cognitive enhancement, and physical enhancement (Shao et al., 2021, p. 2).

At the time of writing, HPE is achieved mainly through performance-enhancing drugs (PEDs) and biomechanical enhancements (exoskeletons). There are two groups especially motivated to use HPE, military and sportsmen. There is sufficient ground to maintain, however, that we are facing the next step to HPE which is gene editing.

Brain doping, like the term *doping* in sports, refers to the illicit use of *prohibited substances*. This subcategory of substances consists of prescription substances used without medical indication and illicit drugs. The list covers drugs presented above (methylphenidate, amphetamines, modafinil, memantine) and others like amphetamine salts, antiementives (acetylcholinesterase inhibitors) and antidepressants (selective serotonin reuptake inhibitors) for the treatment of ADHD, sleep disorders, Alzheimer's disease and depression as well as illicit amphetamines and derivatives (3,4-Methylendioxy-N-methylamphetamin, MDMA, ecstasy) and cocaine. The use of prescription drugs without medical indication as well as the use of illicit drugs for cognitive enhancing purposes is prohibited and can have serious legal consequences, depending on users' sociocultural background (Franke, Lieb, 2013, p. 18).

Since human performance is often an essential feature of military activity which is why enhancement neurotechnologies (e.g., pills, neural implants, and neuroprostheses) are widely administered in the army (Sattler et al., 2022) concerning key areas central to military competition: strength, focus, attention, learning, resistance to fatigue (Scharre, Fish, 2018) and sports competition. Some athletes and individuals use substances or treatments to increase muscle mass, endurance, or overall physical performance. Performance enhancement is situated in the mainstream of military strategies and politics. For example, in the 2021 report for US Department of Defense and Intelligence Community officials prepared by the RAND National Security Research Division (NSRD), human performance enhancement was among such strategic and far-reaching topics such as quantum technology, semiconductor technology, the intersection of artificial intelligence and cybersecurity, deepfake generation and detection, and the use of patent data to assist in understanding global trends in emerging technologies (Blumenthal et al., 2021, p. iii). The modalities of HPE can be grouped into three principal categories: gene editing, applications of artificial intelligence (AI), and networked technologies that are wearable or even implantable (the so-called Internet of Bodies [IoB]) (Blumenthal et al., 2021, p. v). IoB is a subset of IoT devices that interact far more intimately with the human body. They connect the body to an online network through technology that you can wear, ingest, implant, or otherwise link to a human body. Harmsworth (2023) identifies three categories of IoB: *external devices* (external sensors, smart watches), *internal devices* (devices that you can ingest or have implanted to control and monitor various aspects of your health, such as digital pills and smart pacemakers), and *embedded devices* (devices completely merging with your body while maintaining a real-time connection to a remote machine, such as BCIs.

An interesting example of IoB could be a compact supernumerary robotic limb that can augment our body's physical functions and support daily activities with an extra wearable robot arm. It adopts a double-layer scissor unit for the extendable mechanism, which can achieve a distance 2.5 times longer than the forearm length. The proposed device can be mounted on the user's upper arm and transformed into a compact state without any obstruction to wearers (Xie et al., 2022).

An interesting topic deserving to be acknowledged here could be the design and development of sports equipment. Here one may find innovative materials in sports equipment design, which has led to increased energy return and power output during sports performance (Shan, 2023).

2.5.2.4 Cosmetic enhancement

These can alter physical appearance for aesthetic purposes using cosmetic surgery mainly for the facial parts which include the nose, ears, lips, cheeks, eyelids, and others. This procedure is also carried out for other body parts such as hips, breasts, buttocks, and others. It is mainly opted by females as compared to males. This procedure is also done for female reproductive parts such as vaginoplasty, G spot amplification, and labiaplasty. The procedures are carried out in ambulatory surgical facilities, hospitals, clinics, and others. The global cosmetic surgery market size was estimated at $70 billion in 2022 and it is projected to hit around $139.64 billion by 2032. The North American region had the biggest share of the total revenue in 2022 (35.7%) (Precedence Research, 2023). Cosmetic enhancement technologies are developing technologies such as 3D printing. This can also be used (Thomas, Singh, 2020) to create personalised implants or prosthetics (Parthasarathy, 2014).

2.5.2.5 Biohacking

Biohacking can be broadly described as the practice of synthetic biology outside formal institutions by individuals who may or may not have had formal scientific training (Elgabry, Camilleric, 2021, p. 2). Biohacking has been enabled by synthetic biology or the engineering science of re-programming living organisms to create new products and processes in medicine, agriculture, and the environment. Nowadays synthetic biology is becoming an increasingly democratised phenomenon. Biohacking includes do-it-yourself biology and self-experimentation to enhance physical appearance, such as implanting radio-frequency identification (RFID) chips or using subdermal implants located mainly in fingers, hand webbing, skin near the armpit, arm, and hand/forearm. The motivations of biohackers include cybernetic exploration, personal data acquisition, and advocating for privacy rights and open-source medicine (Yetisen, 2018). The bio-hacking community is a part of hidden populations commonly defined by their unknown sizes, with dozens of privacy/access issues which often accompany research, and policy or practice related to these groups (Elgabry, Camilleric, 2021, p. 2).

2.5.2.6 Sensory enhancements

A sense is a biological system used by an organism for sensation, the process of gathering information about the world through the detection of stimuli. Although in some cultures five human senses were traditionally identified as such (namely sight, smell, touch, taste, and hearing), many more are now recognised.

Sensory augmentation is attained by multisensory information processing for enhancement of the ability to perceive external stimuli (Dilmegani, 2023). The most rudimentary example of visual sensory augmentation technology could be navigational aids used by people with visual impairment. Practical examples can be found on Peter Joosten's blog. One refers to a Canadian man who lost his sight at the age of 20 due to two accidents and then volunteered for an experiment in 2002. The researcher developed a prosthesis consisting of a pair of glasses that had a small camera mounted on the frame. The images from the camera were converted into electrical pulses, which connected to his virtual cortex through a hole in his skull. As Peter Joosten puts it: 'He was the first person in the world to have bionic eyes' (https://www.peterjoosten.org/human-enhancement-technologies, accessed 3.07.2023). The second concerns a Dutch man who lost his sight due to a genetic disease. In this case an advanced chip was placed on his retina. As the connection between his retina and his visual cortex was still intact, he was eligible for a chip. A small camera was placed in a pair of glasses and connected to a small computer converting the images to signals that were then wirelessly transmitted to the chip which in turn converted the pulses to the brain. As a result, the man can see now 60 pixels which allows him to recognise contours and pretty lights again.

Hearing augmentation, such as a hearing aid, is a kind of sensory augmentation that enhances its users' hearing ability. Devices or technologies can be used to enhance human senses, such as cochlear implants (having the ability to take over the function of the sensory cells in the inner ear, and electronically stimulate the auditory nerve; it consists of an external part and an internal part that is implanted in the inner ear) for improved hearing or devices that enable infrared or ultraviolet vision. Hearing augmentation, such as a hearing aid, is a kind of sensory augmentation that enhances its users' hearing ability. However, the technology for sensory augmentation does not only involve impaired skills. Night-vision goggles are great examples of visual augmentation. More advanced sensory augmentation would be the technology that alters perception, such as virtual reality (VR), augmented reality (AR) or mixed reality (Dilmegani, 2023).

Peter Joosten introduced another man representing an interesting mix or blending of sight and hearing. He was born colour-blind but is now able to hear colours using a brain implant. He can hear not only the spectrum of colours that healthy people can see but is also able to hear colours such as infrared and ultraviolet (https://www.peterjoosten.org/human-enhancement-technologies, accessed 3.07.2023).

While in the above-presented cases of visual and hearing augmentation, one may question their classification as enhancement, no doubt hearing infrared and ultraviolet by humans fits with the definition of enhancement.

There is some ground to believe that in the future infrared could not only be heard but also seen by humans. Thomson et al. (2013) showed that adult rats can learn to perceive otherwise invisible infrared light through a neuroprosthesis that couples the output of a head-mounted infrared sensor to their somatosensory cortex (S1) via intracortical microstimulation. Rats readily learned to use this new information source and generated active exploratory strategies to discriminate among infrared signals in their environment.

2.5.3 Mood enhancement

One should start with the statement that the current understanding of the regulation of mood is still rather limited (Germani et al., 2021) because the mental status of a human being is influenced by several interacting factors, biological (e.g., genetic, epigenetic, neurodevelopmental), behavioural (e.g., lifestyle), and socioeconomic and cultural nature (e.g., social relations or poverty). One may add to these dietary and physiological factors, such as physical exercise, and sleep. Scientific achievements in this respect are moderate despite decades of using human intracranial electrophysiology (HIE) to characterise seizures in patients with epilepsy and using electrodes implanted intracranially to investigate mechanisms of human cognition (Guillory, Bujarski, 2014).

As indicated earlier, mood enhancement can be achieved mainly through nootropics and pharmaceuticals. Some examples are indicated in Section 2.5.1.2.2 and can be extended to others. First is Rhodiola rosea, an adaptogenic herb that helps your body handle stress more effectively. Several studies have found that Rhodiola rosea supplements can improve mood and decrease feelings of burnout in both anxious and highly stressed individuals (Olsson et al., 2009). Taking small daily doses of Rhodiola rosea has been shown to reduce mental fatigue and increase feelings of well-being in college students during stressful exam periods (Spasov et al., 2000). Second are lysergic acid diethylamide (LSD) and psilocybin ('magic') mushrooms. They can be regularly used of sub-perceptive threshold doses (microdosing psychedelics) (Liokaftos, 2021).

Apart from nootropics, smart drugs and pharmaceuticals, other non-invasive methods are used for mood enhancement, including different mood induction techniques. They can be grouped into three categories:

- visualisation of a material selected for its emotional impact (images, films, or music pieces),
- imagery techniques (consisting of recalling or reactivating past emotional experiences or writing emotionally charged scenarios/phrases to enter the corresponding emotional state),
- and pre-set interactions better known as virtual reality (which allows for the creation of a real-life environment with which the individual has to interact) (Di Pompeo et al., 2023).

One should acknowledge here that an evidence-based approach to the evaluation of the risks and benefits of pharmacological cognitive enhancement is very rare (Repantis, 2013).

There is some evidence, however, that mood may improve with invasive forms of neurostimulation (Chan et al., 2018). For example, targeting the circadian system informed by mechanistic molecular advances is considered one of the three promising areas in circadian-clock-based therapeutics in mood disorders (Bhatnagar et al., 2023).

One should also notice that the results of research on mood enhancement do not always lead to unambiguous and positive results. For example, stimulating the dorsolateral prefrontal cortex (DLPFC) which plays a key role in mood, emotional processing, and attentional processing of emotional information using non-invasive brain stimulation (NIBS) led to ambiguous results. NIBS over the DLPFC can modulate emotional processing and attentional processing of emotional stimuli, without specifically influencing mood (Mondino et al., 2015).

There is a general trend in the research towards targeted interventions of specific neural circuits for modulating brain networks that support affective or cognitive functions. It has resulted in an emerging class of stimulation devices referred to as ‘electroceuticals’, a new category of therapeutic agents which act by targeting the neural circuits of organs. The therapy involves mapping the neural circuitry and delivering neural impulses to these specific targets (Mishra, 2017; Forster, 2023). One important concept for achieving more precise and adaptive electroceutical interventions is closed-loop stimulation systems, that is, devices that can both sense neural activity or neurochemical signatures and adapt their stimulation parameters accordingly (Germani et al., 2021).

There is sufficient base to maintain that in the coming years, the development of in-brain devices that could regulate or self-regulate the emotional needs of a person will be achievable (Germani et al., 2021).

2.5.4 Moral enhancement

Enhancement can target not only cognitive, physical, and emotional capacities as presented above but also complex human behaviours such as morality (Darby, Pascual-Leone, 2017) which is simplified and reduced in this book to evaluate whether an action (or person acting) is good or bad. Moral enhancement is understood as improving moral or social behaviour.

Leaving the intuitive typology of moral enhancement distinguishing between traditional (moral education: learning, training, habituation) and non-traditional (biotechnologies) methods of moral enhancement apart, we may stay with the distinction between invasive (pharmacological enhancement, brain stimulation, biotechnologies) and non-invasive (moral education, animal-assisted interventions, drama-based interventions, etc.) methods of moral enhancement (Sokólska, 2018). This book focuses on invasive interventions.

Pharmacological moral enhancement involves the use of drugs to enhance cognitive abilities. The most commonly used drugs for this purpose have already been discussed and include stimulants such as caffeine, nicotine, amphetamines, and smart drugs such as methylphenidate, piracetam or modafinil. This list can be extended to *oxytocin*, also known as the cuddle hormone (or the moral molecule), which has been shown to improve altruism, cooperation, and trusting behaviour and promote pro-social attitudes in general (Zak, 2013) and *Phenibut* (a synthetic derivative of the neurotransmitter gamma-aminobutyric acid (GABA). It is sometimes used to reduce anxiety and improve mood. While it might indirectly influence mood and anxiety-related moral decisions, it can also have adverse effects.

Recently, the enhancement-purposive use of neuroscience, neuroenhancement, has also been a concern. Neuroenhancement refers to interventions in the central nervous system by using various pharmaceutical means, surgery, and technology to improve cognitive function, memory, mood, or overall brain performance (Tachibana, 2017). One should acknowledge that while brain stimulation has the potential to alter moral behaviour, such alteration is unlikely to improve moral behaviour in all situations and may even lead to less morally desirable behaviour in some instances (Darby, Pascual-Leone, 2017). One may conclude that using brain stimulation for moral enhancement is still a topic of scientific debate, and its effectiveness remains largely unproven (Lavazza, 2019).

The complexity of normal moral behaviour makes it unlikely that morality is a single capacity that can be enhanced. One must keep in mind that moral behaviour results from multiple, interacting cognitive-affective networks in the brain. This, however, does not stop the use of biomedical interventions to improve moral behaviour through non-invasive brain stimulation. With the complicated and multidimensional nature of morality, the moral enhancement debate inevitably takes on a relatively philosophical and speculative, rather than empirical and demonstrative, colouration (Tachibana, 2017). One of the topics discussed in this debate is our freedom which – according to some discussants – would be in jeopardy if we allowed interventions at our genetical level to predispose us to a certain kind of behaviour, even if that behaviour would be moral (Cioiu, 2020).

One may conclude that due to limited empirical research specifically addressing the use of brain stimulation for moral enhancement (*most studies have focused on the effects of brain stimulation on cognitive function, mood regulation, or social behaviour*), the complexity of the subject (*morality is a multifaceted and complex aspect of human behaviour influenced by various factors, including cultural, societal, and individual values*), individual variations (*what may enhance moral behaviour in one person may not have the same effect in another, and it could even have unintended negative consequences*), and no sufficient information on long-term effects and risks (*interventions that affect brain function should be thoroughly studied for safety and effectiveness*), moral enhancement is not well understood. Consequently, interventions that affect brain function should be thoroughly studied for safety and effectiveness.

Despite the lack of empirical data on the effectiveness of moral bioenhancement, some researchers are reasoning that it ought to be compulsory (Crutchfield, 2019).

2.6 HE trends

Having presented the growing scope and various forms of human enhancement, one may try to catch trends in HE development.

Generally speaking, trends in HE are not monitored by scientists and researchers in a systematic, continuous and organised way due mainly – but not exclusively – to the lack of access to complete and reliable data. One of the few exceptions is the Springer book series *Trends in Augmentation of Human Performance*[11] which presents qualitative analyses of the subject.

The trends in HE can be described according to economic and functional criteria.

Human enhancement considered a part of the healthcare market is dynamically increasing pushed by advances in technologies, artificial intelligence, materials, information systems, and human science. Publicly available sources estimated the shipment volume of the global human enhancement market to register a compound annual growth rate (CAGR) of 19.98% over the period 2023–2028 (Mordor Intelligence, 2023). The Asia-Pacific (APAC) region is projected to witness the most rapid human enhancement market growth.[12] There are smartwatches which drive the market growth. Not only do modern smartwatches have several applications similar to that of smartphones and tablets, but also additional applications for measuring/monitoring certain functions of the human body like blood pressure, irregularities in heartbeat rhythms, sleep stages, blood oxygen levels, electrocardiography, and continuous glucose monitoring. The HE market is competitive and consists of several existing and emerging players. Some key players are Vuzix Corporation, Ekso Bionics Holdings Inc., Google LLC, B-Temia Inc., and Samsung Electronics Co. Ltd. As confirmed by market analysts, the defence sector drives a prominent share of the research and development investment due to the sheer number of applications, and subsidised offerings for prosthetics and exoskeletons are fuelling the growth (Mordor Intelligence, 2023).

The quantitative side of human enhancement remains anecdotal and incomplete, especially concerning invasive methods.

There is one invasive method which seems to be relatively easy to approximate. Simple logic suggests that if we can estimate the supply of radio-frequency identification (RFID and near-field communication (NFC) chips which can be implanted under the skin, it could be possible to estimate the number of HE procedures with RFID and NFC. Unfortunately, it is not so easy because RFID and NFC have dozens of other uses among others in production, transport, and storage. To make the story worse, RFID and NFC chips can be injected on a do-it-yourself (DIY) basis, that is, outside of the healthcare system. On the internet, there are many offers of ready-to-use special packages containing appropriately chosen chips, special syringes and needles, and guides on how to use them. The available estimation of the number of chips implanted worldwide ranges considerably from 3,000–10,000 (European Parliament, 2018, p. 7).

There is also anecdotal information available. We may learn for example that in Sweden '… every fifth employee of a TUI subsidiary already carries a microchip in their hands and uses it for their daily work' (ThyssenKrupp, 2020). Also, Peter Joosten presents his experience with a small NFC chip[13] implanted in his hand and interviews three young individuals who implanted themselves with various electronic devices allowing for the extension of perception of colours beyond the visual spectrum through vibrations (Neil Harbisson), to feel sense negativity of the planet, for example, earthquakes (Moon Ribas), and an extra sense allowing for feeling atmospheric pressure changes (Manel Munoz) (https://www.peterjoosten.org/human-enhancement-technologies). The rising interest of individual people in HE can be perceived as one of the outcomes of the democratisation of science which is now available to citizens in their own homes. Citizens are free to choose how to use it for their benefit. It can be done through DIY biology or biohacking activities (Gaspar et al., 2019).

In general, it is relatively easy to measure and monitor methods of human enhancement that have occurred but it is hard to accurately estimate its future use.

More technologically advanced invasive methods of cognitive enhancement like DBS or optogenetics, as well as non-invasive TDCS or TMS elude economic and market analysis.

Judging by appearances, one may say that many different forms of human-enhancing technologies are either on the way or are currently being tested. A few of these emerging technologies include human genetic engineering (gene therapy), neurotechnology (neural implants and BCIs), cyberware, strategies for engineered negligible senescence, nanomedicine, and 3D bioprinting. Human enhancement methods may be used also for modifying '… human physiology to better adapt to other worlds' atmospheric conditions' (Haleem et al., 2023, p. 72).

Such a long-term perspective of using HE to modify human physiological mechanisms may be confronted with potential physiological problems caused by HE interventions themselves. For example, current research shows that anionic nanoplastic contaminants promote Parkinson's disease (Liu et al., 2023) so the potential use of plastic components in biomechanical enhancements[14] may endanger human health in the long run. Staying with human physiology in the context of HE, it is also worth mentioning the interesting results of studies on the placebo effect of HE. Villa et al. (2023) showed (*an experiment with thirty naïve participants who were told to be augmented with a cognitive augmentation technology or no augmentation system while conducting a Columbia Card Task*) the presence of a placebo effect. All of the above support the necessity of further in-depth research on HE.

The chapter has shown that HE is a rising phenomenon. HE research is undertaken both by civilian organisations (universities, research institutes, etc.) and by entities and institutions connected to the military. Researching

HE remains a challenge due to several reasons including but not limited to a lack of a common definition of HE and no data on HE procedures being the most urgent. As discussed in this chapter, HE is hard to measure, monitor, and assess thus its methodology requires further elaboration without unnecessary delay. In such a context, a lack of appropriate legal regulations regarding HE is easily explained (this topic will be further elaborated in Chapter 4).

Despite all these limitations, research on HE is progressing. It should be emphasised that humanistic and social disciplines dominate HE research (with their qualitative methods) at the expense of science and engineering (where quantitative methods take the lead). This chapter reveals that various examples of cognitive, physical, mood, and moral HE are documented in the most recent research. The references and findings presented in the chapter allow us to maintain that HE is gaining in importance and a few trends in technology development only strengthen such an assessment.

One may conclude that all the above put an interesting perspective on Kurzweil's question concerning the human transgression of the limits of biology and the times of singularity (Kurzweil, 2017). This, in turn, entails an outlook on the healthcare system where emerging HE is rooted which is the topic of the following chapter.

Notes

1 A spin-off of Project RAND, a former partnership between Douglas Aircraft Company and the United States Air Force.
2 An obvious bias on this list is the overrepresentation of journals aimed at human genetics which partly could be explained by the leading role of genetic engineering in human enhancement. The last column was added to identify the most current publications on HE.
3 Ethical, legal, and social issues.
4 An example of such a project, the European Union SIENNA (Stakeholder-informed ethics for new technologies with high socio-economic and human rights impact) project can be mentioned. It aims to provide frameworks to help develop research ethics protocols, professional ethics codes and better legal rules on human genomics, human enhancement and AI/robotics. The SIENNA project will be analysed in Chapter 4.
5 See, for example, *Human Enhancement: Three Perspectives*, Royal Institute of Philosophy Workshop, Birmingham branch, May 31, 2013, University of Birmingham, https://philevents.org/event/show/10290one.
6 See, for example, *Bitesize Ethics: Human Enhancement*, The Oxford Uehiro Centre for Practical Ethics, March 26, 2023, https://www.practicalethics.ox.ac.uk/event/bitesize-ethics-enhancement.
7 On March 12–13, 2023, such a conference was organised at the University of Glasgow.
8 A random search in ClinicalTrials.gov on September 21, 2023, using 'human enhancement' as a keyword revealed 115 studies out of which only 3 (Enhancing Medication-based Analgesia in Humans; The Efficacy and Safety of SGF200 on Immune Enhancement: Human-like Robotic Controllers for Enhanced Motor Learning) were connected with HE as defined in this book.

9 This division is not disjoint, because, for example, internal interventions can be (and usually are) carried out using hardware/software.
10 Forms of the pharmaceuticals indicated below were inspired by ChatGPT (OpenAI, 2023) and examples of specific drugs were retrieved from Erica Julson, *The 14 Best Nootropics and Smart Drugs Reviewed*, https://www.healthline.com/nutrition/nootropics,Updated on March 13, 2023.
11 One can be surprised that this series no longer publishes new content. Between 2013 and 2015 three books were published: *Cognitive Enhancement. An Interdisciplinary Perspective* (2013); *From Brain Machine Interfaces to Rehabilitation Robotics* (2014), and *Recent Progress in Brain and Cognitive Engineering* (2015) (https://www.springer.com/series/10849/books).
12 A good example is South Korea. It has 25% of the global market of cosmetic surgery (https://english.visitkorea.or.kr/svc/contents/infoHtmlView.do?vcontsId=139792). In South Korea, 14% of women have undergone plastic surgery. This percentage is 30% for women around 20 years old.
13 The chip can only communicate at a short distance with a device that can read the chip, for example, an apartment lock, a locker, a printer, etc.
14 This is pure speculation because Liu et al. (2023) focused on nanoplastic pollution in the environment.

References

Adamczyk, A.K., Zawadzki, P. (2020). The memory-modifying potential of optogenetics and the need for neuroethics. *Nanoethics*, 14, 207–225, 10.1007/s11569-020-00377-1.

Almeida, M., Diogo, R. (2019). Human enhancement: Genetic engineering and evolution. *Evolution, Medicine, and Public Health*, 1, 183–189, 10.1093/emph/eoz026.

Anomaly, J. (2020). *Creating Future People: The Ethics of Genetic Enhancement*. Routledge.

Bateman, S., Gayon, J., Allouche, S. (Eds). (2015). *Human Enhancement: Interdisciplinary and International Perspectives*. Palgrave Macmillan.

Bhatnagar, A., Murray, G., Ray, S. (2023). Circadian biology to advance therapeutics for mood disorders. *Trends in Pharmacological Sciences*, 44(10), 689–704, 10.1016/j.tips.2023.07.008.

Bjekić, J., Živanović, M., Filipović, S.R. (2021). Transcranial direct current stimulation (tDCS) for memory enhancement. *Journal of Visualized Experiments*, 18(175), 10.3791/62681.

Blumenthal, M.S., Hottes, A.K., Foran, C., Lee, M. (2021). *Technological Approaches to Human Performance Enhancement. Research Report*. RAND Corporation, https://www.rand.org/pubs/research_reports/RRA1482-2.html.

Bostrom, N., Sandberg, A. (2009). Cognitive enhancement: Methods, ethics, regulatory challenges. *Science and Engineering Ethics*, 15(3), 311–341, 10.1007/s11948-009-9142-5.

Buchanan, A. (2011). *Beyond Humanity? The Ethics of Biomedical Enhancement*. Oxford University Press.

Cai Chen, S., Bluhmb, R., Achtyes, E.D., McCright, A.M., Cabrera, L.Y. (2023). Looking through the lens of stigma: Understanding and anticipating concerns about the responsible development and use of psychiatric electroceutical interventions (PEIs). *SSM Mental Health*, 4, 100261, 10.1016/j.ssmmh.2023.100261.

Canellopoulou-Bottis, M. (2018). *The Greek Law on Human Enhancement*, 10.2139/ssrn.3295619, accessed 5.09.2023.

Chadwick, R. (2024). The meaning of enhancement in the post-COVID-19 world. In Jotterand, F., Ienca, M. (Eds). *The Routledge Handbook of the Ethics of Human Enhancement*, Routledge, pp. 309–318.

Chan, A.Y., Rolston, J.D., Rao, V.R., Chang, E.F. (2018). Effect of neurostimulation on cognition and mood in refractory epilepsy. *Epilepsia Open*, 3(1), 18–29, 10.1002/epi4.12100.

Cheng, H., Vepachedu, V. (2016). Recent development of transient electronics. *Theoretical and Applied Mechanics Letters*, 6(1), 21–31, 10.1016/j.taml.2015.11.012.

Cioiu, A.G. (2020). Is freedom compatible with moral neuroenhancement? *BRAIN. Broad Research in Artificial Intelligence and Neuroscience*, 11(2), Sup. 1, 82–98, 10.18662/brain/11.2Sup1/96.

Claes, L.E. (2022). Biomechanical enhancement of fracture healing. In *Mechanobiology of Fracture Healing: From Basic Science to Clinical Application.* SpringerBriefs in Bioengineering. Springer, pp. 65–80, 10.1007/978-3-030-94082-9_5.

Clarke, S., Savulescu, J., Coady, C.A.J., Giubilini, A., Sanyal, S. (Eds). (2016). *The Ethics of Human Enhancement: Understanding the Debate*. Oxford University Press.

Coeckelbergh, M. (2011). Humans, animals, and robots: A phenomenological approach to human-robot relations. International Journal of Social Robotics, 3(2), 197–204, https://doi.10.1007/s12369-010-0075-6.

Coeckelbergh, M. (2013). *Human Being @ Risk. Enhancement, Technology, and the Evaluation of Vulnerability Transformations.* Philosophy of Engineering and Technology 12. Springer.

Coenen, C. (2024). Spotlights on the history of human enhancement discourse. In Jotterand, F., Marcello Ienca, M. (Eds). *The Routledge Handbook of the Ethics of Human Enhancement*, Routledge, pp. 18–29.

Crutchfield, P. (2019). Compulsory moral bioenhancement should be covert. *Bioethics*, 33(1), 112–121, 10.1111/bioe.12496.

Daniel, C. (2020). *Human enhancement.* January 2020, 10.13140/RG.2.2.16648.44805/1.

Darby, R.R., Pascual-Leone, A. (2017). Moral enhancement using non-invasive brain stimulation. *Frontiers in Human Neuroscience*, 11, 10.3389/fnhum.2017.00077.

David, S., Bačić, B., Richter, C., Mundt, M. (2022). Editorial: Artificial intelligence to enhance biomechanical modelling. *Frontiers in Sports and Active Living*, 5, 10.3389/fspor.2023.1188035.

Di Pompeo, I., D'Aurizio, G., Burattini, G., Bisegna, F., Curcio, G. (2023). Positive mood induction to promote well-being and health: A systematic review from real settings to virtual reality. *Journal of Environmental Psychology*, 91, 102095, 10.1016/j.jenvp.2023.102095.

Dilmegani, C. (2023). *What is human augmentation? (With examples and technologies).* Updated on December 29, 2023, https://research.aimultiple.com/human-augmentation, accessed 7.09.2023.

Dresler, M., Sandberg, A., Bublitz, C., Ohla, K., Trenado, C., Mroczko-Wąsowicz, A., Kühn, S., Repantis. D. (2019). Hacking the brain: Dimensions of cognitive enhancement. *ACS Chemical Neuroscience*, 10(3), 1137–1148, 10.1021/acschemneuro.8b00571.

Druckman, D., Bjork, R.A. (1994). *Learning, Remembering, Believing: Enhancing Human Performance.* National Academy Press.

Edgren, N., Dubljević, V. (2023). The ubiquity of the fallacy of composition in cognitive enhancement and in education. *Theoretical Medicine and Bioethics*, 44(1), 41–56, 10.1007/s11017-022-09595-y.

Elgabry, M., Camilleric, J. (2021). Conducting hidden populations research: A reflective case study on researching the biohacking community. *Futures*, 132, 102769, 10.1016/j.futures.2021.102769.

Engelbart, D.C. (1962). *Augmenting Human Intellect: A Conceptual Framework. AFOSR-3233 Summary Report*, October 1962, http://csis.pace.edu/~marchese/CS835/Lec3/DougEnglebart.pdf, accessed 21.09.2023.

Erden, Y.J., Brey, P.A.E. (2022). Ethics guidelines for human enhancement R&D. Technologies to improve human performance raise ethical concerns. *Science*, 378(6622), 835–838, 10.1126/science.add9079.

Erler, A., Müller, V.C. (2021). AI as IA: The Use and Abuse of Artificial Intelligence (AI) for Human Enhancement through Intellectual Augmentation (IA), https://www.researchgate.net/publication/352157558_AI_as_IA_The_use_and_abuse_of_artificial_intelligence_AI_for_human_enhancement_through_intellectual_augmentation_IA?channel=doi&linkId=60bb9f07299bf10dff9c5dd8&showFulltext=true, accessed 14.09.2023.

European Parliament (2018). *The Use of Chip Implants for Workers. Study*. Directorate General for Internal Policies Policy Department A: Economic and Scientific Policy, IP/A/EMPL/2017-12 PE 614.209, January 2018.

Evans, N.G., Reynolds, J.M., Johnson, K.R. (2021). Moving through capacity space: Mapping disability and enhancement. *Journal of Medical Ethics*, 47(11), 748–755, 10.1136/medethics-2019-105732.

Fanelli, A., Ghezzi, D. (2021). Transient electronics: New opportunities for implantable neurotechnology. *Current Opinion in Biotechnology*, 72, 22–28, 10.1016/j.copbio.2021.08.011.

Fisher, J.A. (2021). *Enhancing 'Human Nature': The Human Enhancement Debate in U.S. Bioethics*. Columbia University ProQuest Dissertations Publishing, 28771817, https://www.proquest.com/openview/18b7ac5951b0280a54df392ab7aa5c63/1?cbl=18750&diss=y&loginDisplay=true&pq-origsite=gscholar, accessed 17.09.2023.

Forsberg, E.-M., Shelley-Egan, C., Thorstensen, E., Landeweerd, L., Hofmann, B. (2017). *Evaluating Ethical Frameworks for the Assessment of Human Cognitive Enhancement Applications*. SpringerBriefs in Ethics. Springer.

Forster, R.J. (2023). Wirefree electroceuticals: 3D electrical and electrochemical stimulation of biological systems. *Current Opinion in Electrochemistry*, 39, 101297, 10.1016/j.coelec.2023.101297.

Fox, K.C.R., Fitz, N.S., Reiner, P.B. (2016). The multiplicity of memory enhancement: Practical and ethical implications of the diverse neural substrates underlying human memory systems. *Neuroethics*, 10, 375–388, 10.1007/s12152-016-9282-7.

Franke, A.G., Lieb, L. (2013). Pharmacological neuroenhancement: Substances and epidemiology. In Hildt, E., Franke, A.G. (Eds). *Cognitive Enhancement: An Interdisciplinary Perspective, Trends in Augmentation of Human Performance 1*, Springer Science+Business Media, Dordrecht: Springer, pp. 17–27.

Gallagher, S. (2021). Deep brain stimulation, self and relational autonomy. *Neuroethics*, 14, 31–43, 10.1007/s12152-018-9355-x.

Garasic, M.D., Lavazza, A. (2024). Clinical practice and human enhancement. Blurred borders and ethical issues. In Jotterand, F., Ienca, M. (Eds). *The Routledge Handbook of the Ethics of Human Enhancement*. Routledge, pp. 319–330.

Gaspar, R., Rohde, P., Giger, J.-C. (2019). Unconventional settings and uses of human enhancement technologies: A non-systematic review of public and experts' views on self-enhancement and DIY biology/biohacking risks. *Human Behavior and Emerging Technologies*, 1(4), 295–305, 10.1002/hbe2.175.

Gauttier, S. (2019). Enhancing oneself with an exosense: Learning from users' experiences. Human Behavior and Emerging Technologies, 1(4), 317–340, https://doi.org/10.1002/hbe2.174.

Germani, F., Kellmeyer, P., Wäscher, S., Biller-Andorno, N. (2021). Engineering minds? Ethical considerations on biotechnological approaches to mental health, well-being, and human flourishing. *Trends in Biotechnology*, 39(11), 1111–1113, 10.1016/j.tibtech.2021.04.007.

Glazier, P.S. (2021). Beyond animated skeletons: How can biomechanical feedback be used to enhance sports performance? *Journal of Biomechanics*, 129, 110686, 10.1016/j.jbiomech.2021.110686.

Goonoo, N., Bhaw-Luximon, A. (2022). Piezoelectric polymeric scaffold materials as biomechanical cellular stimuli to enhance tissue regeneration. *Materials Today. Communications*, 31,103491, 10.1016/j.mtcomm.2022.103491.

Gordon, E.C., Dunn, L. (2021). Pharmacological cognitive enhancement and cheapened achievement: A new dilemma. *Neuroethics*, 14, 409–421, 10.1007/s12152-021-09477-5.

Greenbaum, D., Cabrera, L.Y. (Eds). (2020). *ELSI in Human Enhancement: What Distinguishes It from Therapy?* Frontiers Media SA, 10.3389/978-2-88966-221-0.

Guillory, S.A., Bujarski, K.A. (2014). Exploring emotions using invasive methods: Review of 60 years of human intracranial electrophysiology. *Social Cognitive and Affective Neuroscience*, 9(12), 1880–1889, 10.1093/scan/nsu002.

Haleem, A., Javaida, M., Singh, R.P., Rab, S., Suman, R. (2023). Applications of nanotechnology in medical field: A brief review. *Global Health Journal*, 7(2), 70–77, 10.1016/j.glohj.2023.02.008.

Harisa, G.I., Faris, T.M., Sherif, A.Y., Alzhrani, R.F., Alanazi, S.A., Kohaf, N.A., Alanazi, F.K. (2023). Gene-editing technology, from macromolecule therapeutics to organ transplantation: Applications, limitations, and prospective uses. International Journal of Biological Macromolecules, 253(5), 127055, https://doi.org/10.1016/j.ijbiomac.2023.127055.

Harmsworth, M. (2023). How human are you? The internet of bodies is here, but are we ready? Taylor Wessing, January 30, 2023, https://www.taylorwessing.com/en/interface/2023/iot---next-gen/how-human-are-you-the-internet-of-bodies-is-here-but-are-we-ready, accessed 29.09.2023.

Hecht, K.A., Schnackenberg, J., Nair, A., Lignell, Å. (2021). Astaxanthin for improved muscle function and enhanced physical performance. In Ravishankar, G.A., Rao, A.R. (Eds). *Global Perspectives on Astaxanthin*, Academic Press, pp. 447–467, 10.1016/B978-0-12-823304-7.00033-7.

Hoang, K.B., Cassar, I.R., Grill, W.M., Turner, D.A. (2017). Biomarkers and stimulation algorithms for adaptive brain stimulation. *Frontiers in Neuroscience*, 11, 10.3389/fnins.2017.00564.

Howell, A. (2015). Resilience, war, and austerity: The ethics of military human enhancement and the politics of data. *Security Dialogue*, 46(1), 15–31, 10.1177/0967010614551040.

Jebari, K. (2013). Brain machine interface and human enhancement – an ethical review. *Neuroethics*, 6(3), 617–625, 10.1007/s12152-012-9176-2.

Joosten (2023). Peter Joosten blog, https://www.peterjoosten.org/human-enhancement-technologies, accessed 3.07.2023.

Jotterand, F., Ienca, M. (Eds). (2023). *The Routledge Handbook of the Ethics of Human Enhancement*. Routledge.

Juengst, E., Moseley, D. (2019). Human enhancement. In *Stanford Encyclopedia of Philosophy Archive*, https://plato.stanford.edu/archives/sum2019/entries/enhancement, accessed 5.09.2023.

Julson, E. (2023). *The 14 Best Nootropics and Smart Drugs Reviewed*. Updated on March 13, 2023, https://www.healthline.com/nutrition/nootropics, accessed 23.09.2023.

Kamenjasevic, E. (2022). Defining human enhancement for policymaking and lawmaking purposes. *Revue Droit et Santé*, Forthcoming 2023, Available at SSRN: https://ssrn.com/abstract=4301033 or 10.2139/ssrn.4301033.

Kaschel, R. (2011). Specific memory effects of Ginkgo biloba extract EGb 761 in middle-aged healthy volunteers. *Phytomedicine*, 18(14), 1202–1207, 10.1016/j.phymed.2011.06.021.

Kitporntheranunt, J., Kitporntheranunt, M. (2022). Transhumanism: The next step in human enhancement. *Thailand Journal of Health Technology*, 3(2), 46–50, https://thaihta.org/journal/file/files/ThaiHTJ_3-2-06.pdf.

Kongkeaw, C., Dilokthornsakul, P., Thanarangsarit, P., Limpeanchob, N., Scholfield, N.C. (2014). Meta-analysis of randomized controlled trials on cognitive effects of Bacopa monnieri extract. *Journal of Ethnopharmacology*, 151(1), 528–535. 10.1016/j.jep.2013.11.008.

Koops, B.-J. (2013). Conclusion: The debate about human enhancement. In Koops, B.-J., Lüthy, C.H., Nelis, A., Sieburgh, C., Jansen, J.P.M., Schmid, M.S. (Eds). *Engineering the Human. Human Enhancement between Fiction and Fascination*. Springer.

Koops, B.-J., Lüthy, C.H., Nelis, A., Sieburgh, C., Jansen, J.P.M., Schmid, M.S. (Eds). (2013). *Engineering the Human: Human Enhancement between Fiction and Fascination*. Springer.

Kubikova, N., Keefe, D.J., Wells, D., Oktay, K.H., Feinberg, E.C. (2023). Should we use CRISPR gene editing in human embryos? *Fertility and Sterility*, 120(4), 737–744, 10.1016/j.fertnstert.2023.08.009.

Kurzweil, R. (2017). *Nadchodzi osobliwość. Kiedy człowiek przekroczy granice biologii (The Singularity Is Near: When Humans Transcend Biology)*. Kurhaus Publishing.

Lavazza, A. (2019). Transcranial electrical stimulation for human enhancement and the risk of inequality: Prohibition or compensation? *Bioethics*, 33(1), 122–131, 10.1111/bioe.12504.

Leuner, K., Kurz, C., Guidetti, G., Orgogozo, J.M., Müller, W.E. (2010). Improved mitochondrial function in brain aging and Alzheimer disease – the new mechanism of action of the old metabolic enhancer piracetam. *Frontiers in Neuroscience*, 4, 10.3389/fnins.2010.00044.

Lima, V., Belk, R. (2022). Human enhancement technologies and the future of consumer well-being. *Journal of Services Marketing*, 36(7), 885–894, 10.1108/JSM-09-2021-0363.

Linssen, A.M., Sambeth, A., Vuurman, E.F., Riedel, W.J. (2014). Cognitive effects of methylphenidate in healthy volunteers: A review of single dose studies. *International Journal of Neuropsychopharmacology*, 6, 961–977, 10.1017/S1461145713001594.

Liokaftos, D. (2021). Sociological investigations of human enhancement drugs: The case of microdosing psychedelics. *International Journal of Drug Policy*, 95, 103099, 10.1016/j.drugpo.2020.103099.

Liu, Z., Sokratian, A., Duda, A.M., Xu, E., Stanhope, C., Fu, A., Strader, S., Li, H., Yuan, Y., Bobay, B.G., Sipe, J., Bai, K., Lundgaard, I., Liu, N., Hernandez, B., Bowes Rickman, C., Miller, S.E., West, A.B. (2023). Anionic nanoplastic contaminants promote Parkinson's disease – associated α-synuclein aggregation. *Science Advances*, 9(46), 10.1126/sciadv.adi8716.

Luber, B., Lisanby, S.H. (2014). Enhancement of human cognitive performance using transcranial magnetic stimulation (TMS). *NeuroImage*, 85(Part 3), 961–970, 10.1016/j.neuroimage.2013.06.007.

Martín, D., Rueda, J., Earp, B.D., Hannikainen, I.R. (2023). Normality and the treatment-enhancement distinction. *Neuroethics*, 16(13), 10.1007/s12152-023-09519-0.

Mercer, C., Trothen, T.J. (Eds). (2015). *Religion and Transhumanism: The Unknown Future of Human Enhancement*. Praeger.

Michaelides, M., Bonci, A. (2022). Optogenetics. In Pfaff, D.W., Volkow, N.D., Rubenstein, J.L. (Eds). *Neuroscience in the 21st Century*. Springer, pp. 3201–3210, 10.1007/978-3-030-88832-9_172.

Mindus, P., Cronholm, B., Levander, S.E., Schalling, D. (1976). Piracetam-induced improvement of mental performance. A controlled study on normally aging individuals. *Acta Psychiatrica Scandinavica*, 54(2), 150–160, 10.1111/j.1600-0447.1976.tb00107.x.

Mishra, S. (2017). Electroceuticals in medicine – the brave new future. *Indian Heart Journal*, 69, 685–686, 10.1016/j.ihj.2017.10.001.

Mondino, M., Thiffault, F., Fecteau, S. (2015). Does non-invasive brain stimulation applied over the dorsolateral prefrontal cortex non-specifically influence mood and emotional processing in healthy individuals? *Frontiers in Cellular Neuroscience*, 9, 10.3389/fncel.2015.00399.

Moore, P. (2008). *Enhancing Me: The Hope and the Hype of Human Enhancement*. John Wiley & Sons.

Mordor Intelligence (2023). *Human Enhancement Market Size & Share Analysis – Growth Trends & Forecasts (2023–2028)*, https://www.mordorintelligence.com/industry-reports/global-human-enhancement-market-industry, accessed 6.10.2023.

NATO (2023). *Biotechnology and Human Enhancement Technologies: Transformational Innovation*. May 18, 2023, https://www.act.nato.int/article/biotechnology-and-human-enhancement-technologies-transformational-innovation, accessed 8.10.2023.

Naveen, N.B., Deckard, E.R., Buller, L.T., Meneghini, R.M. (2020). Enhanced biomechanical performance of a modern polyester surgical mesh for extensor mechanism reconstruction in total knee arthroplasty. *The Journal of Arthroplasty*, 35(11), 3311–3317, 10.1016/j.arth.2020.05.072.

Neznamov, G.G., Teleshova, E.S. (2009). Comparative studies of Noopept and piracetam in the treatment of patients with mild cognitive disorders in organic brain diseases of vascular and traumatic origin. *Neuroscience and Behavioral Physiology*, 39(3), 311–321, 10.1007/s11055-009-9128-4.

Nyholm, S. (2023). Artificial intelligence and human enhancement: Can AI technologies make us more (artificially) intelligent? *Cambridge Quarterly of Healthcare Ethics*, 1–13, 10.1017/S0963180123000464.

Olsson, E.M., von Schéele, B., Panossian, A.G. (2009). A randomised, double-blind, placebo-controlled, parallel-group study of the standardised extract SHR-5 of the roots of Rhodiola rosea in the treatment of subjects with stress-related fatigue. *Planta Medica*, 75(2), 105–112, 10.1055/s-0028-1088346.

OpenAI. (2023). ChatGPT (3.5) [Large language model]. https://chat.openai.com.

Ostrovskaya, R.U., Gruden, M.A., Bobkova, N.A., Sewell, R.D., Gudasheva, T.A., Samokhin, A.N., Seredinin, S.B., Noppe, W., Sherstnev, V.V., Morozova-Roche, L.A. (2007). The nootropic and neuroprotective proline-containing dipeptide noopept restores spatial memory and increases immunoreactivity to amyloid in an Alzheimer's disease model. *Journal of Psychopharmacology*, 21(6), 611–619, 10.1177/0269881106071335.

Ostrovskaya, R.U., Gudasheva, T.A., Zaplina, A.P., Vahitova, J.V., Salimgareeva. M.H., Jamidanov, R.S., Seredenin, S.B. (2008). Noopept stimulates the expression of NGF and BDNF in rat hippocampus. *Bulletin of Experimental Biology and Medicine*, 146(3), 334–337, 10.1007/s10517-008-0297-x.

Parthasarathy, J. (2014). 3D modeling, custom implants and its future perspectives in craniofacial surgery. *Annals of Maxillofacial Surgery*, 4(1), 9–18, 10.4103/2231-0746.133065.

Pase, M.P., Kean, J., Sarris, J., Neale, C., Scholey, A.B., Stough, C. (2012). The cognitive-enhancing effects of *Bacopa monnieri*: A systematic review of randomized, controlled human clinical trials. *The Journal of Alternative and Complementary Medicine*, 18(7), 647–652, 10.1089/acm.2011.0367.

Pawar, A., Vaidya, D., Jadhav, Y., Kanade, S. (2023). Super soldiers using AI and machine learning technology.*Vidhyayana: An International Multidisciplinary*

Peer-Reviewed E-Journal, 8(7), 14–20, https://vidhyayanaejournal.org/journal/article/view/802.

Poltavski, D.V., Petros, T. (2006). Effects of transdermal nicotine on attention in adult non-smokers with and without attentional deficits. *Physiology & Behavior*, 87(3), 614–624, 10.1016/j.physbeh.2005.12.011.

Precedence Research (2023). Cosmetic Surgery Market, https://www.precedenceresearch.com/cosmetic-surgery-market, accessed 30.09. 2023.

Raisamo, R., Rakkolainen, I., Majaranta, P., Salminen, K., Rantala, J., Farooq, A. (2019). Human augmentation: Past, present and future. *International Journal of Human-Computer Studies*, 131, 131–143, 10.1016/j.ijhcs.2019.05.008.

Reay, J.L., Kennedy, D.O., Scholey, A.B. (2006). Effects of Panax ginseng, consumed with and without glucose, on blood glucose levels and cognitive performance during sustained 'mentally demanding' tasks. *Journal of Psychopharmacology*, 20(6), 771–781, 10.1177/0269881106061516.

Repantis, D. (2013). Psychopharmacological neuroenhancement: Evidence on safety and efficacy. In Hildt, E., Franke, A.G. (Eds). *Cognitive Enhancement: An Interdisciplinary Perspective*. Springer, pp. 29–38.

Rosalia, L., Mossab, S., Roche, E.T. (2022). Devices that enhance the biomechanics of the failing heart. In Karimov, J.H., Fukamachi, K., Gillinov, M. (Eds). *Advances in Cardiovascular Technology: New Devices and Concepts*. Academic Press, pp. 625–640.

Ryan, B.J., Charkoudian, N., Joyner, M.J. (2023). Human performance augmentation: The importance of integrative physiological quantification. *The Journal of Physiology*, 601(3), 407–416, 10.1113/JP283975.

Sattler, S., Jacobs, E., Singh, I., Whetham, D., Bárd, I., Moreno, J., Galeazzi, G., Allansdottir, A. (2022). Neuroenhancements in the military: A mixed-method pilot study on attitudes of staff officers to ethics and rules. *Neuroethics*, 15, 11, 10.1007/s12152-022-09490-2.

Scharre, P., Fish, L. (2018). *Human Performance Enhancement, Super-Soldiers*. Center for a New American Security, http://www.jstor.com/stable/resrep20411, accessed 18.09.2023.

Schläpfer, T.E., Meyer-Lindenberg, A., Synofzik, M., Visser-Vandewalle, V., Voges, J., Coenen, V.A. (2021). Invasive brain stimulation in the treatment of psychiatric illness – proposed indications and approaches. *Deutsches Ärzteblatt International*, 118(3), 31–36, 10.3238/arztebl.m2021.0017.

Shan, G. (2023). Exploring the intersection of equipment design and human physical ability: Leveraging biomechanics, ergonomics/anthropometry, and wearable technology for enhancing human physical performance. *Advanced Design Research*, 1(1), 7–11, 10.1016/j.ijadr.2023.04.001.

Shao, S., Wu, J., Zhou, Q. (2021). Developments and challenges in human performance enhancement technology. *Medicine in Novel Technology and Devices*, 12, 100095, 10.1016/j.medntd.2021.100095.

Shim, J-S, Rogers, J.A., Kang, S-K. (2021). Physically transient electronic materials and devices. *Materials Science and Engineering: R: Reports*, 145, 100624, 10.1016/j.mser.2021.100624.

Sokólska, M. (2018). Non-invasive means of moral improvement – a critical review of selected methods. *Rocznik Kognitywistyczny*, 11, 1–16, 10.4467/20843895RK.18.001.9755.

Sparrow, R. (2019). Yesterday's child: How gene editing for enhancement will produce obsolescence-and why it matters. *The American Journal of Bioethics*, 19(7), 6–15. 10.1080/15265161.2019.1618943.

Spasov, A.A., Wikman, G.K., Mandrikov, V.B., Mironova, I.A., Neumoin, V.V. (2000). A double-blind, placebo-controlled pilot study of the stimulating and adaptogenic effect of Rhodiola rosea SHR-5 extract on the fatigue of students caused by stress during an examination period with a repeated low-dose regimen. *Phytomedicine*, 7(2), 85–89, 10.1016/S0944-7113(00)80078-1.

Tachibana, K. (2017). Neurofeedback-based moral enhancement and traditional moral education. *Humana.Mente. Journal of Philosophical Studies*, 33, 19–42, https://philarchive.org/archive/TACNME.

Taraska, P.A. (2017). *How Can the Use of Human Enhancement (HE) Technologies in the Military Be Ethically Assessed?* (Doctoral dissertation, Duquesne University), https://dsc.duq.edu/etd/148, accessed 17.08.2023.

Thomas, D.J., Singh, D. (Eds). (2020). *3D Printing in Medicine and Surgery: Applications in Healthcare*. (Woodhead Publishing Series in Biomaterials). Elsevier, 10.1016/C2017-0-01048-0.

Thomson, E., Carra, R., Nicolelis, M. (2013). Perceiving invisible light through a somatosensory cortical prosthesis. *Nature Communications*, 4, 1482, 10.1038/ncomms2497.

ThyssenKrupp (2020). *The Top Tech Trends 2020: From Multi-Experience to Human Augmentation*, https://www.thyssenkrupp.com/en/stories/the-top-tech-trends-2020-from-multi-experience-to-human-augmentation, accessed 6.10.2023.

Tomasi, D., Volkow, N.D., Wang, G.J., Wang, R., Telang, F., Caparelli, E.C., Wong, C., Jayne, M., Fowler, J.S. (2011). Methylphenidate enhances brain activation and deactivation responses to visual attention and working memory tasks in healthy controls. *Neuroimage*, 54(4), 3101–3110, https://doi.org/10.1016/j.neuroimage.2010.10.060.

Trothen, T.J., Mercer, C. (Eds). (2017). *Religion and Human Enhancement: Death, Values, and Morality*. Palgrave Studies in the Future of Humanity and its Successors. Palgrave Macmillan.

Vicario, C.M., Nitsche, M.A., Hoysted, I., Yavari, F., Avenanti, A., Salehinejad, M.A., Felmingham, K.L. (2020). Anodal transcranial direct current stimulation over the ventromedial prefrontal cortex enhances fear extinction in healthy humans: A single blind sham-controlled study. *Brain Stimulation*, 13(2), 489–491, 10.1016/j.brs.2019.12.022.

Villa, S., Kosch, T., Grelka, F., Schmidt, A., Welsch, R. (2023). The placebo effect of human augmentation: Anticipating cognitive augmentation increases risk-taking behaviour. *Computers in Human Behavior*, 146, 107787, 10.1016/j.chb.2023.107787.

Vorobyov, V., Kaptsov, V., Kovalev, G., Sengpiel, F. (2011). Effects of nootropics on the EEG in conscious rats and their modification by glutamatergic inhibitors. *Brain Research Bulletin*, 85(3-4), 123–132, 10.1016/j.brainresbull.2011.02.011.

Wilsher, C., Atkins, G., Manfield, P. (1979). Piracetam as an aid to learning in dyslexia. Preliminary report. *Psychopharmacology*, 65(1), 107–109, 10.1007/BF00491989.

Xie, H., Ding, Z., Yoshida, S., Chong, T., Torii, T., Fukusato, T. (2022). *Augmenting Human with Compact Supernumerary Robotic Limbs*. AH2022: 13th Augmented Human International Conference May 2022 Article 8, 1–4, 10.1145/3532525.3532531.

Yetisen, A.K. (2018). Biohacking. *Trends in Biotechnology*, 36(8), 744–747, 10.1016/j.tibtech.2018.02.011.

Zak, P.J. (2013). *The Moral Molecule. The New Science of What Makes Us Good or Evil*. Transworld Publ. Ltd. UK.

Zvejniece, L., Svalbe, B., Veinberg, G., Grinberga, S., Vorona, M., Kalvinsh, I., Dambrova, M. (2011). Investigation into stereoselective pharmacological activity of phenotropil. *Basic & Clinical Pharmacology & Toxicology*, 109(5), 407–412, 10.1111/j.1742-7843.2011.00742.x.

3 Challenges of contemporary healthcare systems

3.1 Identification of challenges of healthcare systems on a global, supranational, and national level

The challenges faced by modern health systems are complex and require some sorting out. These challenges can be identified according to two criteria: the level and the subject formulating them. Concerning the first of these two criteria, challenges can be divided into those formulated at the national, supranational, and global levels. Using the second criterion, it is possible to identify the most important stakeholders of the healthcare system and examine which challenges are crucial for them. These stakeholders may include but not limited to:

- national healthcare administrators (usually Ministry of Health or equivalent),
- managers of healthcare units (hospitals, clinics, ambulatory and primary care facilities, etc.) together with their employees,
- various medical associations, media (with a special emphasis on social media),
- and the patients.

3.1.1 Global level

On the global level healthcare challenges are formulated by the World Health Organization (WHO). At the time of this publication, WHO released a list of 13 urgent health challenges the world will face over the decade 2020–2030. The list highlights a range of issues including:

1. the climate crisis,
2. healthcare delivery in areas of conflict and crisis,
3. healthcare equity,
4. access to treatments,
5. infectious disease prevention,
6. epidemic preparedness,
7. unsafe products,

DOI: 10.4324/9781003449584-4

8 underinvestment in health workers,
9 adolescent safety,
10 improving the public trust of healthcare workers,
11 capitalising on technological advancements,
12 the threat of antimicrobial resistance and other medicines,
13 healthcare sanitation (Advisory Board, 2020).

It is significant that technological progress, which is a determinant of the development of human enhancement, is placed at the bottom of this list. This may indicate that HE is not perceived by WHO as a challenge.

Global healthcare challenges are identified also by researchers representing public health. They maintained that although in 2022 COVID-19 remained the primary public health concern, other viral infectious diseases, such as monkeypox and Ebola, emerged as public health concerns. They shared the WHO's concern regarding climate change and political conflicts impacting global health and identified the following key priority areas for 2023:

- health systems,
- the mental health crisis,
- substance abuse,
- infectious diseases,
- malnutrition and food insecurity,
- sexual and reproductive health challenges,
- environmental pollution,
- the climate crisis, cancer, and diabetes (Lucero-Prisno et al., 2023).

3.1.2 Supranational level

An example of healthcare challenges formulated on the supranational level could be healthcare priorities identified at the European Union (EU) level. Established by Regulation 2021/522, *EU4Health* defines four general objectives which can be linked with the main challenges:

1 improve and foster health (through health promotion and disease prevention, especially cancer, and international initiatives and cooperation),
2 protect people (prevention, preparedness and response to cross-border health threats; complementing national stockpiling of essential crisis-relevant products; establishing a reserve of medical, healthcare and support staff),
3 access to medicinal products, medical devices and crisis-relevant products (ensuring that these products are accessible, available and affordable),
4 strengthen health systems (reinforcing health data, digital tools and services, digital transformation of healthcare; enhancing access to healthcare; developing and implementing EU health legislation and evidence-based decision making, and integrated work among national health systems (EU, 2021).

The urgent health priorities needing investment were the response to the COVID-19 crisis and reinforcing the EU's resilience to cross-border health threats; *Europe's Beating Cancer Plan*, and *the Pharmaceutical Strategy for Europe*. Other areas, such as health systems' digitalisation, reducing the number of antimicrobial-resistant infections, and improving vaccination rates will also be boosted (EU, 2021).

Challenges are also reported by important European healthcare systems stakeholders. For example, the European branch of WONCA[1] reports that excessive workload, early burnout, and the shortage of the primary care workforce represent the most formidable challenge of the near future (WONCA, 2023).

3.1.3 National level

Moving on to the national level and key stakeholders, one must acknowledge the existence of substantial differences between healthcare systems concerning their organisation settings, financing, and operation. Leaving a more systematic analysis of various health challenges aside and being forced to focus on just a few examples, let us present the situation of the US healthcare system. Such a choice/bias can be explained in three ways. First of all, the US health segment of the national economy is the largest sector in the global economy and has changed dramatically over the last 30 years. Healthcare spending totalled $4.1 trillion in 2020, representing 19.7% of the US gross domestic product (Trilliant Health, 2022, p. 4). Second, the American health economy creates more data than any other part of the economy (Trilliant Health, 2022, p. 2) thus theoretically if data on human enhancement is gathered and collected, it could be available in the United States. Third, the United States has the biggest potential for HE development.

The US Department of Health and Human Services identifies five broad strategic goals for the period between 2022 and 2026:

1 to protect and strengthen equitable access to high-quality and affordable healthcare,
2 to safeguard and improve national and global health conditions and outcomes,
3 to strengthen social well-being, equity, and economic resilience,
4 to restore trust and accelerate advancements in science and research for all,
5 to advance strategic management to build trust, transparency, and accountability (HHS, 2022).

As of the time of this publication, there was no reference to human enhancement or the 4IR.

For the position of leading stakeholders, one may refer to the opinion of over 100 American healthcare executives and c-suite decision-makers interviewed in late 2020. As the three leading challenges of the US healthcare system, the respondents named: (1) financial limitations, (2) the availability of a skilled workforce, and (3) implementing new technology (Healthcare Transformers, 2021). The diagnosis of US healthcare practitioners requires attention because it includes financial and technological factors.

The issue of financial constraints of the US hospitals, especially rising costs, is broadly acknowledged and intensively researched but there are also others. A report dated June 2022 identifies the following:

1 lack of interoperability,
2 optimising clinical workflows,
3 personnel shortages and burnout,
4 keeping up with advances in medical science and information,
5 advancing health equity,
6 patient safety (Wolters Kluwer, 2022).

Out of these six challenges, the fourth one is directly connected to human enhancement. One may agree with Davis et al. (2021) that digital medicine products, gene therapy, nanomedicine, mRNA research and other emerging areas are beginning to transform not only the American healthcare system but the society as a whole. In the context of would-be HE financing, it should also be acknowledged that in 2022 several non-traditional investors moved into the US healthcare market to create new channels and markets and to advance the new hybrid healthcare environment (BCG/BCG-X, 2023). These moves may, directly and indirectly, contribute to the development of HE.

With input from stakeholders across the industry, *Modern Healthcare* outlines six challenges the US health care is likely to face in 2023. These include:

1 financial difficulties,
2 health system mergers,
3 recruiting and retaining staff,
4 payer-provider contract disputes,
5 investment in digital health,
6 health equity efforts (Advisory Board, 2023).

It is significant, that American healthcare system stakeholders place financial constraints in front of the challenges (Healthcare Transformers, 2021; Advisory Board, 2023). One should emphasise, however, that financial constraints in the healthcare system constitute an important obstacle in many other countries.

In conclusion, as of the time of this publication, one may maintain that human enhancement is not considered the healthcare system's significant challenge. It seems to be ignored even as a phenomenon since it is absent in national plans and/or strategies. Having said that, let us have a look at the financial side of contemporary healthcare systems. Let us start from the demand side.

3.2 Growing demand for high-quality medical services

Demand for medical services should be preceded by a concise presentation of the specifics of both the health services market and the health services.

3.2.1 Distinguishing characteristics of the healthcare market

Concerning the market one should acknowledge four characteristics that distinguish the healthcare market from other standard goods and services markets:

- intangibility (five senses are incapable of evaluating medical services; the patient can only rely on subjective feelings of pain/discomfort or lack thereof after the treatment),
- inseparability (production and consumption of a medical service take place simultaneously),
- inventory (medical professionals cannot provide a list of different services to meet demand during busy times),
- inconsistency (the variety, composition, and quality of medical services are very different; although different people may see a doctor simultaneously, there are various reasons for visiting a doctor) (Ghorbani, 2022).

The above features should be taken into account when analysing the health services market in general, and when formulating recommendations based on comparisons to other sectors and their functioning in particular.

3.2.2 Demand for healthcare services

There are a few distinctive features of demand for healthcare services. First, the demand for healthcare is self-satisfying. Healthcare itself does not lead to satisfaction since healthy people do not demand healthcare services. Consequently, the demand for healthcare is a derived demand. Second, patients' needs are strongly influenced by physicians and healthcare providers who sometimes can use their competitive advantage over patients resulting from information asymmetry. Third, healthcare is highly heterogeneous thus each patient needs to purchase a fairly different package of care with uncertainty about its effectiveness in meeting the need. Fourth, many health services are paid for by third parties or insurance companies which may lead to ethical risks and increase demand for services that patients may not need. Fifth, health can be considered as both a consumer good and a capital good (Ghorbani, 2022).

The demand for healthcare services is influenced by a variety of factors that can be categorised into several determinants. The research of estimating the demand for health services should be preceded by the presentation of factors shaping the demand for health services. The demand for health services is a function of the factors directly and indirectly affecting health.

Following WHO's methodology one may specify three basic fields from which the sources of demand for health services: the social and economic environment, the physical environment, and the person's characteristics and behaviours (WHO, 2017).

Understanding these determinants of demand for healthcare services is essential for policymakers, healthcare providers, and insurance companies to design effective healthcare systems and services that meet the needs of the population. This three-part typology can be illustrated by a few examples.

The *social environment* covers such elements as government policies (the provision of public healthcare services or regulations on the healthcare industry), and social support networks (families, relatives, friends, social circles, and peer influence) determining our psychological well-being. Then we have culture, customs and traditions supported and partially supplemented by education (including health literacy). The *economic environment* refers among others to employment and working conditions, income (impacting social status), and health insurance coverage.

The *physical environment* refers to the availability of clean and safe drinking water, clean air, adequate housing, healthy workplaces, safe neighbourhoods and streets, and geographic location (impacting access to health services).

The person's characteristics mean age, gender, and individual genetic factors. Behaviours refer to a broadly defined style of life, including diet and nutrition, physical activity, substance use and abuse (tobacco, alcohol, and drugs).

From the human enhancement perspective, the economic environment and the person's characteristics and behaviours seem to be the leading determinants of demand.

3.2.2.1 External and internal factors of healthcare demand

Demand for healthcare services is generated by objective (external) and subjective (internal) factors. The first category refers to medical (physiological or psychiatric) dysfunctions of the human body caused primarily by external factors and incidents (various illnesses, accidents, injuries) and is aimed at regaining health. The second concerns the patient's own (internal) decisions made not to regain health, but to improve his or her health or appearance (sophisticated stomatology, cosmetic surgery) or increase individual biological and physical capabilities (human enhancement).

Demand for health services caused by external factors is difficult to predict and estimate so epidemiology (with its specific methods) and historical healthcare providers' activity data are frequently used (NHS, 2022). The diverse nature of health demand results in, among other things, a long list of metrics used to assess the activity of service providers. In the case of the National Health Service (NHS) in the United Kingdom, we are talking about a dozen or so indicators ranging from an average length of stay, through a referral to treatment maximum wait for non-emergency care of 18 weeks, a four-hour maximum wait in acute and emergency care units to waiting times (Faculty of Public Health, 2023).

Among factors affecting the demand for healthcare, one can find needs based on patient perceptions, patient preferences, price or cost of use, income, transportation cost, waiting time, and quality of care (Ghorbani, 2022).

In the context of human enhancement, it is worth referring to Grossman's concept of combining the human capital theory with the demand for healthcare. According to human capital theory, people invest in themselves through education and health. Consumers buy health services from the market and combine them with their efforts to improve health, such as diet and exercise to increase their income (Grossman, 1999). From such a perspective, human enhancement services can be perceived as a tool granting a competitive advantage to those who decide to acquire HE.

3.2.2.2 Demand for healthcare in the United States, France, and the United Kingdom

One may maintain that the total demand for healthcare in the United States is growing but the situation differs between various levels of care and specialisations. For example, COVID-19 merely accelerated a long-term secular decline in acute and surgical care, despite a growing burden of disease and increasing obesity. Jain (2022) argues that the demand for healthcare services in the United States is tepid and does not correlate with the burden of disease. Demand measured by health expenditures reveals very large differences in the share of health expenditure of different groups of patients. As stated by Ortaliza et al. (2021):

> In 2019, 5% of the population accounted for nearly half of all health spending. The 5% of people with the highest health spending had an average of $61,000 in health expenditures annually; people with health spending in the top 1% have an average spending of over $130,000 per year. At the other end of the spectrum, the 50% of the population with total health spending below or equal to the 50th percentile accounted for only 3% of all health spending; the average spending for this group was $374 in 2019.

Staying with the Trilliant Health report it is worth acknowledging certain trends from *the 2022 Secular Trends Shaping the Health Economy* from that report. On the demand side, it is Trend 6: *Individuals Are Increasingly Making Healthcare Decisions Like Consumers* (declines in trust in doctors and hospitals, lower provider loyalty, especially in competitive markets) and on the supply side, it is Trend 9: *Low Acuity Commoditisation* (retailers like Walmart, CVS and Walgreens offer commodity healthcare services like an office visit, flu test, strep test, or lipid panel; also Amazon further expands its healthcare footprint), and Trend 13: *More Provider Competition* (in the United States this refers to emerging one-day-hospitals aka minute clinics) (Trilliant Health, 2022).

Trend 6 identified in the United States can be observed also in France. Using detailed data from 17 million inpatient stays admitted in France during 2019, Milcent (2023) shows that three-quarters of patients travel past their local hospitals to seek better quality care if they can choose between competing for-profit, non-profit, research, and local hospitals. Only one-quarter of them go to the nearest hospital. They are the most vulnerable patients (i.e., those socio-economically deprived, and very aged) and are mostly treated in local public hospitals with the lowest quality service level (Milcent, 2023).

The position of the US health sector on the global scene notwithstanding, one must agree that trends observed there cannot be extrapolated to other countries because there are developed countries where demand is growing, for example, in the United Kingdom (NHS Providers, 2018).

There is sufficient ground to maintain that despite the trends in demand for healthcare, patients as more aware consumers are paying more attention to the quality of health services. As in the case of healthcare demand, it should be acknowledged that the quality of healthcare is determined by a wide range of factors, including but not limited to:

- the care process (preventative care measures, safe care, coordinated care, and engagement and patient preferences),
- access (affordability and timeliness),
- administrative efficiency, equity,
- and healthcare outcomes (population health, mortality amenable to healthcare, and disease-specific health outcomes) (World Population Review, 2023).

One may conclude that the demand for healthcare differs from the demand for standard goods and services because it is influenced by several factors and is hard to measure, thus healthcare expenditures are a widely used proxy. Findings from the United States and the analysis of current trends show that patients increasingly behave like consumers choosing from competitive offers and are focused on obtaining health services of ever higher quality. The quality of health services, on the other hand, is identified as one of the most important challenges facing healthcare providers. This trend matches fully with human enhancement which can be linked to the internal, subjective sources of healthcare demand based on individual decisions of patients with only limited influence of third parties, namely physicians and insurers since related costs are paid on an out-of-pocket basis. In such a context, financial challenges identified by healthcare providers can be also treated as challenges for the patients willing to experiment with HE treatments.

3.3 Healthcare systems efficiency

Even if efficiency is narrowly defined as the maximisation of output relative to input, it is difficult to apply this concept to a healthcare system.

3.3.1 Output and outcome efficiency

By expanding on this basic concept of efficiency, the OECD methodology introduces differentiation into output efficiency and outcome efficiency. The first category is represented by such outputs as the number of patients treated, hospital discharges, doctor consultations, etc., while the second covers outcomes like an increase in quality and length of life (either at the system level or for specific diseases (OECD, 2016, p. 10).

There are challenges in ensuring that the systems, providers, and patients evaluated are sufficiently comparable and that resources are properly attributed to outputs and outcomes (Cylus et al., 2016a). This refers not only to international comparisons but also to internal comparisons of healthcare providers in a particular country because the production processes underlying health systems are intrinsically complex and poorly understood, making it difficult to develop measures that reliably capture efficiency. Identifying the costs of health care is intrinsically complex, especially in the hospital sector where many costs are fixed and shared across many patients (Cylus et al., 2016a, p. 237). When assessing the efficiency of health care, three types of efficiency can be distinguished: *technical*, *productive*, and *allocative* (Palmer, Torgerson, 1999).

3.3.1.1 Technical efficiency

Technical efficiency is a comparison of the achieved results of medical activities with the inputs used for this purpose (including, first of all, the work of medical professionals). This type of efficiency does not take into account the ultimate effect, that is, changes in health (outcomes), but only the process of health services delivery measured as output. An example of an indicator used to measure technical efficiency in healthcare is the average length of stay used in hospitals.

A recent systematic review of the articles on the key input, process, and output indicators commonly used in measuring the technical efficiency of the hospital, based on 1,537 studies published between 2010 and 2019 (Imani et al., 2022) led to the distinction of three initial types of hospital efficiency indicators: *context/input indicators*, *process/throughput indicators*, and *output/outcome indicators*. Such a division matches the simplistic viewpoint of efficiency defined as the ratio of the inputs an organisation consumes to the valued outputs it produces (Cylus et al., 2016b, p. 10). A complete typology of hospital efficiency factors is presented in Figure 3.1.

The content of Figure 3.1 and the appearance of the drawing itself in a brief format, show the entire complexity of the issue of efficiency in the

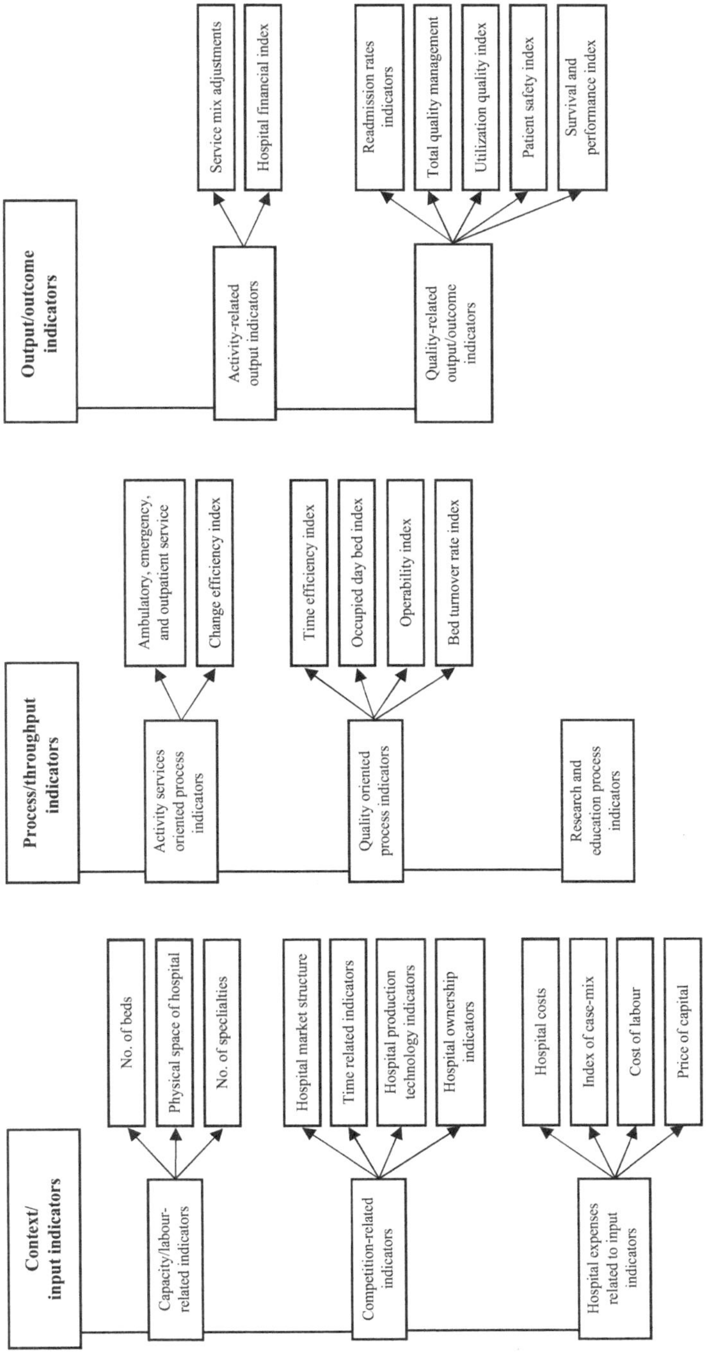

Figure 3.1 A typology of hospital efficiency indicators.

Source: Author's own based on Imani et al. (2022).

healthcare sector. It should be remembered that Figure 3.1 shows the situation of only one (but the most important) component of the healthcare system which is hospitals.

3.3.1.2 Productive efficiency

The concept of productive efficiency refers to maximising the health effect using given inputs (resources) or minimising the resources used to achieve a given health effect. Examples of productive indicators in health care include the survival period after treatment (e.g., in surgery), the number of lives saved, life years gained, or quality-adjusted life years (QALYs).

3.3.1.3 Allocative efficiency

Allocative efficiency additionally refers to the distribution of health effects achieved in society. It allows everyone to assess whether the distribution of health effects is even with spatial (geographic) or demographic (age and gender) criteria being adopted as equalisation criteria. One may conclude that allocative efficiency is achieved '... when resources are allocated so as to maximise the welfare of the community' (Palmer, Torgerson, 1999, p. 1136). Allocative efficiency also helps to analyse the occurrence of exclusion in the area of health effects, which in turn can be treated as the fourth type of efficiency, that is, social efficiency.

From the perspective of medical professionals, efficiency can be measured at two points: efficiency of delivery and efficiency of outcome (Keshishian, 2021).

3.3.2 Indicators of efficiency

Some common indicators of efficiency that are often used as dashboard indicators or to benchmark different providers and/or countries include per-case expenditure, duplicate tests, generic prescribing, emergency readmissions, average length of stay for particular conditions, and operations per specialist. None of them is free of limitations and thus requires further development (Cylus et al., 2016a, pp. 32–36). Also, healthcare efficiency as a subject needs to be intensively researched thus any new frameworks should be welcome.

Here one may refer to a framework for thinking more clearly about what a specific efficiency indicator tells, and for identifying the respects in which the indicator may be informative, misleading or only partial proposed by Cylus et al. (2016b). They assess five aspects of any efficiency indicator:

- the entity to be assessed (what to evaluate?),
- the outputs (or outcomes) under consideration (what are the outputs under consideration?)
- the inputs under consideration (what are the inputs under consideration?),

- the external influences on attainment (what are the external influences on performance?),
- the links with the rest of the health system (Cylus et al., 2016b, pp. 11–18).

Addressing the above questions could help to examine questions such as:

- Is the correct actor being targeted for the efficiency metric under consideration?
- To what extent are the outputs of the entity fully captured in the metric?
- To what extent are the inputs of the entity fully captured in the metric?
- Are the external (uncontrollable) influences on attainment fully taken into account?
- Are there potential influences on the rest of the health system that the metric does not take into account? (Cylus et al., 2016b, p. 241).

All these, in turn, could lead to improving the process of using efficiency metrics for policy purposes.

In practice, efficiency analyses of health sectors as such are rare. More often we find analyses on specific segments of the healthcare system like hospitals (Tiemann, Schreyögg, 2012; Nistor et al., 2017; Alatawi et al., 2020; Asbu et al., 2020), primary health care (Starfield, 2012; Mei et al., 2023; Zhao et al., 2023), or ambulatory care (Conrad, 2002; Kumar, Parthasarathy, 2020; Rocha et al., 2021; Luengo-Fernandez et al., 2022; Seeralan et al., 2023).

As far as the efficiency of primary health care is concerned, some may notice some inconsistency in findings. For example, Zhao et al. (2023) reported that the productivity of Chinese primary healthcare services showed a decreasing trend, mainly due to slowing technology change, while Mei et al. (2023) maintain that the efficiency of primary healthcare institutions in China showed a rising trend in general, but the overall average efficiency was still at a low level, and there were significant geographical differences.

Considering the efficiency of primary health care, one may mention the vital signs profile (VSP) built upon a conceptual framework constructed by the Primary Health Care Performance Initiative (PHCPI). VSP uses dozens of indicators to visualise primary healthcare data across health systems. Interestingly enough, the performance pillar of VSP includes three domains: *access*, *quality*, and *coverage*. Efficiency is placed in outcomes (together with *health status*, *responsiveness to people*, *equity*, and *resilience of health systems*) (PHCPI, 2019, p. 6) and unlike all other indicators is not described and explained.

In an unofficial beta-version second-generation VSP in the performance pillar, among quality indicators, one may find efficiency and effectiveness. The first is represented by *provider caseload* while the second by *admissions for ambulatory care sensitive conditions* (PHCI, 2023). Needless to add, there is no further explanation available on the particular indicators concerning the efficiency of primary care.

Keeping in mind that measuring the efficiency of primary health care is not free from limitations and weaknesses. It is worth mentioning that in the opinion of many researchers and practitioners, investing in and developing primary health care can lead to an increase in the efficiency of the entire healthcare system (WHO, 2023a). OECD also considers primary health care as '... the cornerstone of an efficient, people-centred, and equitable health system' (OECD, 2023a, p. 166).

Radley et al. (2023) in their ranking 2023 for state health system performance use 58 measures grouped into five areas:

- access and affordability,
- prevention and treatment,
- avoidable hospital use and cost,
- healthy lives,
- reproductive care and women's health (Radley et al., 2023).

As a result of a state's performance based on the five areas above, Massachusetts, Hawaii, and New Hampshire placed at the top, and Oklahoma, West Virginia, and Mississippi placed at the bottom of the list. They also reported a decline in Americans' health (Radley et al., 2023).

There is enough evidence to suggest that inefficiency is a major problem in all health systems (Cylus et al., 2017). In such a case, examining the variability of the efficiency of healthcare systems is of great importance, especially in the context of the struggle of the vast majority of healthcare systems with limited resources, mainly financial and human.

Medical professionals rightly point out the need to revise and adjust the terms of efficiency and effectiveness used primarily in management and economics to the conditions prevailing in the healthcare sector (Burches, Burches, 2020).

Empirical findings related to healthcare systems' performance indicate several challenges. The 2017 OECD Survey on Performance Measurement Systems in the Health Sector and Responsibilities across Levels of Government conducted between November 2017 and May 2018 in 23 OECD countries is a good example. The survey revealed that the most common challenges for performance measurement systems were technical such as the quality of data, the comparability of data (including the standardisation of coding) and measuring service outcomes and service quality. This means that the most challenging issue is a lack of commonly accepted and used methodology. Other issues such as vested interests, non-cooperation by sub-national governments and cost concerns were identified as much less problematic (Beazley et al., 2019, p. 63).

Beazley et al. (2019) concluded that government systems were focused mainly on monitoring the performance of hospitals and providers of ambulatory care[2] while providers of ancillary services, retailers and other providers of medical goods, and providers of preventive care were much less likely to be monitored under a specific performance framework (Beazley et al., 2019, p. 64).

3.4 Healthcare systems effectiveness

This issue should be preceded by a delimitation between healthcare effectiveness and healthcare efficiency.

3.4.1 Effectiveness and efficiency of health care

Effectiveness is defined as doing the right things or delivering quality with the available resources. Here it is worth recalling two textbook differences between efficiency and effectiveness. First, efficiency focuses on the process or resources, while effectiveness focuses on the outcomes. Second, efficiency is restricted to the present state, while effectiveness involves thinking long term. Needless to add healthcare providers have to be both effective and efficient to be successful.

3.4.1.1 Effectiveness of healthcare systems

The effectiveness of healthcare systems can be analysed based on the results of patient surveys and the basis of the position in the rankings of healthcare systems. Both should be interpreted as proxies and interpreted with necessary care.

When it comes to surveys, the analyses carried out by the Commonwealth Fund and Europe Health Consumer Index are good examples.

In the United States, the Commonwealth Fund 2023 International Health Policy Survey collected data from nationally representative samples of noninstitutionalised adults aged 18 and older in Australia, Canada, France, Germany, the Netherlands, New Zealand, Sweden, Switzerland, the United Kingdom, and the United States. In such a comparative perspective, the US health system shows considerable weaknesses out of which two categories seem to be the most important here. These are financial barriers to access to health care and income-related disparities. These two issues can be illustrated by the following findings from the 2023 International Health Policy Survey:

- Americans are most likely to have medical bill problems, regardless of income.
- Respondents from the United States, adults with higher incomes are more likely to have healthcare affordability problems, including cost-related access issues and medical bill problems, than their counterparts in most other countries.
- Adults in the United States with lower or average incomes are among the most likely to skip getting mental health care because of the cost.
- American respondents face wider income-related disparities in healthcare affordability compared to adults in other high-income countries. The fact

is that US citizens fare relatively worse on affordability and access to primary care than those in other countries, and income-related disparities across domains are relatively greater throughout, which was confirmed in other publications (Doty et al., 2020).

- Americans with lower or average incomes are more likely to skip needed medical care and have problems paying medical bills than all other countries in this analysis.
- Adults in the United States with lower or average incomes are most likely to skip or delay getting needed health care because of the cost.
- In seven of nine countries, adults with lower or average incomes are more likely to skip dental care than those with higher incomes.
- In six of nine countries, about one-third of adults with lower or average incomes reported at least one social service need (Gunja et al., 2023a).

Systemic disadvantages of the US healthcare system in international comparisons were also presented in other publications, especially regarding outputs and outcomes. Here one may refer to the findings from the 2020 Commonwealth Fund International Health Policy Survey, which covered 13 highly developed countries: Australia, Canada, France, Germany, the Netherlands, New Zealand, Norway, Switzerland, Sweden, the United Kingdom, and the United States. Data, as of 2023, were collected from nationally representative samples of noninstitutionalised adults aged 18 and older. This comparison shows that:

- the United States is a world outlier when it comes to healthcare spending;
- the United States spends three to four times more on health care than South Korea, New Zealand, and Japan;
- but the United States is the only high-income country that does not guarantee health coverage.

Some other outcomes indicate low effectiveness of the US healthcare system, for example:

- US life expectancy at birth is three years lower than the OECD average;
- avoidable deaths per 100,000 population in the United States are higher than the OECD average;
- the United States has the highest rate of infant and maternal deaths;
- rates of suicide are the highest in the United States, Japan, and South Korea;
- deaths from assault are highest in the United States;
- the United States obesity rate is nearly double the OECD average;
- adults in the United States are the most likely to have multiple chronic conditions;
- the United States has the highest rate of death because of COVID-19;
- the United States has among the lowest rates of physician visits and practising physicians.

Some of the US indicators also raise concern, for example:

- low rate of practising physicians;
- the lowest number of hospital beds per 1,000 population;
- more frequent use of magnetic resonance imaging (MRI) compared to the OECD average (and to countries with a higher number of MRIs, such as Norway and Germany) (Gunja et al., 2023a).

This may suggest the existence of American competitive advantage in healthcare efficiency over other high-developed countries (at least in the areas indicated above) refers only to inputs and outputs of hospitals which will be presented below.

3.4.1.2 Healthcare system efficiency

The issue of the US healthcare system's efficiency should be developed further. Sticking to the simple definition of efficiency as maximising effects while minimising the resources used to achieve them, it must be stated that the American healthcare system uses comparatively fewer human and tangible (material) resources than other systems. This, however, does not apply to prices for health services. As diagnosed by Gunja et al. (2023b), in the United States, high prices for health services continue to be the primary driver of elevated spending. Such a judgement was earlier presented by Anderson et al. (2019) who analysed the US healthcare system performance between 2000 and 2015. They used observations about healthcare spending, resources, and utilisation to make inferences about the role of prices in explaining spending differences partly because the available OECD data do not include information about the prices of specific healthcare goods and services, which are very difficult to measure comparably across countries (Anderson et al., 2019, p. 88). Price data from other published articles were also used.

In 2015 or 2016 (depending on the availability of data), the United States had fewer nurses, physicians, and hospital beds per capita (20%, 19%, and 26%, respectively) than the median OECD country in 2015 (Anderson et al., 2019, p. 93).

Fewer resources used, however, did not mean lower expenses. For example, according to data from the Commonwealth Fund on hospital care, the United States spent $21,063 per hospital discharge in 2014, compared to the OECD median of $10,530 and $5,900 per hospital discharge in Germany (28% of the US cost) (Anderson et al., 2019, p. 90).

The high prices in US hospitals may to a great extent explain the dominance of American hospitals in the ranking of hospitals with the highest average revenues. Data from the Statista Health Market Outlook shows that nowhere hospital care is more profitable than in the United States. The hospital sector includes hospitals, including general hospitals (including public and private), psychiatric hospitals, and specialist hospitals, which provide various services to inpatients, ranging from diagnostics to medical treatments and surgical treatments to nursing and specialised accommodation to other medical services. Long-term care facilities, ambulatory care providers, and medical retailers are excluded from the estimates. In the United States the estimated average annual revenues per hospital in 2022 was $116.4 million compared to $44.9 million in Australia and Oceania, $36.7 million in Europe, $15.1 million in Asia, $8.6 million in South America, and $1.7 million in Africa (Armstrong, 2022).

Anderson et al. (2019) concluded that 'Because the differential between what the public and private sectors pay for medical services has grown significantly in the past fifteen years, US policymakers should focus on prices in the private sector' (Anderson et al., 2019, p. 87).

The last ranking is the Euro Health Consumer Index (EHCI) prepared by the Health Consumer Powerhouse since 2005. It is worth mentioning since it focuses on patients as consumers. The latest survey contained six subdisciplines:

1 patient rights and information,
2 accessibility (waiting times for treatment),
3 outcomes,
4 range and rich of services provided,
5 prevention,
6 pharmaceuticals (Björnberg, Yung Phang, 2019).

Forty-six indicators were assigned to each of the six subdisciplines (10, 6, 9, 8, 7, and 6, respectively) (Björnberg, Yung Phang, 2019). Two of the limitations of the EHCI should be acknowledged. First, it covers (as stated in the title) only European countries, and second, the latest issue available covers data from 2018. EHCI 2018 showed significant differences between European countries. The best healthcare system from the customer/consumer's point of view in 2018 was the Swiss one (total of 893 scores of a maximum of 1,000) and the worst was the Albanian one (544 of 1,000).

Keeping in mind the existing challenges for international and national comparisons of healthcare system efficiency (i.e., comparisons among various hospitals and other healthcare providers in a given country), let us move to international rankings of healthcare systems. International rankings use a whole range of indicators where system efficiency is only one of several used in the evaluations thus they can be considered only as a proxy. Here, the concept of a 'high-performing health system' could be useful. The American Medical Group Association identified it through the following traits: quality improvement, team-based care, technology tools, incentivised compensation, cost consciousness, and physician leaders (Westgate, 2012). It can also be treated as a surrogate for the effectiveness of the system.

3.4.2 Selected healthcare systems rankings

There are many rankings of the best healthcare systems (apart from EHCI mentioned above). As an illustration, four rankings will be introduced: *the Commonwealth Institute ranking*, *the Legatum Institute ranking*, *the Health Care Index of Ceoworld Magazine*, and *the Expatriate Group's ranking*.

In 2021, *the Commonwealth Institute* examined the healthcare systems in 11 high-income countries (Australia, Canada, France, Germany, the Netherlands, New Zealand, Norway, Sweden, Switzerland, the United Kingdom, and the United States). The measurements took into account how easily people can access care, administrative procedures and equity around this care, and the quality of healthcare outcomes. Norway, the Netherlands, and Australia were the countries with the best healthcare. The United States was ranked 11th, close to the bottom of this list (International Citizens Insurance, 2023).

The Legatum Institute, a London-based think tank, has also evaluated where to find the best healthcare in the world. Its 2023 report included a 'Health pillar' that is based on how healthy a society is and whether people can access tools to maintain their health, including healthcare services. In most countries, you'll need a travel insurance plan for short visits for up to one year or an international medical insurance plan if you want long-term medical coverage for a year or more to access these services. The best healthcare systems in the world in 2023 were Singapore, Japan, South Korea, Taiwan, China, Israel, Norway, Iceland, Sweden, and Switzerland (International Citizens Insurance, 2023).

There are significant differences between these two rankings. For example, the United Kingdom was ranked fourth by the Commonwealth Institute (out of 11 countries, but before Switzerland, France, and Canada) but by the Legatum Institute was ranked 34th (out of 104 countries and after Switzerland, France, and Canada) (International Citizens Insurance, 2023). As concluded in the recent report on the UK healthcare system: 'The NHS, which sits at the core of the UK health system, is neither a leader nor a laggard when compared to the health systems of 18 similar countries' (Anandaciva, 2023, p. 3).

There are other rankings where two industry groups get attention. This is because both of them seem to take into account the growing migration of people. The first is the Health Care Index of *Ceoworld Magazine* and its ranking for 2023, and the second is Expatriate Group's ranking for 2022.

According to the 2023 edition of *the Ceoworld Magazine Health Care Index*, which ranks 110 countries according to factors that contribute to overall health, Taiwan had the best healthcare system in the world. The Health Care Index is composed of three groups of indicators: *healthcare infrastructure and healthcare professionals' competencies, quality medicine availability and cost, and government readiness*. It also takes into consideration other factors including environmental issues, access to clean water, sanitation, and government readiness to impose penalties on risks such as tobacco use and obesity. The rest of the top ten healthcare systems were South Korea, Australia, Canada, Sweden, Ireland, the Netherlands, Germany, Norway, and Israel (Dimitropoulou, 2023).

The Expatriate Group's ranking for 2022 was interesting because it took into account the conditions defined by national healthcare systems for migrants considering returning to their home countries. In such cases, a country's healthcare system can be the deciding factor in deciding whether or not to move to a country. The ranking for 2022 showed the following ten best countries: South Korea, Taiwan, Denmark, Austria, Japan, Australia, France, Spain, Belgium, and the United Kingdom (Expat Health & Safety, 2022).

The differences between the rankings notwithstanding, one may conclude that the South Asian countries of South Korea, and Taiwan, as well as the Netherlands, Denmark, and Sweden, are highly rated as effective. It is worth noticing that the US healthcare system is comparatively low-rated compared to its revenues. The US healthcare system had the highest revenues in the world in 2021 ($4.3 trillion or $12,914 per capita) and had the highest share of health spending in GDP (18.3% in 2019) in the world (AMA, 2023).

Having acknowledged the existence of methodological and operational challenges related to comparisons of healthcare systems' effectiveness one may share the opinion that: 'There is little evidence that one individual country or model of health care system performs consistently better than another across a range of performance indicators' (Anandaciva, 2023, p. 4).

3.5 Financial constraints of healthcare systems

Healthcare expenditures are driven by several factors. They can be perceived as sector-specific (prices of pharmaceuticals, medical devices, technologies, and medical professionals' salaries), macroeconomics (GDP growth, inflation, labour market issues), and social ones (inflation, rising incomes, ageing, etc.). As to the latter, one should remember that rising health expenditures can lead to an increase in life expectancy, which in turn forces the need to increase spending on health due to growing demand.[3]

As indicated above, financial difficulties are a considerable challenge that healthcare systems are facing. The majority of healthcare systems experience financial constraints albeit in various degrees and related to different healthcare system components. Here a simplistic distinction between developed and developing countries will be useful.

As far as developing countries are concerned, one of the most important financial (but also organisational) challenges is the introduction of Universal Health Coverage (UHC). UHC, embedded within the United Nations Sustainable Development Goals, is defined by the WHO as all individuals having access to required health services, be of sufficient quality, and without suffering financial hardship. UHC implementation remains the challenge especially in the Southeast Asian region (Lim et al., 2023) and sub-Saharan Africa (Ifeagwu et al., 2021). According to WHO estimates, in 2021, about 4.5 billion people were not fully covered by essential health services (WHO, 2023b). Apart from the introduction of UHC, further financial support for primary care remained a priority in developing countries (Zhao et al., 2023). It is worth noticing that UHC and primary health care are intertwined since 90% of essential UHC interventions can be delivered through a primary healthcare approach (WHO, 2023b).

Rising health expenditures accompanied by health deprivation continue to persist in Brazil, Russia, India, China, and South Africa (BRICS) leading to the growing demand for health financing. The BRICS' proportion of global health spending has been continuously increasing and if the current global economic trend holds, the BRICS per capita will most likely equal or exceed the OECD average in the coming decades (Sahoo et al., 2023). As in other countries, population ageing, rising noncommunicable diseases, and advancement in medical treatment are behind rising BRICS' health expenditures. Despite the growth in spending, inadequate healthcare systems and cost-effective allocation of scarce resources continue to be a major concern for BRICS countries. As diagnosed by Sahoo et al. providing comprehensive healthcare through public funding alone has become exceedingly difficult for these countries. It is worth acknowledging that the importance of the private sector in BRICS' healthcare has grown, and the size of government financing of health has been exceeded by private spending coming mainly from out-of-pocket payments (OOP), which often lead to impoverishment (Sahoo et al., 2023). OOPs are defined as expenditures borne directly by a patient where neither public nor private insurance covers the full cost of the health good or service. They include cost-sharing and other expenditures paid directly by private households, and should also ideally include estimations of informal payments to health providers (OECD, 2023a, p. 106). OECD data show that the share of household out-of-pocket payments[4] in gross domestic product between 2015 and 2020 had been rising in Brazil and China reaching, respectively, 2.3% and 2.0% of GDP and remained steady in South Africa (0.5% of GDP). India recorded a decrease in this share from 2.3% in 2015 to 1.5% in 2020 (OECD, 2023b).

Rising health expenditures and financial constraints are diagnosed also in developed countries like Canada and the United States.

In Canada, federal healthcare funding has long been a source of policy debate and the situation was exacerbated by the COVID-19 pandemic. Canadian premiers called for a large expansion of the Canada Health Transfer and an increase in federal healthcare funding. This is because healthcare systems across Canada are expected to face increasing strain in the coming years due to ageing and increasing healthcare costs, which are putting additional fiscal pressure on provincial and territorial governments (Béland, Tombe, 2023).

In the United States at the end of 2022, several health systems reported higher expenses and losses from investments contributing to sizable net losses for 2022. A part of the US healthcare system (20 health systems throughout the United States) reported losses that amounted to over $13.6 billion (Condon, Thomas, 2023).

Although American hospitals' average revenues make them world leaders, equally high and growing are their expenses. US hospital expenses were projected to continue a dramatic increase of $135 billion over 2022: labour expenses by $86 billion, and non-labour expenses by $49 billion (AHA, 2023). Probably, 2022 was projected to be the worst year for American hospitals not only since the beginning of the pandemic but, according to some hospital managers, 40 years of increasing staffing shortages, sky-rocketing labour costs, continuing supply chain disruptions, inflation, rising interest rates, and volatile markets (Robinson, 2022).

Global Health Expenditure Database showed that between 2000 and 2020 the global trend in health spending (defined as a share of GDP) increased in all countries: high-income, upper-middle-income, low-income, and lower-middle income ones. Thanks to the growing trend of the share of health expenditure in GDP, each of the four groups of countries moved up to a higher level crossing the line of (respectfully) 9%, 7%, 6%, and 5% (WHO, 2023c).

OECD countries spent an average of 9.2% of GDP on health in 2022. It declined from a peak in 2021 (9.7%) but was still higher than pre-pandemic levels. The share of GDP going to the healthcare sector remained the highest in the United States (16.6%) followed by Germany (12.7%), and France (12.1%) (see Table 3.1).

Among other 11 high-income OECD countries all spent more than 10% of their GDP on healthcare in 2022 (OECD, 2023b).

As shown in Table 3.1 in 2022 the share of current expenditures on health in GDP as compared to 2015 was higher in 29 OECD countries (Austria, Belgium, Canada, Chile, Columbia, Czechia, Estonia, Finland, France, Germany, Greece, Iceland, Israel, Italy, Japan, Korea, Latvia, Lithuania, Luxembourg, New Zealand, Poland, Portugal, Slovak Republic, Slovenia, Spain, Switzerland, Türkiye, United Kingdom, and United States) and slightly lower in nine countries (Australia, Costa Rica, Denmark, Hungary, Ireland, Mexico, Netherlands, Norway, and Sweden). This means that in the majority of OECD countries, expenditures on health were higher, which supports the statement of the growing trend in health expenditures in OECD countries.

Assessing tendencies in current expenditures on health in GDP one should keep in mind that, due to its nature presented in Chapter 2, HE cannot be financed from a universal health coverage or any other standard health insurance scheme. The only source of HE financing remains private sources, OOPs. This issue will be further developed in Chapter 4.

One may conclude that healthcare systems in developed countries are confronted with several challenges with increasing costs and patients' expectations being the primary ones. Concerning developing countries, the introduction of UHC seems to be the most urgent. Developed countries are

Table 3.1 Share of the current expenditure on health (all functions) in GDP (2015–2022) (in %)

Country	*2015*	*2016*	*2017*	*2018*	*2019*	*2020*	*2021*	*2022*^{E}
Australia	10.2	10.1	10.1	10.1	10.2	10.7	10.6	9.6
Austria	10.4	10.4	10.4	10.3	10.5	11.4	12.1	11.4
Belgium	10.8	10.8	10.8	10.9	10.8	11.2	11.0	10.9
Canada	10.7	11.0	10.9	10.9	11.0	13.0^{D}	12.3^{DP}	11.2
Chile	8.4	8.6	9.1	9.2	9.4	9.7	9.3	9.0
Colombia	7.5	7.5	7.7	7.6	7.8	8.7	9.0	8.1
Costa Rica	7.6	7.3	7.0	7.3^{B}	7.2	7.8	7.6	7.2
Czechia	7.4	7.4	7.4	7.5	7.6	9.2	9.5	9.1
Denmark	10.3	10.2	10.1	10.1	10.2	10.6	10.8	9.5
Estonia	6.6	6.7	6.6	6.7	6.8	7.6	7.5	6.9
Finland	9.6^{B}	9.4	9.1	9.0	9.2	9.6	10.3	10.0
France	11.4	11.5	11.4	11.2	11.1	12.1	12.3	12.1
Germany	11.2	11.2	11.3	11.5	11.7	12.7	12.9	12.7
Greece	8.2	8.4	8.1	8.1	8.2	9.5	9.2	8.6
Hungary	6.9	7.0	6.7	6.6	6.3	7.3	7.4	6.7
Iceland	8.1	8.1	8.3	8.4	8.6	9.6	9.7	8.6
Ireland	7.3	7.5	7.1	6.9	6.7	7.1	6.7	6.1
Israel	7.0	7.1	7.2	7.2	7.2	7.7^{P}	7.9^{BDP}	7.4
Italy	8.9	8.7	8.7	8.7	8.7	9.6	9.4	9.0
Japan	10.8	10.7	10.7	10.7	11.0	11.0	11.3^{P}	11.5
Korea	6.6	6.9	7.0	7.5	8.2	8.4	9.3	9.7
Latvia	5.7	6.1	6.0	6.2	6.6	7.2	9.0	8.8
Lithuania	6.5	6.6	6.5	6.5	7.0	7.5	7.8	7.5
Luxembourg	5.1	5.1	5.1	5.3	5.5	5.7	5.7	5.5
Mexico	5.7	5.6	5.5	5.4	5.4	6.2	6.1	5.5
Netherlands	10.3	10.3	10.1	10.0	10.1	11.2	11.3	10.2
New Zealand	9.3^{P}	9.2^{P}	9.0^{P}	9.0^{P}	9.1^{E}	9.7^{E}	10.1^{E}	11.2
Norway	10.1	10.5	10.2	10.0	10.4	11.2	9.9^{P}	7.9
Poland	6.4	6.6	6.6	6.3	6.5	6.5	6.4	6.7
Portugal	9.3	9.4	9.3	9.4	9.5	10.5	11.1	10.6
Slovak Republic	6.8	7.0	6.8	6.7	6.9	7.1	7.8	7.8
Slovenia	8.5	8.5	8.2	8.3	8.5	9.4	9.5	8.8
Spain	9.1	8.9	8.9	9.0	9.1	10.7	10.7	10.4
Sweden	10.8	10.9	10.8	10.9	10.8	11.3	11.2^{P}	10.7
Switzerland	10.8	11.0	11.0	10.8	11.1	11.7	11.8	11.3
Türkiye	4.1	4.3	4.2	4.1	4.4	4.6	4.6	4.3
United Kingdom	9.8	9.7	9.6	9.7	10.0	12.2	12.4	11.3
United States	16.5	16.8	16.8	16.6	16.7	18.8	17.4	16.6
Non-OECD Economies	10.2	9.0	10.4	9.5	9.4	10.0	...	...

Source: OECD, https://stats.oecd.org/Index.aspx?DatasetCode=HEALTH_STAT.

B: Break.
E: Estimated value.
D: Difference in methodology.
P: Provisional value.

confronted with rising demand for high-quality health services and rising costs fuelled by technological progress, sophisticated medical technologies, and the increasing ageing of populations (which was presented in Chapter 1). A separate problem is measuring, monitoring, and controlling the efficiency and effectiveness of the healthcare systems. These challenges remain. There is also room for improvement regarding the methodology of effectiveness and efficiency in healthcare systems, especially indicators used in day-to-day operations. All these are leading to an increase in financial constraints.

Notes

1 WONCA is an acronym comprising the first five initials of the World Organization of National Colleges, Academies and Academic Associations of General Practitioners/Family Physicians.
2 This can be explained by the biggest share of inpatient care in health expenditures.
3 Senior citizens and children are groups with the highest share in health expenditure.
4 Current expenditure on health (all functions), all providers.

References

Advisory Board (2020). *The 13 biggest threats to global health, according to WHO*, January 15, 2020, https://www.advisory.com/daily-briefing/2020/01/15/who-health-challenges, accessed 13.10.2023.

Advisory Board (2023). *The 6 challenges facing health care in 2023 – and how to handle them*, Daily Briefing, January 4, 2023, https://www.advisory.com/daily-briefing/2023/01/04/healthcare-2023, accessed 15.10.2023.

AHA (2023). *The current state of hospital finances: Fall 2022 update*. American Hospital Association, KaufmanHall, September 15, 2022, https://www.aha.org/guidesreports/2022-09-15-current-state-hospital-finances-fall-2022-update, accessed 24.11.2023.

Alatawi, A.D., Niessen, L.W., Khan, J.A.M. (2020). Determinants of technical efficiency in public hospitals: The case of Saudi Arabia. *Health Economics Review*, 10, 25, 10.1186/s13561-020-00282-z.

AMA (2023). *Trends in health care spending*. American Medical Association, March 20, 2023, https://www.ama-assn.org/about/research/trends-health-care-spending, accessed 16.10.2023.

Anandaciva, S. (2023). *How does the NHS compare to the health care systems of other countries?* The King's Fund, June 2023, https://www.kingsfund.org.uk/sites/default/files/2023-06/How_NHS_compare_2023.pdf, accessed 21.11.2023.

Anderson, G.F., Hussey, P., Petrosyan, V. (2019). It's still the prices, stupid: Why the US spends so much on health care, and a tribute to Uwe Reinhardt. *Health Affairs*, 38(1), 87–95, 10.1377/hlthaff.2018.05144.

Armstrong, M. (2022). *Where hospitals are lucrative operations*, October 21, 2022, https://www.statista.com/chart/28511/avg-revernue-per-hospital-by-world-region, accessed 4.11.2023.

Asbu, E.Z., Masri, M.D., Al Naboulsi, M. (2020). Determinants of hospital efficiency: A literature review. *International Journal of Healthcare*, 6(2), 44–53, 10.5430/ijh.v6n2p44.

BCG/BCG X (2023). *The future of digital health*. Boston Consulting Group, Boston Consulting Group X, January 2023, https://web-assets.bcg.com/55/9b/a892017e4b87ae3a79341d9daf73/bcg-the-future-of-digital-health-jan-2023.pdf, accessed 2.11.2023.

Beazley, I., Dougherty, S., Penn, C., Philips, L., James. C. (2019). Performance measurement systems in the health sector and their budgetary implications. *OECD Journal on Budgeting*, 19(3), 41–66, 10.1787/d94fd384-en.
Béland, D., Tombe, T. (2023). Reforming Canada's federal health-care funding arrangements. *Canadian Public Administration*, 66, 28–44. 10.1111/capa.12514, accessed 24.11.2023.
Björnberg, A., Yung Phang, A. (2019). *Euro Health Consumer Index 2018. Report.* Health Consumer Powerhouse Ltd. https://healthpowerhouse.com/publications, accessed 14.11.2023.
Burches, E., Burches, M. (2020). Efficacy, effectiveness and efficiency in the health care: The need for an agreement to clarify its meaning. *International Archives of Public Health and Community Medicine*, 4, 035, 10.23937/2643-4512/1710035.
Condon, C., Thomas, N. (2023). *20 health systems reporting losses in 2022*, March 2, 2023, https://www.beckershospitalreview.com/finance/20-health-systems-reporting-losses-in-2022.html, accessed 18.11.2023.
Conrad, D.A. (2002). Ambulatory care efficiency: A conceptual essay and empirical assessment. *Journal of Ambulatory Care Management*, 25(1), 1–11, https://journals.lww.com/ambulatorycaremanagement/abstract/2002/01000/ambulatory_care_efficiency__a_conceptual_essay_and.3.aspx.
Cylus, J., Papanicolas, I., Smith, P.C. (2016a). Conclusions. In Cylus, J., Papanicolas, I., Peter C. Smith, P.C. (Eds). *Health System Efficiency: How to Make Measurement Matter for Policy and Management.* European Observatory on Health Systems and Policies, Health Policy Series 46, pp. 225–242. World Health Organization.
Cylus, J., Papanicolas, I., Smith, P.C. (2016b). A framework for thinking about health system efficiency. In Cylus, J., Papanicolas, I., Peter C. Smith, P.C. (Eds). *Health System Efficiency: How to Make Measurement Matter for Policy and Management.* European Observatory on Health Systems and Policies, Health Policy Series 46, pp. 1–20. World Health Organization.
Cylus, J., Papanicolas, I., Smith, P.C. (2017). *How to make sense of health system efficiency comparisons?* Health Systems and Policy Analysis. Policy Brief 27. European Observatory on Health Systems and Policies. WHO.
Davis, B., Ahmed, A., Elsner, N., Miranda, W. (2021). *Personalized therapies in the future of health. Winning with digital medicine products.* Deloitte Insights. A report from the Deloitte Center for Health Solutions and the Digital Medicine Society, Deloitte Development, LLC.
Dimitropoulou, A. (2023). *Revealed: Countries with the best health care systems, 2023*, August 25, 2023, https://ceoworld.biz/2023/08/25/revealed-countries-with-the-best-health-care-systems-2023, accessed 3.11.2023.
Doty, M.M., Tikkanen, R.S., FitzGerald, M., Fields, K., Williams II, R.D. (2020). Income-related inequality in affordability and access to primary care in eleven high-income countries. *Health Affairs*, 40(1), 113–120, 10.1377/hlthaff.2020.01566.
EU (2021). *EU4Health programme 2021–2027 – a vision for a healthier European Union*, https://health.ec.europa.eu/funding/eu4health-programme-2021-2027-vision-healthier-european-union_en, accessed 16.10.2023.
Expat Health & Safety (2022). *The top 10 healthcare systems in the world 2022*, July 21, 2022, Expat Health & Safety, https://www.expatriatehealthcare.com/the-top-10-healthcare-systems-in-the-world-2022, accessed 3.11.2023.
Faculty of Public Health (2023). *Measures of supply and demand*, https://www.healthknowledge.org.uk/public-health-textbook/research-methods/1c-health-care-evaluation-health-care-assessment/measures-supply-demand, accessed 3.11.2023.
Ghorbani, A. (2022). Demand for health and healthcare. In Agrawal, A., Kosagi, S. (Eds). *Healthcare access.* IntechOpen, 10.5772/intechopen.98915.

Grossman, M. (1999). The Human Capital Model of the Demand for Health. National Bureau of Economic Research. Working Paper 7078, https://doi.10.3386/w7078, http://www.nber.org/papers/w7078.

Gunja, M.Z., Gumas, E.D., Williams II, R.D., Doty, M.M., Shah, A., Fields, K. (2023a). *The cost of not getting care: Income disparities in the affordability of health services across high-income countries. Findings from the Commonwealth Fund 2023 International Health Policy Survey*, Commonwealth Fund, Issue Briefs, November 16, 2023, https://www.commonwealthfund.org/publications/issue-briefs/2023/nov/cost-not-getting-care-affordability-high-income-countries-survey, accessed 22.11.2023.

Gunja, M.Z., Gumas, E.D., Williams II, R.D. (2023b). *U.S. health care from a global perspective, 2022: Accelerating spending, worsening outcomes*. Commonwealth Fund, Issue Briefs, January 31, 2023. https://www.commonwealthfund.org/publications/issue-briefs/2023/jan/us-health-care-global-perspective-2022, accessed 21.11.2023.

Healthcare Transformers (2021). *3 biggest challenges in healthcare transformation according to industry leaders*, https://healthcaretransformers.com/healthcare-business/strategy-and-operations/biggest-challenges-healthcare, accessed 13.10.2023.

HHS (2022). Strategic plan FY 2022–2026, https://www.hhs.gov/about/strategic-plan/2022-2026/overview/index.html#strategic-goals, accessed 28.10.2023.

Ifeagwu, S.C., Yang, J.C., Parkes-Ratanshi, R., Brayne, C. (2021). Health financing for universal health coverage in sub-Saharan Africa: A systematic review. *Global Health Research and Policy*, 6, 8, 10.1186/s41256-021-00190-7.

Imani, A., Alibabayee, R., Golestani, M., Dalal, K. (2022). Key indicators affecting hospital efficiency: A systematic review. *Frontiers in Public Health*, 10, 10.3389/fpubh.2022.830102.

International Citizens Insurance (2023). *Ranking the Best Healthcare in the World by Country*, https://www.internationalinsurance.com/health/systems, accessed 3.11.2023.

Jain, S. (2022). *Projected growth in demand for healthcare services is tepid*, November 6, 2022, https://www.trillianthealth.com/insights/the-compass/projected-growth-in-demand-for-healthcare-services-is-tepid, accessed 12.10.2023.

Keshishian, K. (2021). *What does efficiency in healthcare delivery mean? Examples of two market failures*, https://www.dssurgery.com/what-does-efficiency-in-healthcare-delivery-mean-examples-of-two-market-failures, accessed 10.11.2023.

Kumar, P., Parthasarathy, R. (2020). *Walking out of the hospital: The continued rise of ambulatory care and how to take advantage of it*. September 18, 2020, https://www.mckinsey.com/industries/healthcare/our-insights/walking-out-of-the-hospital-the-continued-rise-of-ambulatory-care-and-how-to-take-advantage-of-it, accessed 22.11.2023.

Lim, M.Y., Kamaruzaman, H.F., Wu, O., Geue, C. (2023). Health financing challenges in Southeast Asian countries for universal health coverage: A systematic review. *Archives of Public Health*, 81, 148, 10.1186/s13690-023-01159-3.

Lucero-Prisno, D.E., Shomuyiwa, D.O., Kouwenhoven, M.B.N., Dorji, T., Odey, G.O., Miranda, A.V., Ogunkola, I.O., Adebisi, Y.A., Huang, J., Xu, L., Obnial, J.C., Huda, A., Thepanondh, S., Dayrit, M.M., Evardone, S.B., Lamawansa, M.D., Ethiopia, S.S., Aziato, L., Adongo, P.B., Samai, M.H., Garcia Jr, F.B., Villaruz, J.F., Karunathilake, I.M., Li, H., Azanza, P.A., Findlay, I., Wong, M.C.S. (2023). Top 10 public health challenges to track in 2023: Shifting focus beyond a global pandemic. *Public Health Challenges*, 2(2), e86, 10.1002/puh2.86.

Luengo-Fernandez, R., Landeiro, F., Hallifax, R., Rahman, N.M. (2022). Cost-effectiveness of ambulatory care management of primary spontaneous pneumothorax: An open-label, randomised controlled trial. *Thorax*, 77(9), 913–918, 10.1136/thoraxjnl-2021-218479.

Mei, K., Kou, R., Bi, Y., Liu, Y., Huang, J., Li, W. (2023). A study of primary health care service efficiency and its spatial correlation in China. *BMC Health Service Research*, 23, 247, 10.1186/s12913-023-09197-x.

Milcent, C. (2023). The sorting effect in healthcare access: Those left behind. *Economics & Human Biology*, 51, 101282, 10.1016/j.ehb.2023.101282.

NHS (2022). *Demand and capacity – a comprehensive guide.* Online library of Quality, Service Improvement and Redesign tools. NHS England and NHS Improvement, https://www.england.nhs.uk/wp-content/uploads/2022/01/qsir-demand-and-capacity-a-comprehensive-guide.pdf, accessed 30.10.2023.

NHS Providers (2018). *The state of the provider sector*, https://nhsproviders.org/state-of-the-provider-sector-05-18, accessed 30.10.2023.

Nistor, C.S., Ştefănescu, C.A., Crişan, A.-R. (2017). Performance through efficiency in the public healthcare system – a DEA approach in an emergent country. *Studia Universitatis Babes-Bolyai Oeconomica*, 62(1), 31–49, 10.1515/subboec-2017-0003.

OECD (2016). *Scoping paper on health system efficiency measurement (cooperation between the OECD and EC in promoting efficiency in health care)*, December 2016. https://www.oecd.org/els/health-systems/Scoping-Paper-Measuring-efficiency-in-health-system.pdf, accessed 21.11.2023.

OECD (2023a). *Health at a glance 2023*. OECD 2023.

OECD (2023b). *Health expenditure and financing*, https://stats.oecd.org/Index.aspx?DataSetCode=HEALTH_ECOR, accessed 26.11.2023.

Ortaliza, J., McGough, M., Wager, E., Claxton, G., Amin, K. (2021). *How do health expenditures vary across the population?* Peterson KFF, November 12, 2021, https://www.healthsystemtracker.org/chart-collection/health-expenditures-vary-across-population/#Share%20of%20total%20health%20spending%20by%20age%20group,%202019, accessed 8.11.2023.

Palmer, S., Torgerson, D.J. (1999). Economic notes: Definitions of efficiency. *The British Medical Journal*, 318(7191), 1136, 10.1136/bmj.318.7191.1136.

PHCI (2023). *Country profiles. Preview: Anatomy of a second-generation vital signs profile*, https://phcdigitalhub.improvingphc.org/country-profiles, accessed 16.11.2023.

PHCPI (2019). *Primary health care vital signs profiles detailed methodology note.* Last updated June 19, 2019, https://www.improvingphc.org/sites/default/files/VSP_Detailed_Methodology_Note.pdf, accessed 16.11.2023.

Radley, D.C., Baumgartner, J.C., Collins, S.R., Zephyrin, L.C. (2023). *2023 scorecard on state health system performance: Americans' health declines and access to reproductive care shrinks, but states have options*, Commonwealth Fund, June 2023, https://www.commonwealthfund.org/publications/scorecard/2023/jun/2023-scorecard-state-health-system-performance, accessed 21.11.2023.

Robinson, L. (2022). *2022 state of healthcare performance improvement report*, October 18, 2022, https://www.kaufmanhall.com/insights/research-report/2022-state-healthcare-performance-improvement-report, accessed 20.11.2023.

Rocha, J.V.M., Santana, R., Tello, J.E. (2021). Hospitalization for ambulatory care sensitive conditions: What conditions make inter-country comparisons possible? *Health Policy OPEN*, 2, 100030, 10.1016/j.hpopen.2021.100030.

Sahoo, P.M., Rout, H.S., Jakovljevic, M. (2023). Dynamics of health financing among the BRICS: A literature review. *Sustainability*, 15, 12385. 10.3390/su151612385, accessed 23.11.2023.

Seeralan, T., Magaard, J.L., Engels, A., Meister, R., Kriston, L., Liebherz, S., König, H., Härter, M. (2023). Effectiveness of a coordinated ambulatory care program for patients with mental disorders or multiple sclerosis: Results of a prospective non-randomized controlled trial in South Germany. *Frontiers in Psychiatry*, 14, 1183710, 10.3389/fpsyt.2023.1183710.

Starfield, B. (2012). Primary care: An increasingly important contributor to effectiveness, equity, and efficiency of health services. SESPAS report 201. *Gaceta Sanitaria*, 26(1), 20–26, 10.1016/j.gaceta.2011.10.009.

Tiemann, O., Schreyögg, J. (2012). Changes in hospital efficiency after privatization. *Health Care Management Science*, 15(4), 310–326, 10.1007/s10729-012-9193-z.

Trilliant Health (2022). *Trends shaping the health economy*, annual report, https://www.trillianthealth.com/insights/reports/2022-health-economy-trends, accessed 22.10.2023.

Westgate, A. (2012). Six characteristics of 'high-performing' health systems. Physicians Practice, October 12, 2012, https://www.physicianspractice.com/view/six-characteristics-high-performing-health-systems, accessed 1.11.2023.

WHO (2017). *Determinants of health*, February 3, 2017, Q&A, https://www.who.int/news-room/questions-and-answers/item/determinants-of-health, accessed 27.10.2023.

WHO (2023a). *Investing in the radical reorientation of health systems towards Primary Health Care: The best and only choice to achieve universal health coverage*, November 9, 2023, https://www.who.int/news/item/09-11-2023-investing-in-the-radical-reorientation-of-health-systems-towards-primary-health-care--the-best-and-only-choice-to-achieve-universal-health-coverage, accessed 21.11.2023.

WHO (2023b). *Universal health coverage (UHC)*, October 5, 2023, https://www.who.int/news-room/fact-sheets/detail/universal-health-coverage-(uhc), accessed 23.11.2023.

WHO (2023c). Global health expenditure database, https://apps.who.int/nha/database/Home/Index/en, accessed 26.11.2023.

Wolters Kluwer (2022). Six challenges to delivering quality healthcare. September 6, 2022, https://www.wolterskluwer.com/en/expert-insights/six-challenges-to-delivering-quality-healthcare, accessed 13.10.2023.

WONCA (2023). *WONCA Europe 2023 Brussels: Shortage of European primary health care workforce statement*. Published on June 19, 2023, https://www.woncaeurope.org/news/view/shortage-of-european-primary-health-care-workforce-the-wonca-europe-statement%C2%A0, accessed 21.11.2023.

World Population Review (2023). *Best healthcare in the world 2023*, https://worldpopulationreview.com/country-rankings/best-healthcare-in-the-world, accessed 30.10.2023.

Zhao, Z., Dong, S., Wang, J., Jiang, Q. (2023). Estimating the efficiency of primary health care services and its determinants: Evidence from provincial panel data in China. *Frontiers in Public Health*, 11, 10.3389/fpubh.2023.1173197.

4 Human enhancement challenges

4.1 Legal regulations: current stage

A presentation of the current state of legal regulations is preceded by a brief reference to health policy. Health policy is understood in this book (following the WHO definition) as *the decisions, plans, and actions that are undertaken to achieve specific healthcare goals within a society*. An underlying assumption regarding decisions and plans taken by healthcare politicians is that they are based on rational assessments and analyses, which, in turn, require clear definitions and preferably unambiguous meanings. All these refer to legal regulations of human enhancement (HE).

The state of legal regulations concerning HE is a function of the current position of HE on the life-cycle curve and other characteristic features of the curve. As indicated in the previous chapters, HE remains at the initial stage of development (*in statu nascendi*) and can be characterised as a multidimensional and highly heterogeneous phenomenon. This, in turn, means that HE and/or human augmentation are/is not a distinguished and separate element regulated by law on the international or national level. However, since HE can encompass a wide range of technologies and interventions, including but not limited to genetic modifications, cognitive enhancements, and physical augmentations, one may link HE to existing international law (especially human rights), medical regulations (medical treatments and interventions), laws governing the use of biotechnology and genetic engineering, and gene editing. This means that some jurisdictions may have specific laws addressing data protection laws and regulations governing the use of personal information in the context of enhancements. This, in turn, leads us to anti-discrimination laws (*to prevent discrimination based on genetic information or physical enhancements and to protect individuals from being unfairly treated in areas such as employment or insurance due to their enhanced characteristics*) and intellectual property rights (*patented inventions, medical technologies and proprietary information*). Because HE is in its initial stage, '... legal frameworks may be continuously adapting to keep pace with technological advancements' (OpenAI, 2023).

One of the most recent analyses of human enhancement legal regulations is the SIENNA research project (SIENNA, 2021).[1] It deserves to be acknowledged

DOI: 10.4324/9781003449584-5

for a couple of reasons. Primarily because it has a wide scope. The SIENNA project analyses HE regulations on three levels:

1 international,
2 regional (European Union, Organization of American States, and African Union),
3 national (Brazil, China, France, Germany, Greece, the Netherlands, Poland, South Africa, Spain, Sweden, the United Kingdom and the United States) (Warso, Gaskell, 2019).

The wide range of research carried out by the SIENNA project (which ended on March 31, 2021) can be inferred from the research questions defined in this project, namely:

- What are the international and regional laws relevant to HE?
- Which rights of individuals (or groups) may potentially be affected by developments of HE? Which human rights standards may be relevant to consider in establishing methods to avoid or alleviate negative impacts and encourage positive impacts of those developments?
- To what extent are the existing legal frameworks adequate to deal with challenges posed by developments of HE?
- How might specific novel legal questions be solved in different jurisdictions according to different legal systems?
- What are the commonalities and differences between national legal systems concerning those questions?
- What are the convergences, divergences, and gaps between national and international legal orders for HE technologies?What are the possible ways to overcome the gaps? (Warso, Gaskell, 2019, p. 9).

Having reviewed the literature, the SIENNA project identified seven main legal issues and human rights challenges of HE technologies:

1 regulating human enhancement technologies: devices and drugs,
2 civil liability for human enhancement technologies: product liability and professional liability,
3 property law: ownership and patents,
4 security and criminal liability,
5 employment law: safe work practices, pressure to enhance and risk of discrimination,
6 family law: children's rights, parental responsibility and authority,
7 human rights challenges (Warso, Gaskell, 2019, pp. 11–22).

The categories above cover all the relevant dimensions of the legal regulation of HE and at the same time show the considerable degree of complexity of the problem of HE regulation. The next paragraph will further discuss the categories above.

4.1.1 *International laws*

Concerning international laws in the SIENNA project the following legal actors and sources of law were identified:

The United Nations (Universal Declaration of Human Rights; International Covenant on Civil and Political Rights; International Covenant on Economic, Social and Cultural Rights; Convention on the Rights of Persons with Disabilities; Convention on the Rights of the Child; Single Convention on Narcotic Drugs; Convention on Psychotropic Substances; Convention Against Illicit Traffic in Narcotic Drugs and Psychotropic Substances; UN Guidelines for Consumer Protection, and Principles for Older Persons, and Convention on the Rights of People with Disabilities),

The United Nations Education Scientific and Cultural Organisation (Declaration on Bioethics and Human Rights),

The World Intellectual Property Organization (Patent Cooperation Treaty; Model Law for Developing Countries on Marks, and Trade Names, and Acts of Unfair Competition),

World Trade Organization (Agreement on Trade-Related Aspects of Intellectual Property Rights) (Warso, Gaskell, 2019, pp. 23–24).

Having acknowledged the lack of regulation concerning *human enhancement* as such in the above-mentioned acts analysed by the SIENNA project, one should mention other international initiatives aimed at regulating areas tightly connected to HE such as neurotechnology. Here *OECD Recommendation on Responsible Innovation in Neurotechnology* (OECD, 2022) should be mentioned. It embodies nine principles that focus on:

1 promoting responsible innovation,
2 prioritising safety assessment,
3 promoting inclusivity,
4 fostering scientific collaboration,
5 enabling societal deliberation,
6 enabling capacity of oversight and advisory bodies,
7 safeguarding personal brain data and other information,
8 promoting cultures of stewardship and trust across the public and private sectors,
9 anticipating and monitoring potential unintended use and/or misuse.

Due to the legal status/nature of *a recommendation*, one may conclude that there are no international regulations concerning neurotechnology. It is not considered an important component of HE (as indicated in Chapter 2). Some actions undertaken by only a few countries about OECD recommendations will be presented in Section 4.1.3.

4.1.2 Regional laws

Regional laws are narrowed down in this book to the European Union (EU) regulations and only basic issues concerning the main legal issues and human rights challenges. These regional laws will be presented below according to the seven main legal issues identified by the SIENNA project. In brackets is the number of directives and other EU regulations, where one can find articles and/or provisions referring – more or less indirectly – to HE.

Human enhancement technologies: human enhancement devices and enhancement drugs (six directives and five regulations),

Civil liability for human enhancement technologies: product liability (two directives) and *professional liability* (one regulation),

Security and criminal liability (two directives and two regulations),

Property law: ownership and patents (one directive, one regulation, the Treaty on the Functioning of the European Union, and EU Charter of Fundamental Rights),

Employment law: safe work practices, pressure to enhance and risk of discrimination (one directive, one regulation, the Treaty on European Union, the Treaty on the Functioning of the European Union, and EU Charter of Fundamental Rights),

Family law: children's rights, parental responsibility and authority (the Treaty on European Union, and EU Charter of Fundamental Rights),

Human rights challenges (the Treaty on European Union, and EU Charter of Fundamental Rights) (Warso, Gaskell, 2019, pp. 35–37).

Concerning genomic technologies, a separate set of recommendations addressed to the European Parliament, European Council and Council of the European Union, the European Commission, Medical Device Coordination Group, European Data Protection Board and European Data Protection Supervisor, and EU Member States was formulated by SIENNA project:

- Address ethics regarding human genomic technologies more stringently and consistently;
- Resolve fragmentation and uncertainties regarding genetic data protection, and work towards removing obstacles to the sharing of data;
- Develop guidance on regulation of human genetics and genomics and enhance human genomics research;

- Address the dual use of genomic technology in an effective manner;
- Capitalise on the EU's fundamental right of data protection and consider establishing a right to gen(omic) data (SIENNA, 2021).

The above bullet points and the numbers show how diverse and dispersed the legal basis for the functioning of HE in the European Union is.

The SIENNA project concluded that neither the international treaties related to the seven main legal issues identified above nor the EU directives, regulations, and treatises mention HE. This means that neither international actors nor the European Union has specific, comprehensive regulations solely dedicated to HE technologies. This applies also to the domestic law of 12 analysed in the SIENNA project countries because neither *human enhancement* nor *enhancement procedures* are recognised per se. Taking into account that cosmetic interventions and doping have been classified in Chapter 2 as enhancement procedures, one must acknowledge that they are regulated by law, even though the term *enhancement* is not used. At this point, the fundamental issue arises, that is, the separation (and division) between therapy and enhancement manifesting itself not only in the EU but also in the domestic legal context. A clear demarcation between treatment and enhancement or medical and non-medical uses remains the challenge leading to the formation of 'grey zones' to which it is not known what regulations to apply. This is compounded by an evolution of the understanding and definition of the concept of good health.

Having acknowledged the existence of objective difficulties in a precise legal regulation of HE and its procedures one may conclude that in the European Union, HE is legally permitted insofar as it is not prohibited. Since the existing regulations do not offer proper guidance on specific aspects of enhancement procedures (such as informed consent, and assessment of risk) this role is often taken up by courts on a case-by-case basis (Warso, Gaskell, 2019, p. 57).

4.1.3 National laws

On a national level (i.e., 12 analysed in the SIENNA project countries) the term 'human enhancement' is not used in legal regulations and the legality of enhancement procedures is not entirely clear-cut. One can see, however, publications on HE policy. For example, the Greek Commission on Bioethics has issued two separate opinions on HE. HE in Greece is defined broadly as interventions upon genetic cells, an embryo, and a born human body to ameliorate appearance, health, strength, memory, perception, and other desirable traits (Canellopoulou-Bottis, 2018).

There are also substantial differences between countries concerning areas connected to HE. An example of this is in the area of enhancement drugs. Here the legality and regulation vary from one country to another, and the safety and efficacy of many of these substances are still subjects of ongoing research (Gaspar et al., 2019). Equally diversified and complicated are regulations on cognitive enhancement in the comparative legal examination (Valera, Bellver, 2024).

Referring back to the OECD *Recommendation on Responsible Innovation in Neurotechnology* (OECD, 2022) one may acknowledge that a few dozen countries have taken steps to consider the regulation of neurotechnology by signing up for the *Recommendation*. Chile became the first country to implement legislation in the form of a constitutional amendment that enshrines the right to the mental integrity of all citizens. The legislation aims to protect mental privacy, free will, equal access to cognitive enhancement technologies and protection against algorithmic bias (Harmsworth, 2023). In 2021 France approved a bioethics law that protects the right to mental integrity, and Spain adopted a 'digital rights charter' with a dedicated section on neuro rights. There was also a discussion in Italy on whether mental privacy is sufficiently covered under the country's privacy rights (Harmsworth, 2023).

One may conclude that HE and HE technologies (except for cosmetic surgery and doping, and partially for drugs) are not regulated by law either on an international, supranational, or national level. This means that HE, which is gaining importance and is potentially a very powerful phenomenon, remains out of the legislative regime.

4.2 Financing HE: current stage

As indicated in Chapter 3, healthcare systems have to cope with financial constraints within universal healthcare insurance. It is also no coincidence that one of the recently published textbooks on health policy starts from the chapter entitled 'The Rise of Medical Expenditures' followed by 'How Much Should We Spend on Medical Care?' (Feldstein, Melnick, 2023, pp. 1–29). It does not matter that the cited book refers mainly to the US healthcare system since the vast majority of health policy challenges indicated in that book apply to each of the OECD countries.

Because HE is a dynamic emerging phenomenon, its financing should also be seen from a dynamic perspective. In such a context, a subjective proposal of the stages of development of the HE financing system can be presented.

4.2.1 The phases of HE financing

According to the author's proposition, HE can be funded in three phases*: the initial phase, (supported) private financing,* and *(possible) governmental financing.*

4.2.1.1 The initial phase

In the first, initial phase, HE treatments are financed mostly from private funds with a small part from government sources (the latter restricted to governmental R&D focused on – but not limited to – military purposes). At this stage, HE procedures are rare and this is partly why they are so expensive due to the economies of scale (or rather lack of them). It can be assumed that in the initial stage, related to the low availability of HE services and high prices, only wealthy individuals accepting the high risk associated with HE treatments will decide to undergo HE treatments. As far as the problem of HE costs is concerned, one must acknowledge, that comparative analyses of cost-effectiveness and finances of innovative healthcare procedures remain rare (Binhammer et al., 2020), and cover mainly developed countries (Sachdev, 2022). As of the time of this publication, no analyses were focusing on HE costs. One of the positive examples of a comparative analysis of costs could be a conclusive paper aimed at comparing operative duration and total hospital costs incurred for patients undergoing elective cranioplasty with a variety of materials (Binhammer et al., 2020). However, this analysis is narrow and limited to a certain category of implants, that is, only one of the forms of HE. Therefore, the picture of HE's finances at the current stage of the development of HE remains incomplete and imprecise.

In the absence of reliable statistics and information, we are doomed to speculation. However, these speculations can be related to proven facts. In this regard, we can cite statistics illustrating the number of wealthy and very wealthy people who could invest in their well-being to gain or/and maintain their competitive position in society. Such a move allows us to make a proxy of a potential demand for HE treatments. Needless to add it will be a rough approximation.

The wealthiest individuals can be divided into two groups: ultra-high-net-worth individuals (UHNWIs) and high-net-worth individuals (HNWIs). UHNWI is a person with a net worth of $1 million or more, including their primary residence, while UHNWI is someone with a net worth of $30 million or more, including their primary residence (Knight Frank, 2023).

Globally, the HNWI population reached 21.7 million in 2022, with a total of $83 trillion in wealth. North America led the world's HNWI wealth with 7.4 million individuals, followed by the Asia-Pacific region with 7.1 million, Europe with 5.6 million, and Latin America with 600,000. The Middle East had 900,000 HNWIs while Africa had 200,000 (Hayes, 2023).

In 2023, UHNWIs totalled 579,625 individuals globally, down 3.8% from 2022, with a total of $12.2 trillion in wealth. The United States had the most UHNWIs (241,253) globally by a large margin (41.6%) followed by Europe (155,996), and China (150,362) (Kenton, 2023).

The above suggests that the United States, Europe, some Asian (China, Japan, Singapore), and the Middle East (the United Arab Emirates, Saudi Arabia, Kuwait, Kattar) countries possess significant financial potential for HE development. Bearing in mind that the effective demand for HE treatments will be reported by people with high-risk tolerance (risk-takers), it can be assumed that Americans will dominate among HE clients.[2]

At the time of this publication, HE financing may be ignored by health politicians for a couple of reasons. The first is that HE is not regulated by law thus it is not a subject of health policy. Second, is the emerging character of HE. As indicated earlier, HE remains at the experimental stage, where military research centres and military-related institutions play a leading role. In this sector, the money for HE comes from various R&D programmes and projects. As indicated above, rare experimental non-military/civil HE treatments are financed by individual private sources thus health politicians may ignore them.

4.2.1.2 (Supported) private financing

It can be assumed that the transition to the second stage of HE financing, that is, supported by private financing, will take place when the supply of HE services is increased (dozens of thousands or hundreds of thousands of patients), and economies of scale are achieved, which will result in lower prices for HE treatments. More affordable prices may lead to a considerable rise in the number of individuals willing to benefit from HE (which over time will be less risky and more predictable). This in turn will create a push on health insurers, both private and public, to cover certain HE procedures and services. This will be a considerable challenge for insurers because they almost always are reluctant to include new medical technologies in the packages they offer. A perfect example could be mitochondrial replacement therapy which based on clinical trials was proven effective, but it is not financed by the British NHS[3] (Rhys-Evans, 2021). This conditional participation of insurers in the HE financing of this phase is indicated by the inclusion of '*supported*' in parentheses.

Even if insurers (either public or elective supplementary private health insurance schemes) participate in HE financing, one may agree that the main financial burden lies on households and individual people. Thus it is reasonable to look at out-of-pocket payments (OOPs). Additionally, it cannot be ruled out that concerning some uniformed services (army, police, fire brigade, etc.), certain professions (medical personnel, teachers, etc.), HE treatments may be co-financed from public funds.

The point of departure of the more quantitative analysis of HE financing at the *supported private financing* phase should be the scope of OPPs (Table 4.1).

As defined by the OECD, OOP payments are expenditures borne directly by a patient where neither public nor private insurance covers the full cost of the health good or service. They include cost-sharing and other expenditures paid directly by private households, and should also ideally include estimations of informal payments to health providers (OECD, 2023a, p. 106). Across OECD countries in 2021, around 3% of total household spending was on healthcare goods and services. The highest spending (over 5%) was in Portugal, followed by Switzerland and Korea. The lowest spending (2% or less) was in

Table 4.1 Share of household out-of-pocket payments for health in GDP (in %) (2015–2022)

Country	*2015*	*2016*	*2017*	*2018*	*2019*	*2020*	*2021*	*2022*
Australia	1.8	1.7	1.7	1.6	1.5	1.6	...	...
Austria	2.0	2.0	2.0	1.9	1.9	1.9	1.9	1.8
Belgium	2.1	2.0	2.0	2.0	2.1	1.9	2.0	...
Canada	1.6	1.7	1.7	1.7	1.7	1.8	1.7	1.7
Chile	2.9	3.0	3.0	3.1	3.1	2.9	2.8	2.7
Colombia	1.2	1.2	1.2	1.2	1.1	1.3	1.2	...
Costa Rica	1.7	1.6	1.5	1.6	1.6	1.6	1.6	...
Czechia	1.1	1.1	1.1	1.1	1.1	1.1	1.2	...
Denmark	1.4	1.4	1.4	1.4	1.4	1.4	1.4	1.2
Estonia	1.6	1.6	1.6	1.6	1.6	1.6	1.7	1.5
Finland	1.8	1.8	1.7	1.7	1.6	1.6	1.7	...
France	1.1	1.1	1.1	1.1	1.0	1.1	1.1	...
Germany	1.5	1.4	1.4	1.5	1.6	1.6	1.6	1.4
Greece	3.0	2.9	2.8	2.9	2.8	3.2	3.1	...
Hungary	1.9	1.9	1.8	1.8	1.7	1.9	1.8	1.9
Iceland	1.4	1.4	1.4	1.3	1.3	1.4	1.4	1.3
Ireland	1.0	1.0	0.9	0.8	0.8	0.8	0.7	0.6
Israel	1.6	1.6	1.6	1.6	1.5	1.6	1.6	...
Italy	2.1	2.0	2.1	2.0	2.0	2.1	2.1	1.9
Japan	1.4	1.4	1.3	1.4	1.4	1.3	1.3	...
Korea	2.3	2.3	2.4	2.5	2.6	2.4	2.7	2.7
Latvia	2.3	2.7	2.5	2.4	2.3	2.3	2.4	...
Lithuania	2.1	2.1	2.1	2.1	2.3	2.1	2.4	2.3
Luxembourg	0.5	0.5	0.5	0.6	0.5	0.5	0.5	0.5
Mexico	2.3	2.3	2.3	2.3	2.3	2.4	2.5	...
Netherlands	1.2	1.2	1.1	1.1	1.1	1.0	1.1	1.0
New Zealand	1.2	1.3	1.2	1.2	...	...	...	...
Norway	1.4	1.5	1.5	1.4	1.5	1.6	1.4	...
Poland	1.5	1.5	1.5	1.3	1.3	1.3	1.3	1.2
Portugal	2.8	2.8	2.8	2.8	2.9	3.0	3.2	3.0
Slovak Republic	1.2	1.3	1.3	1.3	1.3	1.3	1.5	...
Slovenia	1.1	1.0	1.0	1.0	1.0	1.2	1.2	1.1
Spain	2.0	2.0	2.0	2.0	2.0	2.1	2.3	...
Sweden	1.6	1.6	1.5	1.5	1.5	1.5	1.5	1.4
Switzerland	2.5	2.5	2.6	2.5	2.6	2.7	2.6	...
Türkiye	0.7	0.7	0.7	0.7	0.7	0.8	0.7	...
United Kingdom	1.4	1.4	1.4	1.5	1.6	1.5	1.6	1.6
United States	1.9	2.0	1.9	1.9	1.9	1.9	1.9	...
Non-OECD Economies	2.7	2.7	2.7	1.6	2.6	2.4	...	...

Source: OECD, https://data.oecd.org/healthres/health-spending.htm.

Luxembourg, followed by Colombia and Turkey. Pharmaceuticals and other medical goods were the main drivers of household spending, accounting for 43% of OOP spending on health on average in 2021 (OECD, 2023a, p. 106).

As presented in Table 4.1, in 2021, the share of OOP payments in GDP as compared to 2015 was higher in 16 OECD countries (Canada, Czechia,

Estonia, Germany, Greece, Korea, Latvia, Lithuania, Mexico, Portugal, Slovak Republic, Slovenia, Spain, Switzerland, and the United Kingdom), lower in 11 countries (Austria, Belgium, Chile, Costa Rica, Finland, Hungary, Ireland, Japan, Netherlands, Poland, and Sweden), and remained the same in ten countries (Colombia, Denmark, France, Ireland, Israel, Italy, Luxembourg, Norway, Turkey, and the United States). In 2021, the highest share of OOP in GDP was noticed in Portugal (3.2%) followed by Greece (3.1%), and Chile (2.8%). This indicated that there was no clear trend in OOP share in GDP between 2015 and 2021.

While it is difficult to identify a clear trend in OOP in OECD countries, it is easier to trace a trend in global wealth. Here the underlying assumption is that in the private financing stage, there are middle-class individuals who constitute the main group of HE beneficiaries. Statistics covering the years 2000–2022 clearly show that the share of adults, who had less than $10,000 in the global population, diminished (from 80.7% to 52.5%, respectively), and the global middle class (adults with $10,000–100,000 of wealth) has more than doubled, driven by the expansion of emerging economies reaching 34.4% share in the global population in 2022 (Neufeld, 2023). Also, projections for 2027 indicated that the share of the middle class in the global population would be rising (Neufeld, 2023). Such a trend makes private HE financing in the second phase feasible.

4.2.1.3 (Possible) governmental financing

The possible third stage will appear when the competition between augmented and non-augmented populations and individuals is moved to the international level, leveraging competition between nations/states. At this stage in the process, the whole reasoning is purely speculative. This may suggest that HE procedures may be introduced into the national health policies to gain and/or maintain the competitive advantage of a nation/state on the international/global level. These processes may be accompanied by growing competition between augmented homo sapiens and artificial intelligence which may further stimulate HE procedures. This, in turn, may stimulate or force countries to co-finance or even finance HE.

In conclusion, due to its nature, HE does not qualify to be covered either by standard private health insurance or by universal health coverage. Regarding universal health coverage, there are various, often opposite positions on the HE policy influencing the way of its financing. For example, some researchers maintain that one of the forms of HE – moral bioenhancement (MBE) – could be considered compulsory (Crutchfield, 2018). MBE is perceived by Crutchfield as a matter of public health, so ought to be governed by the ethics of public health interventions. Placing MBE among public health interventions opens the door to reasoning that moral bioenhancement could be covered by government programmes or by health insurance.[4]

Consequently, there is enough ground to maintain that there is a certain potential for financing HE from private sources in the first two phases of financing. Unfortunately, nearly all the above-presented assessments and opinions are speculative due to the lack of reliable statistics/sources.

Having briefly discussed the current legal and financial situation regarding HE with only a few references to the future concerning financing, let us move to the near future and try to reflect on what should be done and what we could expect so what are HE perspectives.

4.3 Perspectives of human enhancement

HE perspectives indicating what should be done soon will be structured according to legal, financial, social & societal, managerial, and technical perspectives. The above perspectives illustrate the scale of complexity of the problem. To better illustrate the level of complexity of the HE, in some places, examples of appropriate questions encountered in the literature will be presented.

4.3.1 Legal perspectives: what is needed?

Having concluded that there are no HE-specific law regulations one should consider this gap to be the first to be filled.

In trying to fill this gap one should decide first about a regulatory model. Some have been already mentioned (Valera, Bellver, 2024) thus they could be further analysed, discussed, and then transformed into draft laws. The point of departure for these analyses and discussions should be the HE definition. There are no obstacles to using the definition chosen in Chapter 2 of this book. It will be difficult to decide whether HE procedures are defined as a kind of medical treatment or as a separate category: human enhancement. A clear demarcation between treatment and enhancement or medical and non-medical uses remains the challenge. There is, however, a rationale for classifying HE as a non-medical phenomenon.

Leaving aside the orderly and prioritised list of issues that the legal regulations of the HE should cover, they may be broken down into global, international, and local levels.[5] Let us mention only some of them here.

The first is the issue of monitoring and recording the processes of HE treatments. This means that the devices used in the HE process should be properly marked to allow for their identification at every stage of their use. Also, the process of implanting them into the patient's body should be documented and reported. The SIENNA project with its four proposals to regulate the governance of HE devices (Warso, Gaskell, 2019, p. 12) could contribute in this respect. Out of these four, two namely: no regulation beyond existing product safety requirements (which means: status quo), and the ban on all HE device scan be ignored due to their extreme nature and not corresponding to needs. The remaining two: regulating through the existing legal regime (in the European Union it is *the Medical Devices Directive*), and creating a new regulatory regime specifically for HE can be further considered. The last option seems to be optimal for at least two reasons. The first is HE heterogeneousness which requires special attention and treatment and the second is the existing fragmentation of the legal regulations on HE. This constitutes a big challenge for leading actors and judiciaries on international, regional, and national levels to orchestrate and harmonise actions, leading to coherent and mutually agreed legal regulations.

There are many specific legal issues connected to HE which need to be regulated but only a few will be discussed below:

- databases on HE,
- augmented individuals' responsibilities,
- patents of various HE devices,
- technologies, procedures, and techniques,
- potential risks for human health.

A good example of potential regulatory solutions includes (but may not be limited to) the development, use, and protection of data on HE applications in general and brain data from consumer-directed neurotechnological devices in particular (Kellmeyer, 2021). A practical example could be a discussion of moral bioenhancement (MBE) programmes and the dilemma of whether MBE programmes should be covert or overt (Austin-Eames, 2023). Equally important is the issue of gene analysis and related information deposited in and transferred by the internet from the perspective of privacy issues (Sorgner, 2017).

Another intriguing question concerns the responsibility for actions undertaken by augmented individuals using brain implants. Assuming that a considerable number of human beings' decisions have factual origins one may question the responsibility of an individual for a decision taken that was influenced by a brain implant failure (Klaming, Haselager, 2013). One may add to this issue of advanced prostheses with osseointegration and brain-computer interfaces and then ask about the complexities in the relationship between what is recognisably human and what is considered to be objects. Here a tendency could be observed to treat technologies that are intimately and permanently connected to physical bodies as their parts. This is particularly the case concerning implants, and in some circumstances, for example, the need to protect privacy, this approach may be extended to other devices (Warso, Gaskell, 2019).

Scientifically and technically advanced, cutting-edge HE devices, technologies, procedures, and techniques are tightly connected to patent regulations and regimes. Here few interesting issues emerge. For example, in the European patent system, methods for treatment and diagnostic methods are not protected by patents. This means that if HE is classified as a medical treatment, appropriate HE methods and techniques cannot be protected by patent law. In other words, the patentability of HE will depend on the concept of health, its future evolution and the corresponding public policy choices (Nordberg, 2015).

Connected to all the above is the problem of emerging risks to human health and the environment (Gaspar et al., 2019). This refers first of all to the ethical use of genomic technologies in public health, taking into account existing and not known at the moment limitations of these technologies, risks, and uncertainties involved, stakeholders and their interests, including the most vulnerable who may be affected, and the values guiding the practice of public health genomics (Niemiec, Howard, 2020).

The drafting of new legal regulations should not be postponed because the real world requires them. At the current stage of development, available enhancement technology seems unlikely to change the fundamental humanity of enhanced individuals. However, advanced prostheses with osseointegration and BCIs may blur the boundaries between what is recognisably human and what are considered to be objects. This, in turn, under domestic criminal law, may raise important questions such as at what point does the appropriate charge cease to be assault and become criminal damage (to a prosthesis) and does osseointegration change the calculus? (Dinniss, 2018).

The list of questions can be extended. Just to illustrate the wide scope of problems which have to be solved in the law, let us present those formulated by *The UK Law Society* concerning BCI and related to:

Criminal liability: What if a person commits a criminal act 'under the influence' of an implanted microchip? Who will be responsible? Was the person in control? Staying with responsibility, we can ask questions related to civil law. For example, if a mechanical insert malfunctions and someone is injured, does it fall under personal injury law or product liability?

Employment: Will BCIs be available only to those who can afford them, leading to a world characterised by neurotechnological discrimination where employees with implants will be paid more resulting from their ability to 'download' more desirable skills, or will we have no choice in the matter and wearing a BCI will be a condition of employment?

Data protection: How can the user control what data leaves their BCI? If consent is relied upon, will it be valid? What can that data be used for? How do we ensure that data is kept secure? To date 'hacking' has only been thought of in a traditional computer context, but what about the brain? (Harmsworth, 2023). These questions show how complex the issue of legal provisions for the use of HE in civil practice can be.

Some other doubts may arise when we consider the usage of HE technologies for military purposes with a focus on weapons law, the human rights of 'soldiers 2.0', and individual responsibility for the actions taken while under the influence of enhancements (Dinniss, Kleffner, 2018).

It is both interesting and important to notice that HE technologies can influence the legal system itself. Neuroscientific knowledge is nowadays often considered important for developing the criminal justice system. This may mean replacing retributive punishment practices with more lenient consequentialist ones, assessing defendants' culpability and the reliability of testimonies and that novel neurointerventions could be employed in rehabilitating offenders. As indicated by Varelius it '... has been suggested that neuroenhancements could be used to improve the abilities of criminal justice authorities. Judges could be made more able to make adequately informed and unbiased decisions' (Varelius, 2020, p. 325).

Concluding the legal perspectives point let us come back to the SIENNA project and refer to two things. The first refers to a human being's autonomy in the context of HE. Warso and Gaskel argue that '... as the physical invasiveness and complexity of the enhancement become greater, the easier (i.e. more legitimate, proportionate and necessary) it is to justify limiting individual autonomy' (Warso, Gaskell, 2019, p. 57). This can be food for thought regarding the legal status of HE. The second is the statement that it is too early to draw any far-reaching conclusions, as the data gathered in this report is very limited (Warso, Gaskell, 2019, p. 58). More detailed issues connected to gathering and managing data on HE are in Section 4.3.3.

4.3.2 *Financial perspectives: what one can expect?*

Assuming that the three phases of HE financing remain valid, one may argue that the leading source of HE is, and for a long time will be private money. When such a tendency is placed into a framework of basic macroeconomic indicators, one may maintain that private HE financing is feasible. OECD long-term baseline projections reveal that GDP in OECD countries will grow from the level of $62,558,332 million in 2023 to $97,905,070 million in 2050 (in Purchasing Power Parity – PPP, $ at 2015). As indicated above, projections regarding the middle class (considered as representing the core of the demand for HE) in the global population are positive. This is partly due to the increase in gross disposable incomes[6] between 2015 and 2022 (Table 4.2).

Table 4.2 shows that gross disposable income (in PPP) rose (nearly) continuously between 2015 and 2022 in all countries with only minor decreases. Annual decreases were recorded in only a few countries, including Mexico (in 2017 and 2020), Australia (2017), Costa Rica (2020), Greece (2020), Japan (2017), Slovak Republic (2016), Spain (2020), and Switzerland (2017).

Like GDP, also disposable income projection[7] for 2050 is positive among others for the United States, Canada, Mexico, Brazil, European Union, Russia, Japan, South Korea, Australia and New Zealand, China, and India (IEO, 2023). It is worth acknowledging that the highest average annual percentage change in disposable income from 2022 to 2050 is estimated for India and China (4.4% and 4.0%, respectively). This suggests that the HE market could speed up not only in highly developed but also in Asian countries.

Table 4.2 Household disposable income (gross, incl. social transfers in kind, US$/capita) 2015–2022

Country	*2015*	*2016*	*2017*	*2018*	*2019*	*2020*	*2021*	*2022*
Australia	37,604	39,007	38,870	39,583	40,988	43,837	46,838	..
Austria	34,414	36,228	36,984	38,191	40,663	41,069	45,138	50,159
Belgium	32,596	33,823	34,776	35,933	38,980	40,778	43,871	47,446[E]
Canada	31,940[E]	33,594[E]	34,554[E]	35,339[E]	35,621[E]	38,968[E]	41,527[E]	43,609[E]
Chile	15,767	16,719	16,875	17,978	19,036	21,174	23,061	…
Costa Rica	13,520	14,676	16,130	16,619	17,531	16,408	17,885	…
Czechia	22,313	23,664	25,424	26,771	29,352	30,312	33,482	35,566
Denmark	30,507	31,951	33,441	34,714	36,887	38,213	40,395	42,753
Estonia	19,321	20,727	21,826	23,486	25,541	26,301	28,039	29,220
Finland	30,849	32,273	33,377	34,675	37,067	38,520	40,596	43,616
France	31,891	33,551	34,313	35,280	38,368	40,021	42,771[E]	46,366[E]
Germany	35,492	37,894	39,272	41,170	43,667[E]	45,547[E]	47,696[E]	51,566[E]
Greece	19,593	20,286	20,670	21,203	23,316	22,904[E]	25,348[E]	28,039[E]
Hungary	17,974	18,933	19,791	21,482	23,639	24,237	26,885	29,787[E]
Ireland	25,684	27,203	28,347	29,250	31,504	33,029	35,000	38,293
Italy	27,712	29,475	30,435	31,469	33,745	34,296	36,974	40,415
Japan	30,597	29,290	29,916	30,777	31,340	33,527	33,944	…
Korea	23,958	24,191	24,485	25,737	26,690	28,285	29,942	32,683[E]
Latvia	17,170	18,574	19,951	21,281	23,140	24,345	26,480	28,626
Lithuania	21,186	23,290	24,465	25,808	29,632	32,313	34,778	36,326
Luxembourg	43,476	44,506	46,535	48,794	51,122	52,747	55,014	59,714
Mexico	16,227	17,070	16,884	17,182	17,523	16,745	18,608	20,523
Netherlands	32,194	33,258	34,380	36,264	38,839	40,919	44,129[E]	48,810[E]
New Zealand	25,508	27,383	28,766	29,567	31,950	…	…	…
Norway	36,418	36,933	39,225	40,478	42,734	43,613	47,688	…
Poland	19,961	21,331	22,072	23,177	25,609	27,836	28,796	32,154
Portugal	22,628	23,946	24,508	26,052	28,331	28,407	30,881	34,476[E]

(*Continued*)

Table 4.2 (Continued)

Country	*2015*	*2016*	*2017*	*2018*	*2019*	*2020*	*2021*	*2022*
Slovak Republic	20,430	19,929	20,040	21,195	23,321	25,216	27,108	29,493
Slovenia	21,849	23,388	24,666	26,142	28,624	30,550	33,157	36,564
Spain	24,641	26,018	27,136	27,753	30,447	29,925	32,442[E]	34,478[E]
Sweden	31,746	32,921	33,389	34,174	36,405	37,096	40,394	43,912
Switzerland	40,101	41,098	40,421	41,191	43,707	45,576	47,625[E]	52,017[E]
Türkiye	19,694	20,641	21,800	...	...	...	...	...
United Kingdom	30,792	31,588	32,297	33,158	35,355	37,297	39,407	40,816
United States	47,228	48,258	50,047	52,451	54,747	58,653	62,334	...

Source: OECD, https://data.oecd.org/hha/household-disposable-income.htm.

E: Estimated value.

Private money used for HE treatments raises a serious challenge for health policy. It is the issue of possible growing inequality in a narrow, cognitive, and physiological sense, as well as in a broader, social, and genre range. These issues will be further developed below.

4.3.3 Social and societal perspectives

As mentioned in the Introduction and Chapter 2, there is much rich philosophical, ethical, and sociological literature on HE thus addressing issues similar to those indicated in the title of this section. Consequently, it seems to be necessary to reduce the scope of this section just to a few selected issues. They will be placed within a framework of challenges observed in modern societies such as the democratisation of knowledge, growing individualism accompanied by competition, HE and social stratification, HE and humanness, and HE and posthumanism.

4.3.3.1 Democratisation of knowledge

One of the social phenomena worth noting is changes in science due to extensive information flow on the internet. Two points deserve attention: deinstitutionalisation (*research is being processed outside of formal specialised institutions and laboratories*) and the federalisation of science (*spontaneously formulated groups of people composed of scientists representing various fields and specialisations and people interested in the subject(s), without scientific degrees – enthusiasts with impressive knowledge and readiness to participate in research*).

These processes lead to the emergence of various phenomena, an example being the 'biohacker' movement comprised of 'loose collectives of scientists, engineers, artists, designers, and activists experimenting with biotechnology outside of conventional institutions and laboratories' (Gaspar et al., 2019, p. 296) whose final achievements could contribute to human enhancement. What should be acknowledged is that nowadays individual people may use some biotechnology applications for personal benefit through do-it-yourself (DIY) biology or biohacking activities (Gaspar et al., 2019). This, in turn, means that some human enhancement procedures can be performed outside of healthcare facilities by non-medical staff. These activities cannot be tracked and/or monitored. This means that even if in some cases HE treatments can take place outside of the healthcare system. The people who would be making important decisions on health care may be put in place by politicians. Even if health policies could have regulatory guidelines on HE treatment(s), some potential beneficiaries of HE treatments may not be considered by those who are making policy decisions. This could be an argument for controlling the supply of HE devices (i.e., marking them and monitoring their distribution and usage. For Elgabry and Camilleric, 'biohackers' represent *the hidden populations*. As such they present logistical challenges because the biohacking community is an under-researched catalyst for innovation and social change (Elgabry, Camilleric, 2021). Consequently, due to limited academic research on the subject, it may be necessary to expand the search for information to include 'grey' literature, including modern resources such as podcasts. Here we touch on a fragile issue of academic rigour, reliability, and methodological soundness. For some researchers, they constitute a very useful primary source (Elgabry, Camilleric, 2021). Following such an acceptance of non-academic outcomes such as blogs and podcasts[8] as accessible sources of information, one may quote five main areas of human augmentation and related questions formulated by Tracinski:

Bionics and prosthetics: Would people eventually feel pressure or temptation to remove healthy limbs or organs in favour of enhanced bionic replacements, and would that be a good thing?

Brain-computer interfaces: Will faster, seamless access to information result in an even greater dependence on our devices? Could it lead to a real-life version of this cartoon?

Neurotechnology: What are the side effects and potential long-term consequences of altering our brain functions with implants?

Nootropics: What are the side effects of nootropics? And how big is the benefit? Is this just 'brain training' all over again – a fad that thrives on anecdotal evidence but doesn't have much actual data to show its effectiveness?

Gene editing: There is the risk that in re-engineering our DNA, we will introduce problems instead of improvements and that we won't know this ahead of time (Tracinski, n.d.). This list of questions may be added to the list of issues and questions presented in Section 4.3.1.

A slightly separate but interesting issue is the rationale behind the decision of enhancement and the whole decision-making process, especially in the context of the democratisation of knowledge and CIT development. The underlying assumption is that adults should in principle be able to make rational and informed decisions about enhancing themselves. This, however, can be questioned because a rational and informed choice to enhance oneself may in some cases be impossible (Lyreskog, McKeown, 2022).

4.3.3.2 Individualism and competition

Liberal democracies and market mechanisms (with inherent competition principles in place) prevail in today's world. Within such a framework, individual rights are promoted within the human rights movement. Such an appreciation of individuality is supported and magnified by the intensive usage of the internet and social media. One may maintain that individualism and competition constitute the main driving force for HE development.

Within this framework, several important phenomena and issues can be identified but only a few will be introduced here.

Assuming that HE can provide benefits in terms of increased productivity, improved academic performance, or athletic achievements, one may raise the issue about the potential for misuse of human enhancement drugs, adverse health effects, and ethical dilemmas, particularly when healthy individuals use these substances to gain a competitive advantage. One should keep in mind how deeply competition is rooted in all humans. It has various forms and features. One is the attractiveness of individual people. An extensive survey (39 countries, 93,158 human participants) showed that issues such as applying makeup or using other cosmetics, hair grooming, clothing style, caring for body hygiene, and exercising or following a specific diet for the specific purpose of improving one's physical attractiveness are universal despite all differences in culture, religion, political system, etc. (Kowal et al., 2022). Consequently, various forms of competition should be monitored not only by researchers but also by societies at large.

4.3.3.3 Human enhancement and social stratification

The first and most important social issue is the stagnation of a social structure and the strengthening of social stratification. As argued above, HE financing is and for long will be based on private sources. Even if regulated by law it will lead to growing inequality in a narrow, cognitive, and physiological sense, as well as in a broader, social, and genre range. Such an approach seems to collide with the assumptions often presented in ethical debates. A good example of an ethical debate is the discussion around genetic enhancement and the reasoning that the technology will eventually be fairly accessible once available, and its distribution will be equal and equitable. This depends upon fair environments guaranteed by society so any argument that the distribution of genetic enhancements will be fair and that the technology is therefore morally permissible is mistaken (Prince, 2023). Such an assessment is supported by Carapeto Raposo (2022) who tries to weaken the inequality argument against genetic enhancement because it will create a 'genetic apartheid'. She argues that the dichotomy of treatment versus enhancement can be questioned because the differences between the two are unclear, and that human enhancement is part of human nature. She also maintains that possible genetic equality is not, per se, a value to which we ought to aspire if it leads us to a uniform community of downsized human beings (Carapeto Raposo, 2022). Not only genetic enhancement may lead to inequality. The rapid development in neurotechnologies also raises questions such as how will these new neurotechnologies change personality and society (Stieglitz, 2021). Similar doubts about the deepening of differences in society are raised concerning cognitive enhancement (McCall, Dubljević, 2024).

The equality issue could be developed further from a theoretical perspective. If human enhancement is being explored from a political philosophy perspective, as a problem of distributive justice, then some questions may be asked. For example, should the enhancement of human intellectual functioning be rejected on distributive grounds of equality? Or does distributive justice require such enhancement? (Walsh, 2021).

The subject of monitoring should also consider a public attitude to and perception of augmented individuals who – by definition – possess certain competitive advantages (especially regarding cognitive skills) over not augmented peers. This applies but is not restricted to labour market policies and practices. Since there is no appropriate research yet, an interpretation of the results could be the outcome of a survey of the American public's attitudes towards cybernetic soldiers. It revealed that respondents were quite divided. The main findings were that the more religious a person was, the more likely he/she rejected the idea of cyber soldiers. Also, the greater an individual's understanding of these technologies, the more likely he/she was to accept cybernetic soldiers (Emanuel et al., 2019). Also, a survey among US staff officers revealed that attitudes towards neuroenhancement in the military varied considerably among respondents (Sattler et al., 2022).

What gets attention in this study is the proposal for recontextualisation of the relationship between military and civilian ethics. Even if we agree that the military sector performs specific duties and tasks, such a delimitation of ethics may raise doubts as leading to the relativity of ethical principles. Equally controversial is the distinction between normative and experimental bioethics (Rodríguez López, 2023).

4.3.3.4 *Human enhancement and humanness*

Finally, assuming progress in the field of HE in the coming years and decades, it is worth introducing the issue of humanness and recalling some questions posed by researchers in this context. We must admit that the use of artificial intelligence and HE technologies causes a rapid acceleration in human evolution. Designing humanity out of ourselves through human enhancement and moving towards singularity may pose significant harm to our existence: total annihilation of our inner human qualities and humanness (Al-Amoudi, 2022; Eski, 2023; Karlan, 2023).

4.3.3.5 *Human enhancement and posthumanism*

Another interesting perspective on HE development is a discussion of posthuman and postbiological civilisation(s) in parallel with the renewed interest in the entire field of future studies. Some further questions originating from such an approach regarding the long-term future of human enhancement are:

- How far human enhancement can go?

- Is human enhancement a further step towards building a true postbiological civilisation?
- Should we actively participate and help shape this process?
- Is the future of humanity 'typical' in the same Copernican sense as our location in space and time is typical in the galaxy?
- If so, can we derive important insights about the evolutionary pathways of postbiological evolution from astrobiological and Search for ExtraTerrestrial Intelligence (SETI) studies? (Ćirković, 2017).

Due to the potential negative effects on societal equality and/or fairness, the issues mentioned above seem to support the statement that HE must be monitored and controlled.

4.3.4 Managerial perspectives

Monitoring and controlling are managerial functions. They could be effectively carried out if we can measure HE. The problem is as indicated earlier (see Section 2.3) there is no comprehensive system of information and data on human enhancement and its assessment. One may maintain then that the managerial perspective constitutes one of the biggest HE challenges.

One of the most important questions here (assuming that HE has been already defined) could be *who is supposed to be in charge* (which institution/organisation) of managing HE on global, supranational, and national levels. Concerning *what should be measured* one may point to the demand and supply side of the HE market.

On the demand side, we should have the number of individuals undergoing HE treatments divided into those who got it and those who are willing and capable of receiving them. On the supply side, we should have the record of medical specialists and special medical devices used in HE technologies (the latter with appropriate certifications).

An answer to the question of *how HE should be managed* depends on several factors which, in turn, depend on how HE is defined and the socioeconomic profile of the country concerned. It is therefore too complicated to be presented in this section.

To illustrate how challenging HE management could be, let us mention just a few of the difficulties from various areas.

Let us remember that the literature shows that quantitative evaluation of HE remains at the initial stage (Ryan et al., 2023). This refers to several HE applications such as BCI robotics for hand rehabilitation after a stroke where large heterogeneity in reporting was identified. Consequently, it is suggested to develop a standard protocol for assessing technical and clinical outcomes so that the necessary base of evidence on efficiency and efficacy can be developed (Baniqued et al., 2021). One may acknowledge the high heterogeneity of devices, protocols, and applications present in the description of BCI, so a proposition of a standardised glossary for BCI research together with a functional model for BCI presented as late as 2021 (Bianchi et al., 2021) should be welcome.

Similar challenges regarding measuring HE outcomes are observed concerning the efficacy of some HE methods such as deep brain stimulation (DBS) against mental illness. As indicated in the literature, there are no publications on randomised, controlled trials thus the efficacy of DBS has not been confirmed (Schläpfer et al., 2021).

Another example could be gathering, storing, and using data on HE devices. Assuming that some HE procedures require special sophisticated devices, there is a problem with their registration. HE devices can be classified as high-risk, thus earning marketing approval is a prerequisite so is their compulsory registration. Findings from the United States show that obtaining informed consent from trial participants remains a challenge (Kramer, Parasidis, 2022).

If one adds the issue of data privacy (with appropriate reference to existing law regulations), and cybersecurity concerns, the challenges HE management is facing could be even more complex and difficult.

4.3.5 Technological perspectives: what is knocking at the door

As pointed out in previous chapters, the military sector is one of the main drivers for human enhancement research and innovation. HE in the military sector also shows its heterogeneity and complicated nature such as ethical implications and the impact on military values, operational and practical dilemmas, and issues related to military law and the notion of informed consent (Puscas, 2018).

Taking into account the global position of the US military sector and considering the future of HE, it is worth referring to the public release report prepared by a team composed of biologists, bioengineers, multi-media specialists, and other related field experts from the US Department of Defense (Emanuel et al., 2019). The report titled 'Cyborg Soldier 2050: Human/Machine Fusion and the Implications for the Future of the DOD' surveyed a wide range of current and emerging technologies relevant to assisting and augmenting human performance in many domains. It identified four areas as being technically feasible by 2050 or earlier:

- ocular enhancements to imaging, sight, and situational awareness (*overlaying data streams onto a soldier's retinal wall and sent up the optic nerve. The data stream could cover a much larger range of the electromagnetic spectrum than visible light so a soldier might be able to see objects in the infrared range and beyond*);
- restoration and programmed muscular control through an optogenetic bodysuit sensor web (*light receptors are implanted just under the skin and a soldier's critical muscles and nerve bundles are stimulated allowing for an external source of muscle power and even external muscular control over the soldier*);

- auditory enhancement for communication and protection (*it could not only protect a soldier from overexposure such as a blast but also increase sensitivity to low amplitude sounds and even infrasonic and ultrasonic sounds. In the future one may foresee soldiers capable of echo-locating adversaries in the dark and using imperceptible forms of communication with each other*);
- direct neural enhancement of the human brain for two-way data transfer (Emanuel et al., 2019, p.v).

When commenting on the technical perspectives of HE in the future one may mention senses some animals have like magnetoception, echolocation, electroreception, and hygroreception. Theoretically, in the future, a human being through sophisticated HE operations could be equipped with some of the senses found in animals. The question is would it be still a human being?

Notes

1 Stakeholder-informed ethics for new technologies with high socio-economic and human rights impact, the European Union's Horizon 2020 research and innovation programme, grant agreement No. 741716.
2 Such a statement could be supported by the American entrepreneurial spirit and the universally socially recognised and practised principle/virtue of competition.
3 One must remember that the NHS is a publicly funded healthcare system. This in turn may suggest that even public health insurers (i.e., national insurers) are not willing to expand their coverage. This should come as no surprise, as Chapter 3 mentions the financial challenges of modern health systems.
4 Parker Crutchfield himself does formulate such an opinion in the quoted paper.
5 Such a list should be formulated by legal professionals and consulted with healthcare stakeholders, namely health politicians, managers, and patients.
6 Household gross disposable income is the income available to households such as wages and salaries, income from self-employment and unincorporated enterprises, income from pensions and other social benefits, and income from financial investments (less any payments of tax, social insurance contributions, and interest on financial liabilities). Depreciation costs are not subtracted.
7 Unlike in OECD, in the International Energy Outlook data is structured by continents and regions with just several countries called by names. Data come from the US Energy Information Administration and Oxford Economics. Global Economic Model.
8 Non-academic sources were referred to earlier in this book. See Joosten's (2023) blog in Chapter 2 references.

References

Al-Amoudi, I. (2022). Are post-human technologies dehumanizing? Human enhancement and artificial intelligence in contemporary societies. *Journal of Critical Realism*, 21(5), 516–538, 10.1080/14767430.2022.2134618.

Austin-Eames, L. (2023). Should moral bioenhancement be covert? A response to Crutchfield. *Neuroethics*, 16, 21, 10.1007/s12152-023-09529.

Baniqued, P.D.E., Stanyer, E.C., Awais, M., Alazmani, A., Jackson, A.E., Mon-Williams, M.A., Mushtaq, F., Holt, R.J. (2021). Brain-computer interface robotics for hand

rehabilitation after stroke: A systematic review. *Journal of NeuroEngineering and Rehabilitation*, 18, 15, 10.1186/s12984-021-00820-8.
Bianchi, L., Antonietti, A., Bajwa, G., Ferrante, R., Mahmud, M., Balachandran, P. (2021). A functional BCI model by the IEEE P2731 working group: Data storage and sharing. *Brain-Computer Interfaces*, 8(3), 108–116, 10.1080/2326263X.2021.1969789.
Binhammer, A., Jakubowski, J., Antonyshyn, O., Binhammer, P. (2020). Comparative cost-effectiveness of cranioplasty implants. *Plastic Surgery*, 28(1), 29–39, 10.1177/2292550319880922.
Canellopoulou-Bottis, M. (2018). *The Greek law on human enhancement* (December 4, 2018). Available at SSRN: https://ssrn.com/abstract=3295619 or 10.2139/ssrn.3295619, accessed 3.12.2023.
Carapeto Raposo, V.L. (2022). The better I can be: In defence of human enhancement for a new genetic equality. *Canadian Journal of Bioethics/Revue canadienne de bioéthique*, 5(2), 189–202. 10.7202/1089801ar.
Ćirković, M. (2017). Enhancing a person, enhancing a civilization: A research program at the intersection of bioethics, future studies, and astrobiology. *Cambridge Quarterly of Healthcare Ethics*, 26(3), 459–468, 10.1017/S0963180116001134.
Crutchfield, P. (2018). Compulsory moral bioenhancement should be covert. *Bioethics*, 33(1), 112–121, 10.1111/bioe.12496.
Dinniss, H.A.H. (2018). Legal aspects of human enhancement technologies from part II – applying the law to some new technologies. In Boothby, W.H. (Ed.). *New Technologies and the Law in War and Peace*. Cambridge University Press, pp. 230–257, 10.1017/9781108609388.009.
Dinniss, H.A.H., Kleffner, J.K. (2018). Soldier 2.0: Military human enhancement and international law. In Heintschel von Heinegg, W., Frau, R., Singer, T. (Eds). *Dehumanization of Warfare*. Cham: Springer, pp. 163–205, 10.1007/978-3-319-67266-3_10.
Elgabry, M., Camilleric, J. (2021). Conducting hidden populations research: A reflective case study on researching the biohacking community. *Futures*, 132, 102769, 10.1016/j.futures.2021.102769.
Emanuel, P., Walper, S., DiEuliis, D., Klein, N., Petro, J.B., Giordano, J. (2019). *Cyborg Soldier 2050: Human/machine fusion and the implications for the future of the DOD*, Combat Capabilities Development Command Chemical Biological Center-TR-1599, https://community.apan.org/wg/tradoc-g2/mad-scientist/m/articles-of-interest/300458, accessed 14.11.2023.
Eski, Y. (2023). *A Criminology of the Human Species. Setting an Unsettling Tone*. Palgrave Studies in Green Criminology. Cham: Palgrave Macmillan.
Feldstein, P.J., Melnick, G. (2023). *Health Policy Issues. An Economic Perspective*. Eight Edition. Chicago, Illinois: Health Administration Press.
Gaspar, R., Rohde, P., Giger, J.-C. (2019). Unconventional settings and uses of human enhancement technologies: A non-systematic review of public and experts' views on self-enhancement and DIY biology/biohacking risks. *Human Behavior and Emerging Technologies*, 1(4), 295–305, https://onlinelibrary.wiley.com/doi/epdf/10.1002/hbe2.175.
Harmsworth, M. (2023). *How human are you? The internet of bodies is here, but are we ready?* Taylor Wessing, January 30, 2023, https://www.taylorwessing.com/en/interface/2023/iot---next-gen/how-human-are-you-the-internet-of-bodies-is-here-but-are-we-ready, accessed 29.09.2023.
Hayes, A. (2023). *High-net-worth individual (HNWI): Criteria and example*, Updated June 1, 2023, https://www.investopedia.com/terms/h/hnwi.asp, accessed 13.12.2023.
IEO (2023). *International Energy Outlook 2023*. https://www.eia.gov/outlooks/ieo/data/pdf/A_A18_lp_230823.090253.pdf, accessed 14.01.2024.

Karlan, B. (2023). Human achievement and artificial intelligence. *Ethics and Information Technology*, 25, 40, 10.1007/s10676-023-09713-x.
Kellmeyer, P. (2021). Big brain data: On the responsible use of brain data from clinical and consumer-directed neurotechnological devices. *Neuroethics*,14, 83–98, 10.1007/s12152-018-9371-x.
Kenton, W. (2023). *Ultra-high-net-worth individual (UHNWI): Definition and criteria*, Updated June 24, 2023, https://www.investopedia.com/terms/u/ultra-high-net-worth-individuals-uhnwi.asp, accessed 18.12.2023.
Klaming, L., Haselager, P. (2013). Did my brain implant make me do it? Questions raised by DBS regarding psychological continuity, responsibility for action and mental competence. *Neuroethics* 6, 527–539, 10.1007/s12152-010-9093-1.
Knight Frank (2023). *The wealth report 2023*, https://www.knightfrank.com/wealthreport, accessed 13.12.2023.
Kowal, M., Sorokowski, P., Pisanski, K., Valentova, J.V., Varella, M.A.C., Frederick, D.A., et al., (2022). Predictors of enhancing human physical attractiveness: Data from 93 countries. *Evolution and Human Behavior*, 43(6), 455–474, 10.1016/j.evolhumbehav.2022.08.003.
Kramer, D.B., Parasidis, E. (2022). Informed consent and compulsory medical device registries: Ethics and opportunities. *Journal of Medical Ethics*, 48(2), 79–82, 10.1136/medethics-2020-107031.
Lyreskog, D.M., McKeown, A. (2022). On the (non-) rationality of human enhancement and transhumanism. *Science and Engineering Ethics*, 28(6), 52, 10.1007/s11948-022-00410-4.
McCall, I.C., Dubljević, V. (2024). Human flourishing or injustice? Social, political, and regulatory implications of cognitive enhancement. In Jotterand, F., Ienca, F. (Eds). *The Routledge Handbook of the Ethics of Human Enhancement*. Routledge, pp. 389–406.
Neufeld, D. (2023). *Visualizing the pyramid of global wealth distribution*, November 2, 2023, https://www.visualcapitalist.com/global-wealth-distribution/#google_vignett, accessed 12.01.2024.
Niemiec, E., Howard, H.C. (2020). "Genethics" and public health genomics. In Patrinos, G.P. (Ed.). *Applied Genomics and Public Health. Translational and Applied Genomics*. Academic Press, pp. 243–257, 10.1016/B978-0-12-813695-9.00013-3.
Nordberg, A. (2015). Patentability of methods of human enhancement. *Journal of Intellectual Property Law & Practice*, 10(1), 19–28, 10.1093/jiplp/jpu203.
OECD (2022). *Recommendation of the council on responsible innovation in neurotechnology*, OECD/LEGAL/0457, https://www.oecd.org/science/recommendation-on-responsible-innovation-in-neurotechnology.htm, accessed 4.01.2024.
OECD (2023a). *Health at a glance 2023*, OECD 2023.
OpenAI (2023). ChatGPT [Large language model]. https://chat.openai.com, accessed 2.12.2023.
Prince, P. (2023). Gene – environment interaction: Why genetic enhancement might never be distributed fairly. *Journal of Medical Ethics*. Published Online First: June 2, 2023, 10.1136/jme-2023-109101.
Puscas, I.M. (2018). Military human enhancement. In Boothby, W.H. (Ed.). *New Technologies and the Law in War and Peace*. Cambridge University Press, pp. 182–229.
Rhys-Evans, S. (2021). Should mitochondrial replacement therapy be funded by the National Health Service? *Journal of Medical Ethics*, 47(3), 194–198, 10.1136/medethics-2019-106053.
Rodríguez López, B. (2023). Experimental bioethics and the case for human enhancement. In Viciana, H., Gaitán, A., Aguiar, F. (Eds). *Experiments in Moral and Political Philosophy*. Routledge, pp. 270–289.

Ryan, B.J., Charkoudian, N., Joyner, M.J. (2023). Human performance augmentation: The importance of integrative physiological quantification. *The Journal of Physiology*, 601(3), 407–416, 10.1113/JP283975.

Sachdev, V. (2022). 'Beyond' human enhancement – taking the developing country's perspective seriously. *Asian Bioethics Review*, 14(2),169–182, https://link.springer.com/article/10.1007/s41649-021-00193-z.

Sattler, S., Jacobs, E., Singh, I., Whetham, D., Bárd, I., Moreno, J., Galeazzi, G., Allansdottir, A. (2022). Neuroenhancements in the military: A mixed-method pilot study on attitudes of staff officers to ethics and rules. *Neuroethics*, 15, 11, 10.1007/s12152-022-09490-2.

Schläpfer, T.E., Meyer-Lindenberg, A., Synofzik, M., Visser-Vandewalle, V., Voges, J., Coenen, V.A. (2021). Invasive brain stimulation in the treatment of psychiatric illness – proposed indications and approaches. *Deutsches Ärzteblatt International*, 118(3), 31–36, 10.3238/arztebl.m2021.0017.

SIENNA (2021). *Enhancing EU legal frameworks for genetics & genomics research*. SIENNA project Policy Brief #2 (V2.0), February 2021, https://sienna-network.com.gr/wp-content/uploads/2021/11/2.sienna-policybrief-GenomicsFeb21–210218.pdf, accessed 18.12.2023.

Sorgner, S.F. (2017). Genetic privacy, big gene data, and the internet panopticon. *Journal of Posthuman Studies*, 1(1), 87–103, 10.5325/jpoststud.1.1.0087.

Stieglitz, T. (2021). Why neurotechnologies? About the purposes, opportunities and limitations of neurotechnologies in clinical applications. *Neuroethics*, 14, 5–16, 10.1007/s12152-019-09406-7.

Tracinski, R. (nd). *The future of human augmentation and performance enhancement*, https://www.realclearscience.com/articles/2017/04/04/the_future_of_human_augmentation_and_performance_enhancement.html, accessed 18.12.2023.

Valera, L., Bellver, V. (2024). Contemporary bioethical and legal perspectives on cognitive enhancement. In Jotterand, F., Ienca, F. (Eds). *The Routledge Handbook of the Ethics of Human Enhancement*. Routledge, pp. 407–417.

Varelius, J. (2020). Neuroenhancement, the criminal justice system, and the problem of alienation. *Neuroethics*, 13, 325–335, 10.1007/s12152-019-09427-2.

Walsh, A. (2021). Distributive justice, equality and the enhancement of human cognition: A commentary on fairness and 'cognitive doping'. *International Journal of Drug Policy*, 95, 102874, 10.1016/j.drugpo.2020.102874.

Warso, Z., Gaskell, S. (2019). *SIENNA D3.2: Analysis of the legal and human rights requirements for Human Enhancement Technologies in and outside the EU*, 741716-SIENNA- D3.2 Deliverable report, Ref. Ares (2019)2271580 - 29/03/2019, https://zenodo.org/records/4066617, accessed 15.12.2023.

Conclusions

At this point, let us try to point out the most important themes and issues raised in this book.

To begin with, it should be noted that the Fourth Industrial Revolution (4IR) has an ever-expanding and powerful impact on health systems, societies, and the health of individuals.

Some of the 4IR outcomes, namely new medicines, new medical devices, implants, genetic engineering, nanotechnology, neurotechnology, and nanorobotics lead to HE. It is defined as an intervention/modification – a human action of any kind – in the biology or psychology of a person that either increases species-typical normal functioning above the statistically typical levels or produces a new capacity that normal human beings do not possess.

Human enhancement (HE) seems to represent the essence of 4IR understood as 'a fusion of technologies that is blurring the lines between the physical, digital, and biological spheres' (Schwab, 2016). There are sufficient grounds to maintain that HE is on its way up.

HE remains at the very first stage of development (*in statu nascendi*) and is intensively researched both by civil and military institutions. HE is studied mainly by researchers representing the humanities (philosophers/ethicists) and social sciences (mainly sociologists). The share of physical sciences and engineering in researching HE is small. As a result, qualitative methods dominate research. Economic analysis of HE is rare if it exists.

The phenomenon of HE is not unambiguously defined, and its definitions vary. Additionally, HE is not regulated by any current laws. HE is a new step in homo sapiens' evolution and possesses far-reaching consequences for individuals and societies and thus cannot be left unregulated.

HE has many forms. In this book, four basic forms of HE: *cognitive enhancement, physical enhancement, mood enhancement, and moral enhancement* are discussed. Cognitive enhancement (BCI, DBS, optogenetics, TDCS, and TMS) seems to possess a special meaning for individual people as well as societies, and countries.

Rare HE procedures remain in an experimental phase and are covered either by governmental R&D programmes or by individuals (OOP). Private

DOI: 10.4324/9781003449584-6

HE financing will be prolonged for decades due to current financial challenges – only wealthy individuals can afford HE. HE procedures are aimed at extension, not the restoration of or maintaining existing health so they cannot be financed by standard health insurance schemes especially nowadays when health sectors face considerable challenges due to rising costs and patients' expectations. Thus an extension of coverage is questionable.

The dominance of private financing of HE may lead to the deepening and further increase in social disparities and inequalities. Private HE financing raises a serious challenge for health policy. It is the issue of possible growing inequality in a narrow, cognitive, and physiological sense, as well as in a broader, social, and genre that can jeopardise social cohesion principles.

One may argue that the top priority at this phase of HE development should be the creation of proper laws and/or regulations on global, supranational and national scales.

Laws and/or regulations must define HE and the mechanisms of HE management, monitoring, and assessment with a special emphasis on the principles and conditions of the usage of HE technologies. HE procedures should be recorded and stored under proper control. Information about enhanced people should be available. Any enacted laws and/or regulations must be rigorously monitored and enforced at every level.

HE procedures should be treated as inevitable since they are pushed by technological development (that cannot be stopped) and are rooted in the competitive nature of humans (in its Darwinian sense which cannot be eliminated at the current stage of homo sapiens' evolution). Consequently, appropriate regulations must be elaborated on and implemented without unnecessary delays.

One may conclude that due to its potential and only partially identified consequences for individuals, societies, nations, and humanity as a whole, HE enhancement should be a subject of intense exploration not only by scientists but by society as a whole.

Reference

Schwab, K. (2016). *The Fourth Industrial Revolution: what it means, how to respond*, World Economic Forum, https://www.weforum.org/agenda/2016/01/the-fourth-industrial-revolution-what-it-means-and-how-to-respond, accessed 12.02.2023.

Index

Pages in *italics* refer to figures and pages in **bold** refer to tables.